Ferrari Berlinetta Boxer

The Road and Race Legends

Nathan Beehl

Nathan Beehl 70/512

Ferrari Berlinetta Boxer
The Road and Race Legends

© Copyright Nathan Beehl 2007

Published by
Fiorano Publishing
Beds, LU3 1HQ
boxerbook@yahoo.co.uk

ISBN Special Edition 978-0-9555643-1-4

Designed by
David Tokeley

Printed by
The Lavenham Press
47 Water Street, Lavenham,
Suffolk CO10 9RN
01787 247436

Acknowledgements

First and foremost, thanks to my long-suffering wife Roz who has graciously accepted this Ferrari obsession for many years.

Also, my gratitude to all the following who have helped by supplying photos and/or information. In alphabetical order;

John S Allen	Marcel Massini
Steve Biagini	Jon Masterson
Bruno Burri	Simon Phillips
Keith Bluemel	Steven Pickering
David Blumlein	Dave Robidoux
Lee Carducci	Gerald Roush
Lin Chandler	Dave Seibert
Bob Donner Jnr.	Lee Sanders
Dr. Herbert Gerl	Ron Spangler
Peter Grootswagers	Mike Sheehan
Michitake Isobe	Tom Shelton
Chuck Jordan	Mark Tippetts
Fred Lewis	Tom Wiggers

And the many owners, too many to mention, who offered information and photos - Thank you all!

Not forgetting -
For ten years the Ferrari Berlinetta Boxer was raced by private entrants. The vast majority of the expense was borne by owners and enthusiasts with little or no chance of any financial reward.

These men alone represented the name of Ferrari in top-line sports car racing, at tracks such as Le Mans and Daytona where the Ferrari legend was forged. For those enthusiasts who enjoy supporting Ferrari away from the exaggerated hype of Formula One these teams were the only regular sources of involvement. Some of the performances achieved were way beyond what most people expected, and could only add to the Ferrari legend.

I hope that all those owners, mechanics and drivers will accept this work as a token of appreciation for all their efforts whether successful or not.

Nathan Beehl
boxerbook@yahoo.co.uk

Contents

Introduction

Think of all the great sports cars, and one name that inevitably comes to mind is Ferrari. For nearly 60 years, Ferrari has been building cars that impress not only by their performance but also by their stunning appearance.

Enthusiasts around the world have been awed as Ferrari have produced classic after classic. (That's if the term 'classic' as an auto-related description hasn't been totally devalued by its excessive use during recent years.) In the early years, Ferrari produced the Tipo 166 and its many variants, and then the 250GTs, including the beautiful Berlinetta Lusso and the legendary GTO, the 275GTB/4, the 365GTB/4 "Daytona," the superb Dino 246GT, the Berlinetta Boxers, 288GTO, F40, 550 Maranello, F50 and Enzo. This list probably doesn't include your particular favorite.

But Ferrari was, and still is, known first and foremost as a racing car manufacturer. Ferrari has been involved in almost every sphere of international motorsport at one time or another, including rallying and the Indianapolis 500. It is also the only manufacturer to have competed in Formula One every year since the inception of the World Championship back in 1950.

It's also safe to say that where Ferrari competition cars led, the production cars followed. In the early years there was not much to choose between the two types of vehicle. In the later years, as racing became more specialized, the technical advances prompted by competition were incorporated, where appropriate, into the road cars.

Bellancauto's unique BBB heads a pack of mid-field cars at LeMans 1981 (NB Colln)

Therefore, the Berlinetta Boxer was an important step in the Ferrari lineage, having been the first 12-cylinder Ferrari to follow the commonly called mid-engine configuration popularized by Grand Prix cars of the 1960s.

From the earliest days, Ferrari produced competition versions of its top Grand Touring cars. For example, the Tipo 166 that won the Le Mans 24 Hours race in 1949 was also available as a Lusso (luxury) version. In real terms, there was scant difference, although the interior of the Lusso, including the dashboard top, was finished in leather.

Later, as GT racing became more specialized, the difference between the two versions grew, yet their common heritage was still recognizable. Enthusiasts with long memories will recall the racing successes of the 250GT in its many guises, especially the 250GTO, as well as the 275GTB and the 365GTB/4, among others. Younger enthusiasts will be aware of the competition versions of the 550 and 575 Maranellos. The Berlinetta Boxer was no exception, and it competed with varying degrees of success on the race tracks of the world, including Le Mans, Silverstone and Daytona.

This, then, is the story of Ferrari's Berlinetta Boxer – the road and race supercar.

The Ferrari Boxer Engine – History

Another view of the Ferrari Boxer flat-12, showing crackle-finish on cam and timing gear covers.(Ferrari Photo).

The Ferrari Boxer 180° "Flat" engine, but still a V-12. (Ferrari photo).

Interestingly, calling Ferrari's flat-12 engine a "Boxer" is technically incorrect. True, it has a "Boxer" layout, in as much as the pistons lie horizontally rather than at an angle to the vertical. But a true "Boxer" engine is one in which the opposite pistons move simultaneously, both in and out at the same time, like clapping hands. This means that each piston has to have a separate crankshaft pin, which is not only expensive but can also be unreliable as it places added stress on the crankshaft. Ferrari used the more normal V-12 type arrangement of two pistons on a common crank pin, and in so doing endowed the flat-12 with the same super smooth balance as the famous V-12 series of engines. In true technical terms, Ferrari's "Boxer" engine is a 180° V-12, but if Boxer is good enough for Ferrari then it's good enough for me and for you too.

Surprisingly, Ferrari did not invent the Boxer engine. Porsche is well-known for using that type of motor, and back in 1939 Alfa Romeo built a flat-12 engine although it never actually raced. In fact Ferrari's Boxer engine first appeared in its 1964 Grand Prix car. The 1.5-liter 12-cylinder engine produced a reputed 220 bhp at 11,800 rpm. During the course of its year-and-a-half competitive life, its best result was a second-place finish by Lorenzo Bandini in the 1965 Monaco Grand Prix.

Lorenzo Bandini on his way to a second place finish in the 1965 Monaco Grand Prix, the best result recorded by the 1512 Formula One Ferrari (Geoffrey Goddard/The GP Library).

But why did Ferrari build a flat-12 when Ferrari, of all people, had built its reputation on the V-12? The main reason was that the flat-12 would have a lower center of gravity and should therefore, in theory, allow the engineers to build a better handling race car. A beneficial byproduct of the horizontal layout is that the engine ancillaries can be placed above the block thus making it easier for the mechanics to service them when necessary.

For the 1966 Grand Prix season, the governing body of motorsport decided that a new formula was needed, and so the 3-liter capacity formula was brought in. Ferrari had found that the flat-12 engine had offered little, if any, advantage in the previous one-and-a-half-liter formula. So the company reverted to its more usual V-12 layout for the new season.

But the flat-12 story doesn't end there because, in 1967, Ferrari resurrected it as a two-liter engine. During 1968, this new engine was tested in a light-weight, open, two-seater sports racing car, and it was launched in 1969 as the 212E Montagna, entered in the European Mountain Climb Championship. The EMCC was a series of eight events over various European mountains, with the seven best results to count. Ferrari gave the last event a miss, but having won the other seven outright it didn't really matter. The Boxer engine, after a false start in 1964 and 1965, was on its way.

The compact flat–12 2-liter engine designed for the 212E Montagna with which Ferrari dominated the 1969 European Mountain Climb Championship. (Ferrari Photo).

The 212E Montagna undergoing tests at Modena's Autodrome. Chris Amon, in helmet, watches as a mechanic makes final preparations. (Peter Coltrin Photo / The Klementaski Colln).

From 1966 to 1969, Ferrari continued with the V-12 engine in Formula One but with what can only be described as mediocre results. So in late 1969, Ferrari started testing a new 3-liter grand prix engine, the 12-cylinder Boxer. For many years it was assumed that Ferrari returned to the flat-12 engine because then chief engineer, Mauro Forghieri, had been instrumental in the development of the original 1964 engine. Engineer Forghieri tells it differently: "The 12 cylinder that raced at the end of 1969 had been designed at the end of 1968. It was at the wish of Enzo Ferrari that a special development office was set up, which was where the "312" flat engine was designed as a totally new concept. It had nothing to do with the 1964 engine. The configuration was the only thing they had in common, although the basic ideas from which they were developed were closely related to each other . . . There is another thing about this engine; Ing. Ferrari wanted it to be an engine that could be mounted in the wing of an airplane. We had received an order from an American firm for an engine of this kind. The engine was erroneously called a Boxer but it wasn't a Boxer at all; it was a flat engine, 25 cm high in its first version. It had nothing on top of it and could actually be fitted into the wing of an airplane . . . ."

Despite Forghieri's modest explanation of the rebirth of the Boxer engine, it was considered by many to be a technical and sporting success. Lee Carducci, engineer on the 1990 Lamborghini Formula One team, explained: "In May 1987, at the Monaco Grand Prix, I had the great fortune to met Ing. Forghieri [who was then working at Lamborghini] and discuss the possibility of a Chrysler/Lamborghini Formula One engine team. In September of that year, after Chrysler officially purchased Lamborghini, I had a meeting with Ing. Forghieri and Sig. Audetto to discuss my future with Lamborghini. From then on, I was the engineer responsible for the engine electronics department at Lamborghini Engineering, and track engineer for, first, the Larousse and then the Lotus Formula One teams."

Why was Carducci so keen to work with Forghieri? He continued, "When I was young I was vacationing with my parents in my father's hometown in Italy. At that time in my life I was always tearing things apart to try and find out how they worked and, of course, I had a strong passion for cars, especially very fast ones. In Italy the big news that I can remember at the time was about this great engineer called Ing. Forghieri at Ferrari, and about the engine that was going to turn the racing world upside down. Not knowing exactly how this engine functioned I think the biggest interest I had was in how he was able to engineer the Boxer style engine into a competitive race car and, of course, I was a Ferrari nut. I decided that I was going to work for Engineer Forghieri at Ferrari."

Working with Forghieri was everything that Carducci expected. "The opportunity to work for and with Mauro basically seven days a week gave me insight into what makes this man such a great engineer and, for that matter, a great person," he said. "He is the kind of person who does not permit barriers to stop the creativity of his team. He is always pushing his engineers to design/develop new applications. Believe me when I state that you would never hear him say that it can't be done. I believe that is what really makes the Boxer such a great power train package. I have met members of the team that did the design and development work and still cannot believe some of the concepts that were tested during that project. Remember this was more than 30 years ago. They are proud of what they call 'The Application Engineering,' being able to not so much invent but engineer for the specific application. That accomplishment during the project by the team permitted an overall complete power train package. This is what makes the Boxer engine and its related chassis such a great project in my mind.

"When asked if I still consider the car great, I think my response would have to be that there are many engine/car combinations that drastically outperform the greats

The open side of the 312B shows just how shallow the Boxer Formula 1 engine was (Peter Coltrin Photo / The Klementaski Colln).

Enzo Ferrari confers with mechanics, drivers and engineers during testing of the new 312B at the Modena Autodrome in December 1969. (Peter Coltrin Photo / The Klementaski Colln).

from the past, and I'm sure that in the future new technology will permit even greater leaps. But one thing that has to be remembered is the time in which the car came into production and the resource the engineers had to work with. If you could factor that into some sort of an equation then the Boxer engine has to be one of the greatest that will ever exist.

"As for the man, people see Mauro in different ways. Some see him as the madman who constantly pushed the engineers, mechanics and drivers at the race track. Some see him as a charming Italian playboy. Others see him as the great engineer. For me, he is all of the above! He taught me a lot in many different areas of engineering and life. Everybody should have the opportunity to work with a man like Mauro."

Despite Carducci's praise, not everyone had as much faith in Forghieri and his technicians. Testing began in the autumn of 1969 with none-too-promising results. In fact, No.1 driver Chris Amon became so disillusioned with the continual engine breakages that he signed for the fledgling March-Ford team for the 1970 season. This was a pity because Forghieri, with a bit of outside help, solved the reliability problems, and the flat-12 went on to be a great success. The initial unreliability was caused by severe torsional vibration which, in turn, resulted in a number of crankshaft breakages. So Pirelli built a special rubber coupling that fitted between the four main bearing crankshaft and the flywheel, and this, along with a crank manufactured from a single steel billet, eventually conquered the problem.

The first 3-liter, known as the 312B, had a bore and stroke of 78.5 mm x 51.5 mm and an 11.5:1 compression ratio. The valve gear was all in twos – two overhead camshafts, with two inlet and two exhaust valves per cylinder. A Lucas indirect fuel injection system was fitted, and a Magnetti Marelli transistorized ignition system provided the spark. The quoted power was 450 hp at 12,000 rpm.

In 1970, its first year of competition, the 312B took four victories – the Italian Grand Prix for local favorite Clay Regazzoni, while the popular Jacky Ickx won the Austrian, Canadian and Mexican events. This success was in startling contrast to the Boxer's V-12 predecessor, which could only manage three wins in four seasons. Yes, the Boxer had finally arrived.

The Belgian driver Jacky Ickx would spend four years, (1970-1973) racing in Ferrari's flat-12 Formula One car, with mixed degrees of success. (Geoffrey Goddard/The GP Library).

For the 1971 season, the Boxer engine was modified. With an enlarged bore and subsequently reduced stroke, higher revs were possible and power was increased 20 bhp to 470 bhp at 12,600 rpm. Regrettably, only two championship victories were recorded, but this had more to do with poor chassis performance and recurring tire-induced vibration problems than any shortcoming with the engine.

As if 1971 wasn't bad enough, 1972 was even worse. Drivers Ickx and Regazzoni continued to struggle with the 312B2, as the latest Ferrari Grand Prix car was known. Only Ickx's victory at the Nürburgring gave the team anything to smile about. Maybe Ferrari was stretched too far, as it was also competing in the World Sportscar Championship, which coincidentally was also for cars of up to 3-liter capacity. But more about the sports-racers later.

The continued lack of success, despite having an engine that most observers felt was the best in Formula One at that time, led to Forghieri being moved sideways temporarily and the Grand Prix team spending a year in the wilderness. Ferrari even went as far as having three chassis built at TC Prototypes in Northampton, England,

Ickx is seen here driving the Ferrari 312B2 in the 1972 Italian Grand Prix. (Geoffrey Goddard/The GP Library).

In 1974 Niki Lauda replaced Ickx on the Ferrari team. Here he is with an early 1974 version of the revamped 312B3. (Peter Coltrin Photo / The Klementaski Colln).

but to no avail. The next year, 1973, was a disaster as far as Ferrari's Formula One activities were concerned. The engine was slightly modified to produce a claimed extra 15 bhp, but it wasn't enough to override the B2's failings.

Of course, when you're down there's only one way you can go — up. (Although I guess that you might successfully argue that 'out' is a frequent second alternative). For 1974 there was a major shake-up in the house of Maranello. Ferrari abandoned sports car racing, thus allowing nearly all its resources to concentrate on Formula One. Forghieri was brought back into the racing team, and Luca di Montezemolo was appointed by Fiat as team manager with the mandate to do whatever was necessary to restore Ferrari to the top. Ickx left, no doubt disheartened by the lack of success, and coming man Niki Lauda was signed as his replacement. The 1974 car was a totally new design reflecting Forghieri's theories on the polar moment of inertia and other long phrases. The engine, having been basically correct from the start, was virtually unchanged. In the first Grand Prix of the year, at Buenos Aires, Lauda and Regazzoni finished second and third, respectively. Lauda's first win came at the Spanish Grand Prix, and he followed that up with another victory at Zandvoort in Holland. Regazzoni won in Germany, giving Ferrari three victories for the season, a vast improvement on previous years.

Despite the much-improved showing in 1974, di Montezemolo and Forghieri were determined to do better in 1975, and so Ferrari unveiled to the press the new 312T. The Boxer engine remained basically unchanged, although development had resulted in power output being raised to about 500 bhp. The main technical novelty was the change to a Ferrari designed and built transverse gearbox. In this car, Lauda became the 1975 World Champion.

Niki Lauda driving the new 312T to victory in the 1975 Monaco Grand Prix. He would go on to win the driver's championship that year. (Geoffrey Goddard/The GP Library).

The Ferrari 312P sports-racer with the 3-liter Boxer engine was fast but fragile in 1971. At Sebring, this car driven by Jacky Ickx and Mario Andretti had a 4-lap lead when the transmission gave out. (Bill Warner photo).

For 1976, a rules change demanded that the high air box of the 312T be dropped but the basic technical layout remained the same. There's little doubt that Lauda would have been the 1976 World Champion if it hadn't been for a horrific crash at the Nürburgring that nearly took his life. Although given 'last rites' while lying in a hospital bed, he made a gutsy, heroic return to motor racing less than six weeks later, finishing fourth in the Italian Grand Prix. He lost the World Championship to James Hunt by just one point.

Ferrari continued to use the Boxer engine in Formula One with beneficial results. The following year, 1977, Lauda became World Champion yet again, and in 1979 South African driver Jody Scheckter won yet another World Championship for Ferrari. Even so, the Boxer's days were numbered.

Two major developments caused the demise of the Boxer engine in competition. The first was the success of the ground-effects Lotus 78, and the other was the potential shown by Renault's 1.5-liter turbo-charged Grand Prix challenger.

The advent of ground-effects in Grand Prix racing effectively ruled out the flat-12 engine, not because of any deficiency in the engine but because its low, wide layout took away space needed for the all-important, down force producing, underbody venturi sections. A short, narrow V-6 turbo had as much power as the flat-12 (and the potential to produce even more power with further development) as well as being better suited to a high down force design.

So force of circumstances caused the Boxer engine to be quietly withdrawn from Formula One, but during a 10-year period it had proven to be an effective engine. The Boxer engine powered Ferrari to three World Driver's Championships, four Formula One Manufacturers Championships and won 43 Formula One races.

In early 1972, the latest version of the Boxer-engined 312P, which would go on to score considerable success that year, was introduced at Ferrari's brand new Fiorano test track alongside one of Ferrari's first successful racing models, a 166MM Touring Superleggera Barchetta. (Peter Coltrin Photo / The Klementaski Colln).

Along the way, Ferrari had also been busy in sportscar racing — at least for a short period anyway. From 1971 through 1973, it ran the 312P -- often referred to as 312PB but that nomenclature was never officially used by Ferrari -- which also had the three-liter flat-12 engine.

In 1971, the factory ran the flat-12 312P essentially as a development project, but even against the 5-liter Porsche 917s (which incidentally also had flat-12 engines) the 312Ps were competitive, usually being as quick if not quicker but lacking reliability.

All the hard work came to fruition in 1972 when the sports cars were limited to 3-litre engines. Ferrari absolutely dominated the series, winning the 10 Championship races and even two non-Championship events. The next year was less successful, mainly because of handling and chassis inadequacies, but Ferrari still won two of the nine Championship races.

Overall, the Boxer engine was successful for Ferrari, and that it should appear in its top-of-the-range road car at the same time as the successful race cars was not surprising.

365GT4/BB – The Production Engine

Although the 365GT4/BB engine appeared to be new, and even a new concept to some, it was not much more than a widened out and flattened 365GTB/4 Daytona engine. The bore and stroke were the same, the compression ratio was the same, and it even had the same twin cams per cylinder.

While some observers may have expected Ferrari to design and construct a totally new engine for its first mid-engined super car, there are a number of good reasons why this didn't happen.

First, new Ferraris have always been the result of natural progression and improvement. For instance, Ferrari's engines gradually grew in size from the original 1.5-liter V-12 of the late '40s, also becoming technically more adventurous along the way. Ferrari's chassis design advanced at a steady pace as well. In fact, the switch from front-engined to mid-engined layout was probably the most radical technical change in all of Ferrari history up to that point.

Second, another factor was that Ferrari was still in the process of recovering, with Fiat's help, from a major financial crisis that nearly saw the giant American auto manufacturer Ford buying the company. Finally, Ferrari was, as it still is today, only a comparatively small manufacturer of specialist high performance cars.

The carry-over of parts from a model already in production was an understandable economic decision for Ferrari. Certainly there was nothing wrong with the specification and performance of the Daytona engine, and Ferrari's engineers were confident that in its new guise it would maintain Ferrari's reputation as manufacturers of the world's fastest and most desirable cars.

The Daytona's 4.4-liter V-12 produced a claimed (you'll see this word 'claimed' used quite often when it comes to describing Ferrari engine power outputs. Ferrari tended to be rather optimistic about engine power claims) 352 bhp. It powered an automobile that managed to impress even the more jaded and cynical members of the motoring journalist's posse and still continues to do so!

The 365GT4/BB's identical (to the Daytona's) oversquare bore and stroke of 81 by 71 mm created an engine with 365 cc per cylinder (hence the designation "365") and a total capacity of 4390 cc. The cylinder block and crankcase were cast in silumin (an aluminium/silicon alloy), a lustrous, gleaming metal that combines lightness with strength. The cast-iron cylinder liners were deep frozen and shrink fitted into place.

The crankshaft was a machinist's work of art. As was Ferrari's tradition, it was produced from a single billet of hardened and tempered steel and machined down on a lathe. A typical billet would start off weighing more than 300 pounds and yet the finished item would be pared down to about a sixth of that, to just more than 50 pounds. After being machined, it was magnafluxed, heat treated and nitrided to enable it to stand up to the pounding of 12 pistons at 7700 rpm. This complete process required 17 hours of machining and 65 days to complete. Later, the crankshafts and camshafts for the V-12 Ferraris would be foundry cast in KNV steel and machined by computer controlled robots.

The crankshaft ran in seven main bearings, although the 312B racing flat-12 used only four. No doubt the added length, weight and friction losses due to the three extra bearings were considered less important than the need for strength and reliability. Moving out from the center of the power house, the 12 connecting rods, running on thin-wall bearings, were mounted in pairs on each crankshaft throw.

Bolted on to each bank of cylinders was an alloy cylinder head incorporating two camshafts -- one for intake and one for exhaust -- activating two large valves per cylinder. Nowadays, four valves per cylinder seem quite common in a high-performance sports car, but 20 years ago this type of technology was only reserved for out-and-out racing cars.

One major change from previous Ferrari engines was to switch the cam drive from triplex or duplex roller chain to reinforced rubber-toothed belts. While the old system was unlikely to break and was long lasting and reliable, the chains stretched in use and required frequent adjustment. The rubber belts require no lubrication. As a result, they are cheaper and easier to maintain and are also much quieter, an additional benefit as buyers of sports cars became more sophisticated and demanded less noise and more comfort.

Topping off this mechanical concoction were four of Eduardo Weber's famous sculptures -- 40 IF 3C carburetors. Although fuel injection is now all the rage and the letters GTi have taken on an almost mythical significance as far as the average motorist is concerned, most enthusiasts are stirred by the appearance of 12 polished inlet trumpets sitting atop a row of Weber carburetors.

Marelli electronic ignition was specified using a single distributor mounted at the rear of the left hand cylinder bank and driven by the exhaust camshaft. The alternator and air-conditioning pump, to be driven by the cam belts, were mounted at the forward end of the engine.

One strange anomaly was the decision to use a wet sump lubrication system. The Daytona had a dry sump system, and one would have thought that the anticipated higher cornering speeds afforded by the BB's mid-engined layout would have ensured that the Boxer had a similar system. The change to a dry sump system for the 365's successor, the BB512, suggests that the decision to go with a wet sump may have been the wrong one.

The new 4.4-litre flat-12 engine (Ferrari)

This cut-away reveals the internal secrets of the 365GT4/BB engine (Gerald Roush Colln)

Regardless of the rights and wrongs of the sump system, Ferrari claimed that the new BB engine produced 380 bhp at 7700 rpm compared to the Daytona's 352 bhp. However, when the 5-liter BB was launched with a claimed output of 360 bhp -- some 20 less than the 365 despite a larger engine -- questions were raised about the accuracy of the claims for the 365. It was then admitted that the first 365GT4/BB engine had developed a genuine 380 bhp, but that in the interests of reliability and drivability the production engines were slightly less powerful at 360 bhp at 7000 rpm (woe betide the unlucky owner who tried to take his production Boxer round to 7700!) although the sales brochure still quoted the 380 figure. The brochure also quoted a top speed of 188 mph, although in reality it was only 181 mph. Mind you, that's probably only of academic interest to the majority of us.

Apart from the engine layout, the transmission system was another technical innovation. The Ferrari engineers were faced with the problem of how to fit the 12-cylinder engine and the transmission into a limited amount of space. On a racing car this is no problem -- the driver can sit further forward since there's no need to allow space for luggage, spare wheel, etc., so mounting the engine and transmission inline is an acceptable solution. But in a road car, the 12-cylinder engine and an inline transmission would be far too long. Lamborghini overcame this problem by mounting the Miura's V-12 engine sideways in the chassis and by mounting the gearbox in front of the engine in the Countach.

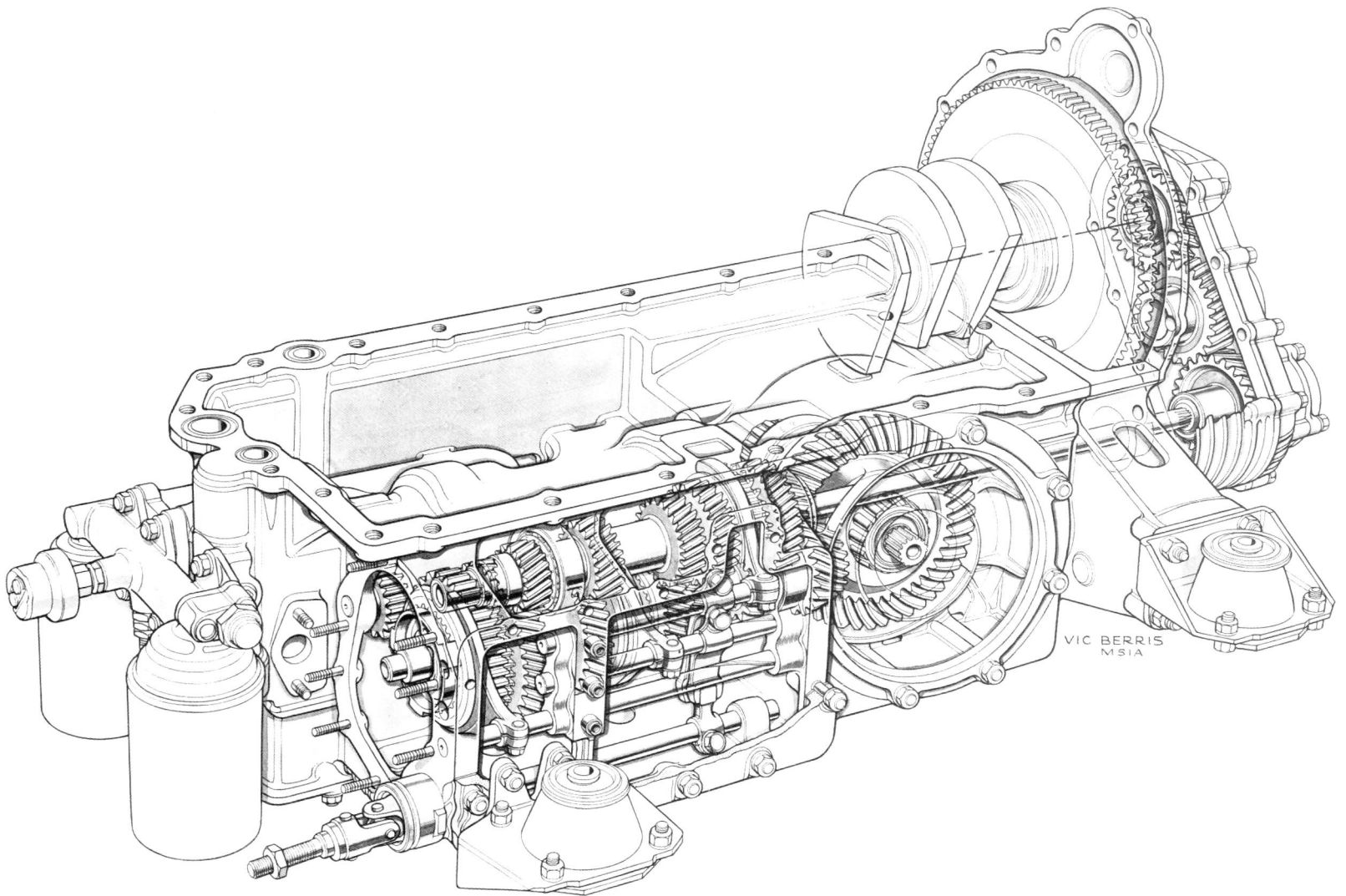

*The unusual transmission arrangement is clearly demonstrated
in this Vic Berris cutaway (Gerald Roush Colln)*

Ferrari overcame their problem by mounting the transmission beneath the engine, practically in the sump. Ferrari engineered this by running the crankshaft drive through the flywheel, through a single plate clutch and then through three step-down helical gears. The third of these gears was attached to a long quill shaft that ran back beneath the crankshaft and was offset to one side. The actual gear cluster was therefore located below the front half-a-dozen cylinders and the final drive below the next four cylinders, leaving the final couple of cylinders to hang out over the back of the rear axle line. Only the Boxer engine configuration made this type of layout a practical consideration. All things considered, this was quite an elegant compromise. Although this arrangement left the crankshaft approximately 20 inches (500mms) above the ground it should be remembered that the bulk of the engine was actually no higher than the crankshaft, unlike a V-12 which obviously has a lower crankshaft but a whole lot more engine stuck above it.

In detail, the gearbox was a two-shaft unit with Porsche-type syncromesh, giving five forward gears and reverse. According to the Ferrari sales brochure, maximum speed attainable in each gear was 54, 80, 108, 138 and 188 mph. Not mentioned in the brochure was the fact that about 60 mph could also be achieved in reverse! The second motion shaft transmits the power through a spiral bevel gear, through a ZF limited slip differential, and then out through universal-jointed driveshafts to Michelin 215/70VR 15XWXs mounted on five-pointed star 15 x 7½ inch alloy wheels.

365GT4/BB –
The Chassis

Although the Berlinetta Boxer was a radical new design for Ferrari, in many ways it was still traditional Ferrari. As we've already seen, the engine, dimensionally and mechanically, followed traditional Ferrari design parameters.

The chassis was to be no different. It too followed standard Ferrari practice as it was a separate frame constructed from oval and rectangular section tubing. The main section of the chassis was of oval construction with the water pipes passing through the center tube, similar to the Dino 246GT. This principal center section was then sandwiched top and bottom with sheet steel welded into place to form a strong rigid platform. This was augmented by two sub frames -- one at the front to carry the suspension, bodywork, spare wheel and other necessary bits and pieces -- and one at the rear to cradle the engine, hang the suspension on and mount the engine cover and bodywork.

The 365GT4/BB chassis in all its naked glory.(Peter Coltrin Photo / The Klementaski Colln)

The chassis tubes extended up into the BB's roof, and by fixing the roof and central bodywork directly to these tubes, Ferrari created an extremely strong, box-like center section. This method of construction served Ferrari well for many years, and a number of owners have had good reason to thank Ferrari for the strength and integrity of its chassis. In some ways Ferraris are perhaps over-engineered, but this means that crashed Ferraris are rarely write-offs. Even if the chassis should be bent, the damaged tubes can usually be cut out and new tubes welded in.

Fitted over the chassis is what is best described as a fiberglass blanket. This separates the chassis and suspension components from the rest of the car and forms the spare wheel housing, the front and rear internal wheel arches, the front and rear passenger compartment bulkheads, as well as the luggage space and battery well. Much of the fiberglass was pre-formed, but some was added after the bodies were fitted in order to close up any gaps, such as in the foot well.

The suspension design stemmed from Ferrari's experience with the mid-engined 250LM and Dino racing cars but differed in detail due to the BB's extra weight. It was independent all-round, using unequal length A-arms and coil-over shock absorbers fixed to the lower suspension arms, with cast-alloy uprights to hold the wheel hubs. The rear was slightly unusual in that the more rearward placement of the engine (compared to the racing cars) put more weight directly over the suspension, so two coil-over shock absorbers were used on each side, placed fore and aft of the driveshafts.

The hand-built aspect of the BB can be appreciated from this photo
(Peter Coltrin Photo / The Klementaski Colln)

Naturally, an important part of any high-performance car is the brake system. Ferrari followed the conventional route, and chose to fit ventilated disc brakes front and rear with four-pot calipers. A servo assisted twin circuit system assured the driver of the BB's ability to stop in a reasonably short space. An interesting, if not incongruous, feature was the small drum brakes cast into the rear discs for the handbrake to operate on.

The steering, as Ferrari traditionalists would expect, was by rack and pinion. Because of the rearward weight bias -- 44/56 -- there was no need for any power assist.

Again, here is an example of Ferrari's evolutionary, rather than revolutionary, advancement.

DICK ELLIS
M.S.I.A.

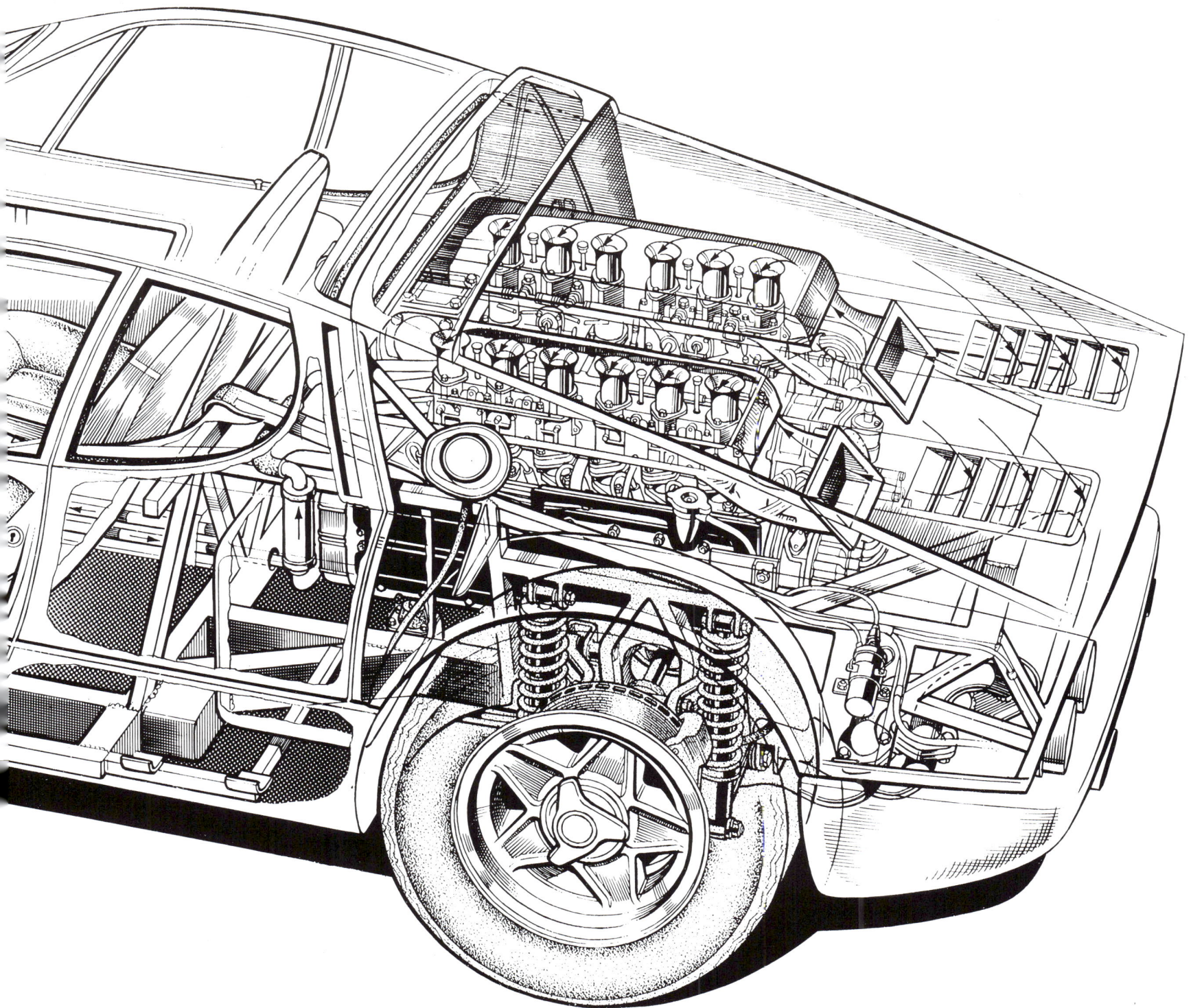

The 365GT4/BB x-ray reveals the chassis and suspension detail, and the unusual air-flow through the engine cover vents to the carburetors.(Gerald Roush Colln)

365GT4/BB – Bodywork

Clothing this marvelous mechanical mélange was another traditional Ferrari trademark -- a Pininfarina body. Looking back in time it seems as if Ferraris have always had Pininfarina bodies, but that wasn't always the case. The earliest Ferraris were usually clad by Carrozzeria Touring, famous for Alfa Romeo designs and the Superleggera (super-light) method of construction, although the Ferrari 166, in its heyday, sported many different body styles by companies such as Zagato, Stabilimenti Farina (not to be confused with Pininfarina), Bertone, Ghia, Allemano, and Vignale to name the better known ones. Even in the mid-seventies-'70s, Ferrari flirted briefly with Bertone, who designed the Dino 246GT's successor, the 308GT4.

Below and Right: These Pininfarina sketches show some of the designs considered for the BB. Whilst none of them look exactly like the production car there are various styling elements that appeared on the final version. (Pininfarina)

These studio shots feature the prototype of the 365GT4BB as it was unveiled at the 1971 Turin show. The side profile shows the Pininfarina concept of continuous evolution. The BB, despite the switch to mid-engine specification, looks like a chopped and stretched Daytona, so many of the styling elements of the BB's front engined predecessor are still evident. (Pininfarina)

The Ferrari/Pininfarina collaboration began in 1952 with the design of a neat, uncluttered convertible based on the 212 Inter chassis. Since then nearly every classic Ferrari you can think of has been a Pininfarina design -- the 250SWB, 250 Lusso, 250 California Spyder, 250LM, 275GTB, 365GTB/4 Daytona, Dino 246, Testarossa, F40 and Enzo. Wow!

Although the production Berlinetta Boxer didn't appear until 1973, the genesis of the design went back five years, to 1968. At the Turin show in October of that year Pininfarina unveiled the Prototipo P6 -- a one-off design for a mid-engined Berlinetta (although the prototype didn't actually have an engine at all!). In this prototype can be seen certain styling elements that were repeated on the BB. For example, the basic side elevation view above bumper level is almost identical to the BB. The line of the nose, side window shape, Kamm-effect tail and also the head-on view are all mirrored in the BB.

A long, close look at photographs of the Berlinetta Boxer will be far more informative than any description that I can give, but it may be of benefit to point out just one or two of the more interesting and perhaps unusual styling elements.

An easy-to-miss feature is the roof height air deflector mounted just aft of the rear window. This served to smooth the airflow off the roof and also to force air down into the carburetor air intakes. - It also looked a bit racy!

Although the headlights looked to be streamlined-in, beneath large, flat Perspex covers they were, in fact, of the pop-up type. These large exposed lights were, not headlights, but very large direction indicator lamps. Auxiliary spot-lights were mounted in the grille.

At first glance, there are no obvious door handles, but a closer examination reveals a small lever mounted at the base of the window frame and painted semi-gloss black to blend in.

Moving to the rear of the car we see a triple theme, in as much as the rear lights are in sets of three, and so are the exhausts. No doubt the use of six exhaust pipes was more for effect than necessity.

The Berlinetta Boxer made its world debut at the 1971 Turin Motor Show. Chuck Jordan, who at that time was head of design at General Motors, was at the launch of the Boxer. Years later he recalled that moment and explained the significance of the Berlinetta Boxer's design;

"To me the thing that sets a Pininfarina design apart is its timelessness," said Jordan. "Now, you have to understand that every coachbuilder tries to create timeless designs. That's a given. The difference is in how Pininfarina succeeds.

"The Boxer is a good example. I remember being at the Turin Show in 1971 the night before it opened, when the bright red Boxer prototype was pushed down the aisle to its featured spot on the Pininfarina stand. The excitement of that first look will never dull in my mind.

"The proportions were the first thing that got my attention. A lot of that, of course, had to do with the basic architecture of a mid-engine layout. But the shape Pininfarina developed over the architecture -- that was magic -- the fast-sloping windshield, the smooth rounded forms -- the sheer grace of the car. The Boxer combined the aggressiveness of the Daytona with the voluptuousness of the Dino and the 275GTB. That's a difficult balance for a designer to achieve, but Pininfarina did it.

"When you look back today and remember that the Boxer was the replacement for the Daytona, it kind of boggles the mind. It's hard to imagine two cars that could be more different and still look like Ferraris. Beyond the proportions, there was the stance. The Boxer seemed wider, lower and more glued to the ground. The biggest difference though was at the back of the car. The louvers, buttresses and those giant carburetor covers told you at a glance that this was where the engine was. They signaled a change.

Ferrari F1 driver Niki Lauda waits to test drive the new BB (G Roush Colln)

"The relationship of the body to the wheels reinforced the message. The Boxer had a long front overhang and a very short rear overhang; just the opposite of the Daytona, and the cab was moved far forward. In the Daytona the cab was where it had always been in Ferrari road cars: as far back as possible. The difference could not have been more pronounced.

"And yet the very fact that the Daytona and the Boxer still clearly had that Ferrari 'look' speaks well of Pininfarina's sense of continuity and history. Pininfarina Ferraris have always looked like Ferraris; they've always been true to the heritage. I can't think of a single relationship between a carmaker and a coachbuilder that's resulted in such a rich and consistent heritage of good design.

"Of course, a beautiful shape is only half the story. To achieve total greatness a car has to do what the design promises and vice versa. It can't just sit there and look pretty.

"The Boxer succeeded on that level as well. I owned one for years and it was an ongoing pleasure. The driving position was just right for me; I could drive for hours without tiring. One of the reasons was that the visibility forward and to the sides was so good. A lot of mid-engined exotics don't give you that; you feel as though you're sitting in the middle of a mailbox. The Boxer wasn't that way. Visibility to the rear was limited and long trips were a little difficult because the luggage area was so small, but the pleasure and satisfaction of driving the car more than made up for its shortcomings. The only part of the Boxer that didn't wear well with me was the rear view. It was a little abrupt, a little cut off. The more subtle and graceful forms that characterized the rest of the car didn't quite carry over to the rear.

"I think it's interesting that we're looking back at the Boxer now. It proves the timelessness of the Pininfarina design.

"You might recall that the Boxer came out around the same time as the Lamborghini Countach and the Lotus Esprit, two outstanding designs that were considered bigger 'breakthroughs' at the time. Everyone was talking about the wedge look in those days. That was supposed to be the coming thing.

"Well, the wedge look came, and went. And as spectacular as those designs were they look a little dated now, but the Boxer doesn't. The Boxer remained fresh. The Boxer endured.

"Enzo Ferrari once said, 'the first time you see a Pininfarina design it seems insignificant. A year later you begin to appreciate them, and then they become more and more beautiful as time goes by.' Except for the first part of that statement (I don't think any Pininfarina design is insignificant) I think he hit it on the head.

"There will always be new Ferraris, but as long as they are being designed by Pininfarina, there will never be a Ferrari that ever truly grows old."

In the Berlinetta Boxer's case it is probably a good thing that Pininfarina's Ferraris "never truly grow old," as it was to be another two years before the production BB was available. In the meantime Ferrari test driver, Giorgio Enrico, had been driving the BB thousands of miles, and the engine characteristics and handling were being refined.

The interior also followed the traditional-but-evolved theme. The slightly bucket-shaped leather seats with strip inserts, the gated gearlever and thin-rimmed steering wheel were already well known to Ferrari owners. The dashboard, though, was updated. Out went the oval dash of the Daytona/Dino to be replaced by a rectangular dash with four black-faced Veglia instruments set with orange figures. In the center were two small dials for the oil pressure and water temperature, with a larger dial set on each side of these two. One large dial was the speedometer, and the other was the 10,000 rpm tachometer, red-lined at 7,700 rpm.

The heating and secondary lighting switches were on the center console next to the gearlever, and the headlight, dimmer, washer and wiper controls were column mounted. The sun visor was a novel, if not complicated, arrangement. Instead of the normal flip-down visor, there was a roller blind mounted in the headlining that could be pulled down as necessary and was held in place with a small suction cup. Release the suction cup and the blind retracted itself back into the headlining.

So although the BB was a new model for Ferrari it still followed Ferrari's well practiced 'gradual development' theory.

365GT4/BB – An Owners View

by Steve Biagini

Service. I have my service performed by an authorized Ferrari dealer, so I can't share any "do-it-yourself" stories. However here are my impressions:

The mechanicals are very robust. My car is 29 years old, and I have owned it for five years but no engine and/or transaxle work has ever been needed other than normal servicing.

365GT4/BBs are reputed to have weak transaxles, but it is my understanding that improvements were made during the production run. My car, being a 1976 model, is one of the last 365s produced and has had the benefit of some upgrades to the transaxle materials.

Another common misconception is that the Weber carburetors need constant adjustment and synchronizing. Once set up properly shortly after my purchase, they have needed no adjustments in my subsequent years of ownership.

I have an occasional backfire upon closing the throttle in higher gears. I haven't yet traced the problem. It is most likely an obscure exhaust leak or something inside the carburetors such as throttle plate/bore alignment.

Performance. I have owned both a BB512i and my current 365GT4/BB, so I have some basis for comparing the two.

The BB512i has significantly more mid-range power due to its higher torque output. However, I believe that the 365GT4/BB has more peak horsepower, as claimed by the factory. To obtain the full power of the 365 requires the engine to be revved up to near its limit, however. There is a lot of additional power produced north of 6,000 rpm and the engine loves to rev up to its redline. The lower midrange torque of the 365GT4/BB is also offset to some degree by its lower gearing (3.75 final drive vs. 3.21). Given the peakier nature of its engine, the 365 is more difficult to launch from a standing start but its performance above 4,000 rpm is substantial.

The 365GT4/BB is probably 100 or 200 pounds lighter than the 512, but when cornering, the 512's wider rear tires negate the weight difference. The mass of the engine in the back can definitely be felt in cornering and it is not as confidence inspiring in these situations as modern cars, such as the F355.

Enjoyment. I would describe the enjoyment factors in three categories: aesthetics, performance and "experience."

From the aesthetics perspective, I admire the sheer physical beauty of the design, from its long, sloping front bonnet to its flying buttresses on the rear deck. The car is delightful to view from various angles and is devoid of so many of the aerodynamic devices that litter modern cars. I prefer the uncluttered lines of the 365 Berlinetta Boxer than those of the later 512s. Even though the front chin spoiler, NACA ducts and wider rear wheels of the 512s provide real performance benefits, in my opinion they detract from the raw simplicity and beauty of the original design.

The acceleration performance is still good by today's standards, but of course it has been eclipsed substantially by the march of progress seen in many of today's performance cars. You will be outclassed by many of these cars, but there is still enough power to provide real driving enjoyment. The Boxers are primarily GT cars and love an open road with long sweeping bends. They are not quite as happy in tight twisty bits with their narrow (by today's standards) tires.

This brings me to what I feel is the most important category: the driving experience. It begins with the delightful process of firing up the engine. The procedure for a cold engine is as follows:

Twist the ignition key to the first position. You will hear the clicking of the fuel pumps as they start delivering fuel to the carburetors. After approximately 15-20 seconds, pump the accelerator pedal to the floor four or five times, squirting lots of fuel into the intakes. Then, while holding the accelerator pedal about a third of the way down, twist the ignition key to the start position. You will hear a deep, exciting, exploding bark as the engine comes to life, accompanied by significant quantities of smoke out the exhaust tips, as the oil that has been resting in the cylinders is burnt. If the ambient temperature is cold and the car has not been driven for a while, the engine may die, necessitating a repeat of the above-described procedure. Once started, the rpms should be kept at 2,000 until the smoke clears, usually in about two or three minutes.

Out on the open road, at low to mid-throttle, the moaning and slurping sound of the Webers is the dominant sensation. The gear change is typical period Ferrari, a bit notchy but still positive and satisfying. When the throttle is opened wide, the result is a massive roar and a seamless delivery of power. The smooth power delivery is deceptive as a glance at the speedometer usually reveals speeds greater than expected. The sound of the engine when extended is exciting and is similar to the sounds emanating from Jody Scheckter's and Gilles Villeneuve's Formula One flat-12s as recorded on the "Ferrari Exhaust Notes" CD.

To summarize, driving my 365GT4/BB is a religious experience, full of sensual inputs that are impossible to achieve in most cars, my F355 included. Even though its ultimate performance has been exceeded by modern cars, its driving experience has not.

Steve's 365GT4/BB – 18745

365GT4/BB – Press Reaction

The motoring press reacted strongly to the new Ferrari. The specification alone was enough to ensure that any red-blooded journalist would be excited about the new Boxer. But it should be remembered that the press reaction was just that -- a reaction to what the car looked like and the written specification. The idea of a journalist being loaned a new Ferrari to road test in those days was just not considered. After all, by 1973 Ferrari only built 1772 cars, and the exposure from racing produced enough publicity for Ferrari.

Occasionally, a motoring magazine arranged to borrow a car from an owner or the importer, and then the proper impressions and true reactions could be gauged. One of the first publications to test the 365GT4/BB was the Australian magazine Wheels in its September 1974 edition. Its conclusion was: "You could drive the Boxer at five-tenths of its capabilities and still be king of the road, but run it out and you know that you are experiencing something whose dynamics are unbeatable and simply beyond the reach of other cars...Of course it is a self-indulgent car but it is also a masterpiece."

The British magazine Motor managed to get its hands on one for the Oct. 25, 1975 issue. The magazine was impressed by the price, pointing out that for the same money one could buy 14 Minis, or 3.5 Jaguars, or even a couple of Porsche 911s. (Quite why anyone should want two Porsche 911s instead of one Ferrari wasn't explained; and I can't think of one logical reason either!) They also caught on to the fact that Ferrari claimed a top speed of 188 mph when the Italian government had the car homologated at 171 mph.

They weren't quite as impressed as their antipodean cousins: "While the Boxer breaks new ground for Ferrari, it is no trendsetter in the idiom of the 246GT or other Ferrari classics like the 275GTB/4, arguably the greatest of them all. Its performance isn't mind-bending or perhaps even quite as brutish as the Daytona's, although it is sufficient to place it firmly in the supercar class. The handling wouldn't compare with, say, the smaller, nimbler 246GT, but it is still pretty impressive for a car of this size and weight. The brake fade was less acceptable. Over less excusable, more niggling details like the inefficient air-conditioning and the lack of luggage space we mustn't dwell too long. Merely remember it is a Ferrari and that alone explains why some of those 50-60 Britons each parted with £17,487."

On the other side of the water, Road & Track published its Berlinetta Boxer feature in June 1975. Because the BB wasn't 'federalized' (great word isn't it? In other words the BB didn't conform to the U.S. regulations) it had to wait until a BB was imported privately. It was reported that Ferrari's attitude was along the lines that if the Americans legislated against cars like the BB then they didn't deserve to have them anyway. The R&T test car was suffering from a slipping clutch, but it still recorded 0-

Parece ser que las personas que ostentan las mismas iniciales para el nombre y el apellido gozan o gozarán de notoriedad, éxito en la vida y que, en pocas palabras, han nacido bajo una disposición particularmente benigna de los astros. Los primeros ejemplos que se nos ocurren son los de C.C., Claudia Cardinale y B.B. como Brigitte Bardot y... ¡el Berlinetta Boxer de Ferrari! Este vehículo ultra-sofisticado, presentado como prototipo por vez primera en Turin en 1971, constituyendo así la "respuesta" del Commendatore al Miura de Lamborghini, está destinado sin duda alguna a dejar una huella inolvidable en la historia del automovilismo deportivo. Según alguien, será también el último auténtico Ferrari a disposición del público. Una vez más, tenemos que dar las gracias a nuestro buen amigo André Barras, prestigioso jugador de golf y aficionado del automovilismo deportivo que siempre tiene en su garaje el último Ferrari, por haber puesto amablemente a nuestra disposición su personal B.B. para este ensayo.

FERRARI 365 GT4/BB

60 mph in 7.2 secs, and 0-100 in 14.8 seconds, with a claimed top speed of 175 mph. That's not a bad performance considering they were changing gears at 7.000 instead of 7,700 rpm. The magazine was impressed with the handling and summed up the BB as having few equals.'

Car and Driver reviewed the Berlinetta Boxer in its January 1976 issue and in its usual inimitable style. The magazine's five-page article was almost exclusively concerned with canvassing Safeway shoppers for their opinion on how much they thought the $50,000 supercar cost.

In its November 1976 issue, Car and Driver decided to treat the Berlinetta Boxer a bit more seriously and tested a Coco Chinetti 'Americanized' (another great word!) version. The smogged, catalyzed (can I say that?) BB knocked out a 0-60 time of 6.1 seconds, 0-100 in 14.1 seconds and a projected top speed of about 176 mph. Making it at that time the fastest street legal production machine ever sold in the United States.

365GT4/BB – Contemporary Competitors

Exactly what the BB's competitors were depends on your point of view. But for the sake of this book, let's make performance the main criteria, and pick out those cars capable of at least 150 mph. To show that there's no bias, we'll take them in alphabetical order.

Aston Martin V8 Vantage -- The small, English concern Aston Martin seems to have been continually in and out of financial problems yet still built, and continues to build, desirable high- performance cars. The Vantage, by virtue of being front-engined, was beginning to look a little out of place technically, but it could still perform. Aston's own 5.3-liter V-8 was topped off by a quartet of twin-choke Weber carburetors and pushed out an estimated 350-375 bhp, although Aston Martin itself offered no output figures. Although basically a 2+2, the Vantage still takes less than six seconds to go from 0-60, and has a top speed up near 170 mph. In some ways it would be fairer to compare the 2+2 with the Ferrari Daytona, as an Aston enthusiast would say that the Vantage is a true GT, whereas the BB is a sports car. Nevertheless, for some the Aston was a viable alternative to the Boxer.

The Aston Martin looked great, and a 5.3l V-8 made sure that there was plenty of performance. (neillb@brucephoto.co.uk)

1974 De Tomaso Pantera
Italian styling + American engine = best of both worlds? (neillb@brucephoto.co.uk)

De Tomaso Pantera -- Alejandro de Tomaso, an Argentinean race driver, immigrated to Italy in 1955 and in 1959 started to build cars. It wasn't long before a small production line was set up and things began to look up with the launch of the mid-engined Pantera in 1971. De Tomaso hooked up with Ford, and a deal was struck whereby the Italian-built car would have the American company's 5.7-liter V-8 engine fitted. Ford also agreed to offer the car through its American dealer network with de Tomaso looking after the rest of the world. The result was a car with Italian looks, a modern mid-engine layout, reliable and easy to service American parts and a particularly attractive price tag. The snobbish Italian aficionados looked down on its American heritage, but thousands of enthusiasts found that 0-60 in less than six seconds and 150+ mph performance figures more than outweighed the stigma of the Ford engine. The general consensus seemed to be that the handling was the equal of any of the other supercars, but the build quality left something to be desired.

Iso Grifo -- This one just about makes the cut although production ended in 1974. This was another Italiano-American hybrid, but this time with a Chevrolet V-8 and the engine in the front. Depending on the state of tune of the V-8, the Iso was a six-second machine with a genuine 170 mph top speed. Although attractively styled by the talented Giorgio Giugiaro, the Iso was already eight years old when the BB appeared and wasn't considered by many potential buyers as a real alternative to the Ferrari.

1972 Lambo Miura P400SV
Almost futuristic; the Miura had a side-mounted V12 and speed to match the looks.
(neillb@brucephoto.co.uk)

Lamborghini Miura -- Oh yes, the old antagonist, Lamborghini set out to be a thorn in Ferrari's side, and succeeded to some extent, especially with the Miura. Here was a dynamic, eye-catching car that was exotic not just to look at but also on paper. Even before Ferrari launched the Daytona, Lamborghini had the mid-engined Miura in production. And it wasn't just any-old mid-engined car. It didn't even have an American engine. No, it had Lamborghini's own 4-liter V-12 mounted sideways in a state-of-the-art chassis. Here was a car that could do 170+ mph and looked like it too. No wonder the BB needed a 188 mph top speed.

Also available at the same time was the Lamborghini Jarama 400GTS, a front engined V-12 capable of 150+ mph. Although the Lamborghinis were certainly capable of matching the Ferraris on performance, most commentators felt that the Ferrari had the better overall package.

Maserati -- This long-established firm had a number of 150+ mph cars in production in 1973. Some were just about at the end of their lives, and others just starting. The Mexico, Ghibli and Indy were all extremely quick cars, but the Boxer's main competitor had to be the Bora. The Bora was a mid-engined machine powered by Maserati's famous twin-cam V-8 in 4.7-liter form, with a body designed by Giugiaro's new Ital Design consultancy. It looked the part. Its 160+ mph top speed, and excellent road manners made it a very attractive proposition. Regrettably, a lack of finance meant that it was never the success that it deserved to be.

Monteverdi -- Swiss industrialist Peter Monteverdi introduced his 375 Series in 1967. The chassis was a Monteverdi design; using a 7.2-liter Chrysler V-8 and a Frua-designed body. The top-of-the-range model was powered by the famous 426 ci Hemi with 450 bhp. This was enough to give the Monteverdi supercar performance and a top speed of more than 150 mph. Despite using a mass produced engine, the still almost totally hand-built car was very expensive and by 1977 had ceased production.

These then were the 365GT4/BB's competitors when it was in production. Of course, during the next few years, companies such as Lamborghini and Porsche would bring out even stronger contenders. Ferrari couldn't afford to stand still.

BB512 – Background

The new BB512 looks very attractive in all red with white interior. (Gerald Roush Colln)

The BB512 shows just a few exterior changes. Notice the spot-lights set behind the grille; the small nose bib; and NACA duct in the lower body (Pininfarina)

At first glance, it would seem that Ferrari replaced the 4.4-liter Berlinetta Boxer with the 5-liter car in order to increase the performance and keep its place as the manufacturer of the world's No. 1 sportscar. Certainly, the appearance in 1974 of the amazing Lamborghini Countach and in 1975 of the rapid and reliable Porsche 911 Turbo meant that Ferrari was up against some serious competition. But further investigation reveals that increasing performance wasn't the main criteria.

As the so-called 'developed nations' became more ecology conscious, the automobile was picked out as being one of the main offenders and destroyers of the world as we know it. The fuel crisis of the early 1970s also made the automobile a prime target of the legislators. The Americans were at the forefront in the battle against the auto, with most of the European nations not too far behind them. Although Ferrari still wasn't too concerned with selling to the United States, it still had to be able to sell its cars on the home continent.

The main problem facing Ferrari, and other motor manufacturers, was how to make each engine more efficient and cleaner -- which is a good thing. In those early days, most manufacturers who were interested in maintaining their performance image took the same route as Ferrari -- they increased the size of their engines. This allowed them to add anti-smog devices and catalytic converters and still keep the performance levels high. Today, manufacturers use far more high-tech methods.

Thus was born the BB512. With the 512, Ferrari changed its type designation method. With the earlier car, the designation indicated the displacement in cubic centimeters of an individual cylinder. Ferrari now went to its contemporary racing car method where the first of the three digits indicated the total engine capacity to the nearest liter and the next two digits indicated the number of cylinders. Hence the designation BB512 -- a five-liter, 12-cylinder engine. The extra engine displacement was obtained by opening the bore out 1 mm to 82 mm and lengthening the stroke by 7 mm to 78 mm, for a total engine displacement of 4942 cc.

With alterations also to the compression ratio and the camshaft timing, the new 5-liter was more tractable than the 365. Some people reveled in the 365's caminess and high rpm limit, but Ferrari's intention with the BB512 was to maintain the performance but improve the drivability. Accordingly, the new car was surprisingly listed as less powerful than the 4.4, with a claimed 360 bhp at 6800 rpm, although the torque was up at 331 ft/lb at 4300 rpm.

But again this enters a contentious area, as these figures are supposed to have been attained by the prototype engine, but they are repeated in the official sales brochure. Interestingly, an official Ferrari publication printed in 1985 lists the BB512 at 340 bhp, and this now seems to be accepted as the more accurate of the two figures presented.

To cope with the increased torque, the clutch was changed from the single plate to an 8.5-inch twin plate, and the final drive ratio was changed to offset the lower rpm limit. Top speed was still a genuine 176 mph, even though the speed through the gears was slightly slower.

Another major change was the switch to a dry-sump engine lubrication arrangement, to counteract any oil-surge problems that might be caused by the 512's higher cornering ability.

The increased cornering potential came from the switch to 225/70VR15 Michelin XWXs on 9-inch wheels at the rear, instead of the 215/70VR15s on 7.5-inch wheels that the 365 used front and rear. The wider rear tires naturally resulted in a wider rear track -- in this case an additional 1.7 inches which, in turn, resulted in wider rear bodywork. In fact, the whole engine cover was subtly redesigned with three sets of louvers inset between, and to each side, of the carb covers. At the back of the car, the six rear lights were reduced to just four, and the exhausts were reduced to two per side. Ferrari changed the appearance at the other end as well, with the addition of a spoiler below the grille to eliminate any tendency to lift at high speed and also to improve stability. The eagle-eyed also spotted the new NACA ducts let into the sills, just ahead of the rear wheels.

So, overall the new 512 retained the look of the original Berlinetta Boxer, but there were numerous detail differences, as well as the major mechanical changes. Again this emphasized Ferrari's policy of change through evolution not revolution.

Fabulous studio photo shows a view few owners will ever see (Ferrari)

Driver's eye view. Speedometer shows 330kph and rev counter is red-lined at 7000rpm (Ferrari)

The rear view shows the change to a double rather than triple theme, and the extra ventilation vents required for the 5-litre engine (Ferrari)

BB512 –
Press Reaction

Any new Ferrari is warmly welcomed by the world's motoring press. On its own, the Ferrari tradition of producing fast and exciting cars is enough to inspire most writers to dig out the thesaurus and look for those obscure and meaningful adjectives. But the real test is the road test.

One of the first to try the BB512 was *Autosport* Technical Editor John Bolster. In the July 9th 1977 issue he called the 512 an "unjustifiable and illogical extravagance," which perhaps was meant as a compliment. Why was it illogical? "How can one justify the ownership of a car that will carry two people and not much luggage at a speed that will give every copper in the country apoplexy?" Well, that's fair enough, but the next comments were probably more telling, "Soon I was driving happily away in what is probably the fastest practical road-going car in the world. By 'practical' I mean that it will crawl in traffic all day without the suspicion of a misfire or the slightest rise in temperature. Meanwhile, the occupants can keep equally cool with refrigerated air-conditioning and the built-in stereo equipment is ready to while away a dreary hour." In fact, Bolster seemed to hardly find anything wrong with the BB512, and he summed up by saying, "For sheer engineering excellence, it is supreme." That's high praise indeed.

Mel Nichols, in *CAR* magazine in January 1977 was also full of praise for the BB512. He reveled in its handling, "There was barely a moment among those hours when I wasn't amazed by the new grip of the car and by how much of its performance could be employed." Dynamically, he found the 512 to be superior to its predecessor the 365 "without losing anything by way of civility, this is a tauter, tidier car." And the engine? "It's as easy to manage as ever...It just sends you gliding along...It's a sustained thrust that goes on and on and on...Such is the smoothness and magnificence of this 5.0-liter engine." Nichols' only criticism seemed to be the lack of luggage space, but even so, he concluded by saying that the BB512 was "a car that, provided you can spare £23,868, will give you the sort of pleasure that seems beyond price."

In 1981, *CAR* magazine went back to the Boxer, and writer Steve Cropley found out that he had a problem. "It is a singular thing, being required to produce the fifth or sixth in a nine-year line of stories about the Ferrari Berlinetta Boxer, when each of the previous authors has been profoundly moved by the car. . . . It is the disquieted scribbler that finds that the die of his story is cast before he begins it; that two-thirds of his adjectival ammunition has been removed before the skirmish can even begin." And so Mr. Cropley adds to the already high pile of adulation, "No longer is it the best and fastest road Ferrari. . . . Now, it is a resounding answer to that most difficult of questions: which single new car would you buy if money were no object? For us it's the Ferrari Boxer. It is, by a very large margin, the most desirable new car available in Britain." Any complaints? Luggage space again, and that was about it.

It was genuinely difficult to find a critical review, except for our old friends at Car and Driver, which said "The Boxer is a genuine silly car, an absolutely enormous Lotus Esprit. The interior is cramped and airless, the driving position is classic Italian lie-down-I-want-to-talk-to-you, and the controls are all placed somewhere that your hands and feet won't go without surgery. Even if you could buy one for ten grand, it wouldn't be any fun to drive." (*Car and Driver* June 1981)

I'll leave you to make up your own mind about those comments. My opinion wouldn't look too good in print!

176.2 mph
FERRARI BB512

"*Well, we really don't have to go into this that much. It feels like what it is and what it's supposed to feel like: a Ferrari. It's just as businesslike as it can be and rather noisy relative to some of the other cars that will go reasonably fast. But when the Boxer decides to really get up and go, it goes. What was its speed—284 kilometers? It just feels tight and race-bred all the way through.*"—Phil Hill

"*This is really a fabulous car. It makes a tremendous noise, which may be nice or not so nice, depending on your preference. It surely must be tiring on a long trip. The suspension is quite firm, and it is beautifully stable at high speeds.*"—Paul Frère

0–60 mph, sec	5.1
0–100	12.2
1/4 mile, sec @ mph	13.5 @ 100.5
Top speed	176.2

46   ROAD & TRACK

BB512 –
Contemporary Competitors

As we did with the 365GT4/BB, we'll use the admittedly arbitrary classification that a competitor of the BB512 was any production automobile capable of 150+ mph and again to avoid the accusation of bias they'll be listed in alphabetical order. So here we go.

Aston Martin V-8 'Vantage' -- In 1977, Aston Martin breathed on the venerable V-8 and introduced the 'Vantage.' Aston's lusty 5.3-liter engine featured a redesigned top-end with larger (48 mm) carburetors, larger inlet valves, new valve timing and modified exhaust system. The body style was still basically that of the V-8 but with a few subtle styling changes, such as a blanked-off radiator grille, front air dam and a trunk-lid mounted spoiler. At the launch, it was claimed, at least by Aston Martin, to be the world's fastest accelerating production car with a 0-60 mph time of 5.3 seconds and a top speed of 170 mph. But in reality the 'Vantage' was still more akin to the Ferrari Daytona than the Boxer. It offered the possibility of squeezing four people in and still having space for some luggage. It was a true Grand Tourer. (Look for it again in the BB512i section).

1978 Aston Martin V8 Vantage
Modified engine, modified bodywork and it still looks great.
(Neill Bruce: neillb@brucephoto.co.uk)

BMW M1 -- When asked to name all the BB512's competitors, this is one that most observers would miss. During its short production run (1978-81), it was overlooked by most enthusiasts, and yet it was a genuine supercar, capable of 0-60 mph in 5.5 seconds and a top speed of 162 mph. It was powered by BMW's famous six-cylinder 3.5-liter engine, mounted lengthways behind the driver as a true mid-engined supercar! Although a BMW, it was, in actual fact, designed and developed by Lamborghini, with bodywork styled by Giorgetto Giugiaro's Ital Design. It was also planned to be built by Lamborghini as well, but its financial problems meant that although the chassis and bodies continued to be made in Italy, the final construction was by Baur in Germany. With Italian design flair and German engineering, it couldn't fail to be great.

That it was originally built to be a competition car only adds to its desirability. Unlike the Berlinetta Boxer, which became a competition car after going into production, the M1 was designed from the outset to take on Porsche and the like in the Group 4 class of the World Sports Car Championship. To qualify, BMW had to build at least 400 cars, and then it was allowed to modify a number of them for racing purposes. The factory soon lost interest in the project as its thoughts turned to Formula One engines, but many private teams competed with M1s at Le Mans and other events. Le Mans enthusiasts will no doubt remember Hans Stuck's electrifying performance in the torrential rain of Le Mans 1980, when he ran as high as second overall. BMW's M1 was, and still is, to some extent, a vastly under-rated sportscar.

1979-80 BMW M1
The forgotten supercar? (Neill Bruce: neillb@brucephoto.co.uk)

De Tomaso Pantera GTS -- With a 5.7-liter Ford V-8, mounted amidships, what the Pantera lacked in 'culture' it more than made up for in power. Since it began production in 1971, it had a number of facelifts along the way and has been referred to, perhaps unkindly, as 'the poor man's Ferrari.' In 1973, De Tomaso unveiled the GTS, a 175 mph contender. This was for the European market only. Americans, due to their anti-smog regulations, only had a poor imitation of the GTS.

Lamborghini Countach -- But of course the BB's main contender was the Lamborghini Countach. As the successor to the astounding Miura, it had already been in production two years when the BB512 was released, so at least Ferrari knew what it was up against. It was just as startling as its predecessor. Marcello Gandini's styling alone ensured that all who saw it were impressed. (If 'Back to the Future' had been made about 15 years earlier, then Michael J. Fox would probably have piloted a Countach instead of a DeLorean). Throughout the years, it has grown, almost as if on steroids, but originally the LP400 Countach had a 4-liter V-12 mounted lengthways behind the driver but with the gearbox in front for better weight distribution and suspension by wishbones and coil springs. It was a genuine 175 mph car, although some considered it to be not quite as civilized as the BB512, but then others considered it to be the ultimate.

Maserati Bora -- Maserati's first and only mid-engined road car was a practical, if rather plain-looking, design. It used Maserati's 4.7-liter four-cam V-8 to push it up to about 160 mph and had a 0-60 mph time of about 6.5 seconds. It had all the right numbers and specifications as well as Maserati's racing heritage, but the low production volume of about 60-65 cars per year and Maserati's financial woes probably worked against it.

1981 Lambo Countach LP400S
If you thought the Miura was futuristic! The Countach was jaw-dropping.
(Neill Bruce: neillb@brucephoto.co.uk)

Porsche 911 Turbo -- Introduced in 1976, the Porsche 911 Turbo lifted the German company into the 150+ mph club. In many ways it was, and still is, a strange breed. The 911 engine isn't in the front. It's not even in the middle. Believe it or not it actually hangs out behind the rear axle! And a flat six engine-- what kind of engine is that for a supercar? And yet here it is, at the time of writing, the biggest selling 150 mph+ car of all time.

The Turbo was launched in 1976 with a 3.0-liter engine, but in 1978 the engine was enlarged to 3.3 liters, and an inter-cooler was added to the turbo-charger system. A 0-60 mph time in the five-second bracket and 150+ mph top speed ensured its longevity, so much so that an updated Turbo is still in production at the time of writing.

1980 Porsche 911 Turbo 3.3
For many the reliable and affordable alternative to the Boxer. (Neill Bruce: neillb@brucephoto.co.uk)

Interestingly, the now sadly demised *Supercar & Classics* magazine did a group-test of the BB512 and its main competitors. Lined up with the Boxer were the BMW M1, Lamborghini Countach, Maserati Bora and the De Tomaso Pantera. All five cars were driven around the highways and byways of Scotland in an attempt to find the best. Mind you, *S&C* by its own admission found it difficult to be objective: "To arrange these five cars in some objective order of merit would be an impertinence based on too many crass assumptions. . . . There's no escaping the old heart-before-head cliché here: you know, it's not what they do but the way they do it." *S&C* continued, "Much as I lusted after the Countach in small doses, I'd sooner have the more civilized Boxer, not least because it is a Ferrari. Rationale denied, I just adore Ferraris. . . . The Boxer doesn't handle as sharply as the Countach, feeling a mite ponderous in fact, but it goes hard, looks a million dollars and has a lovely (air-conditioned) cabin that's as comfortable as it is airy and elegant." But just wait for the sting in the tail, "Yes, I'd have the Ferrari, but be in no doubt that the BMW M1 is a better car...the M1 was the best supercar of its decade."

In a way, that sums up not only the BB512 but Ferraris in general. Other cars may appeal to the intellect, but Ferraris appeal to the heart.

BB512i – Background

Entitled "Now, The Ferrari 512BBi," the press release for the 1981 Motorfair introduced British motoring enthusiasts to the latest update of the Berlinetta Boxer. The press release continued, "The Ferrari 512BBi, flagship of the Ferrari range, now has fuel injection giving it quieter and smoother performance. This classic Pininfarina-styled body, built by Scarlietti [sic], is a pure 2-seater GT of utter luxury.

"Powered by its 4,942 cc flat-12 cylinder engine, the new twin Bosch K-Jetronic fuel injection systems enable it to smoothly surge forward to cover the standing kilometer in 25.1 seconds and 0-400 meters in 14.2 seconds. It produces 330 bhp at 5,700 rpm with a maximum 6,600 rpm.

"The fuel injection has improved fuel consumption figures in official tests - simulated urban driving 12.9 mpg; constant speed driving at 90 kph (56 mph) 25 mpg; constant speed driving at 120 kph (75mph) 19.5 mpg. Not that fuel costs themselves are likely to worry the owner of a Ferrari 512BBi which has a fuel tank capacity of 26.5 gallons giving the car a touring range of around 500 miles without needing to stop to refuel.

The front grille is now shorter so that the spot-lights are exposed, and indicator lights are set into the body just above the spot-lights. Compare this right hand drive version which has the single body colour with the more usual two-tone paint scheme. (NB Colln.)

Down at the trotting track the new injection Boxer shows little change, although the rear valance was tidied up. (Pininfarina)

These drawings from the BB512i handbook show the lubrication system and the cambelt layout. (Ferrari)

1. Inlet camshaft drive gear for cylinders 1-2-3-4-5-6

2. Exhaust camshaft drive gear for cylinders 1-2-3-4-5-6

3. Driving gears

4. Idlers

5. Inlet camshaft drive gear for cylinders 7-8-9-10-11-12

6. Exhaust camshaft drive gear for cylinders 7-8-9-10-11-12

7. Driving dowels

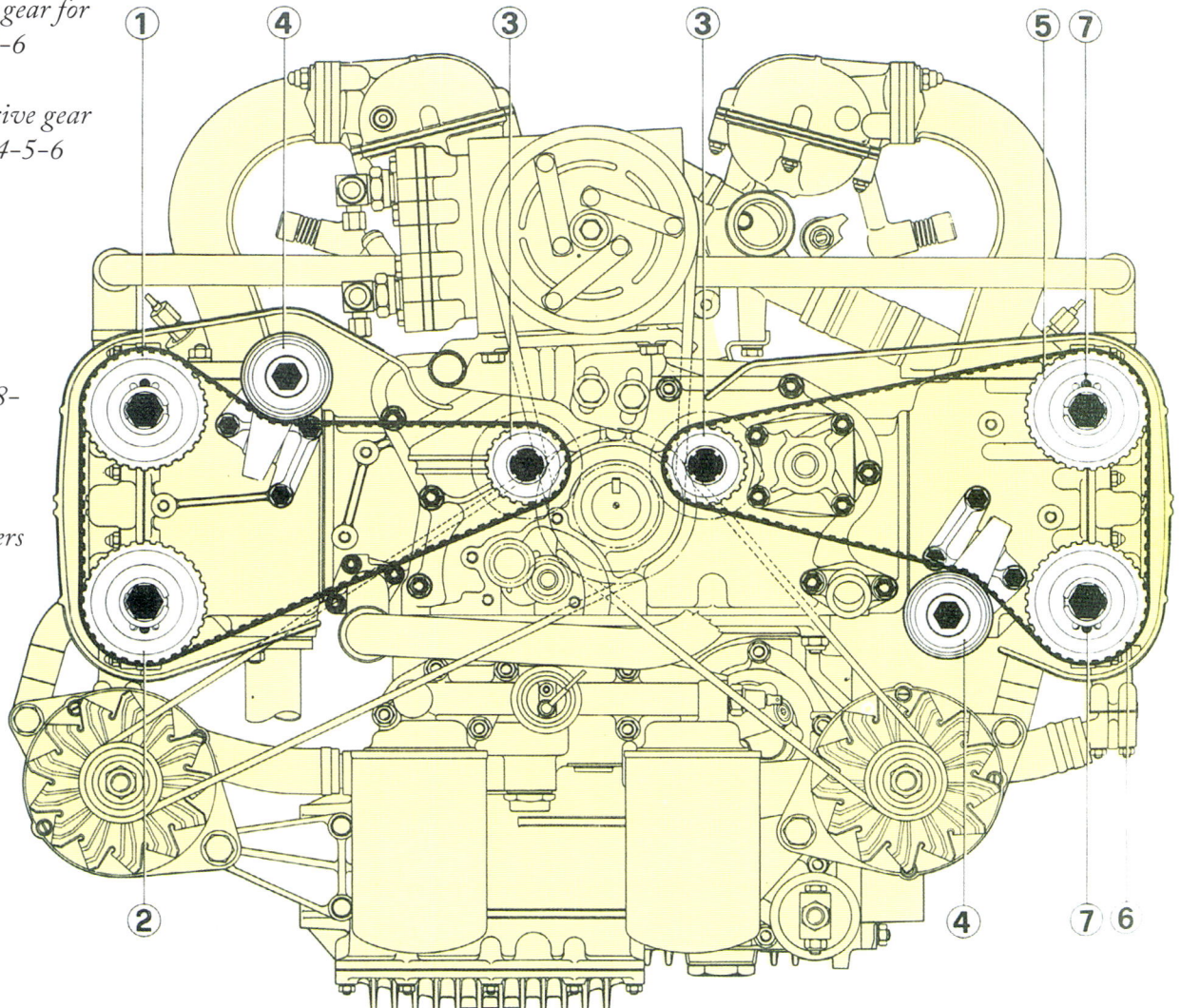

"As one would expect, there is not a list of optional extras - electric windows, air-conditioning, tinted glass, radio/stereo are all fitted as standard. The usual option exercised by customers is that of colour but Ferrari red over black is still the most popular.

"The first right-hand drive 512BBi (sic) is expected to arrive in the UK in about four months' time and the price including car tax and VAT is £39,991 "

Yet the strangest thing is that when Ferrari published the showroom brochure for the BB512i, it wasn't, as one might have expected, the new fuel injection system that was featured but, as the brochure put it, "Control of Corrosion at Ferrari." The brochure continued: "It is certainly easier to define corrosion than to combat it....From the scientific viewpoint, it is possible to consider the breakdown of chemical, physical and mechanical properties of a metallic material due to the interaction with ambient conditions; in other words, the natural spontaneous return of the metal to its origins. Corrosion, therefore, is the exact opposite to extractive metallurgy." So, now you know! Anyway, the brochure went on to explain that Ferrari had gone to enormous lengths to try to combat the onset of "ferric deterioration" (sic).

The brochure also mentioned some other interesting facts, probably the least known being that, "When driving, the human body emits humidity through the skin." To combat this, Ferrari developed special seats of which it was immensely proud: "If the seats are not absorbent, the accumulated vapor gives an unpleasant humid effect. The Zegna cloth can absorb humidity equal to 30% of its weight without negative effects, and also emit heat proportionally to the humidity absorbed and maintain the body dry."

Still no mention of the new fuel injection system! So why did Ferrari switch to fuel injection? Again, it was primarily in order to meet the more-stringent emission regulations rather than for any performance advantage. In fact, the introduction of the BB512i resulted in yet another reduction in power output for the Boxer engine. The power output was now down to 340 bhp at 6,000 rpm with a 6,600 rpm redline.

The new fuel injection system in detail (Ferrari)

A. Mixture Control Unit

B. Warm-up regulator

C. Injection valve

D. Air valve

E. Auxiliary Starting assembly

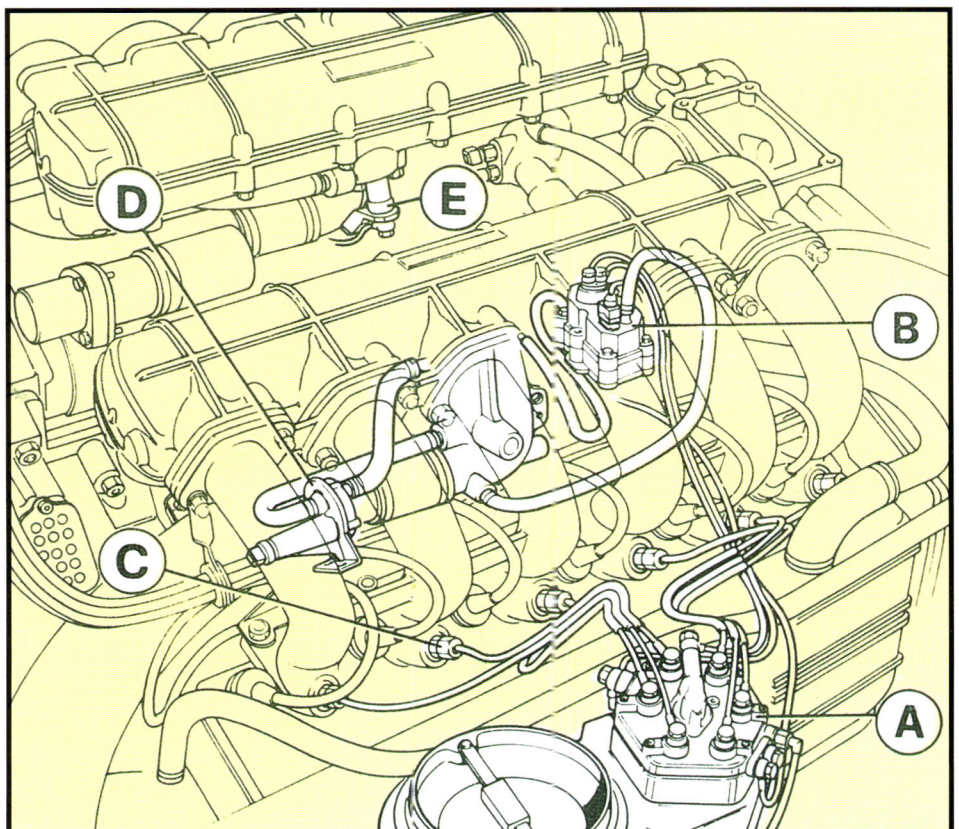

The flat-12 engine was still the same basic unit as the BB512 except for a radical alteration to the camshaft timing and the substitution of fuel-injection for carburetors. The BB512i used two fuel pumps to push the fuel to the injection system via twin filters. The system consisted of a mixture control unit which injected fuel into the cylinders in direct proportion to the volume of air that was metered.

Ignition was a Marelli AEC 104B-660 electronic Dinoplex system with a rev limiter to avoid unintentional damage due to accidental over-revving. The distributor and coil were also by Marelli. In simple terms the ignition system used a 'magic box' to read inputs from the intake manifold and the fly wheel (engine speed) and others that identified tdc (top-dead-center), all of which were then co-related so that a spark could be sent to each plug at exactly the right moment.

Another crucial change centered on the tires, which were now Michelin TRXs. The fitting of these lower-profile tires meant that new wheels were also needed, but more importantly, that the suspension was also modified. The wheels were not radically changed or altered, but adjusted to obtain the best performance from the new rubber.

Externally, the BB512i was barely changed from its predecessor. The front grille was shortened slightly, revealing the previously hidden fog lights, and turn indicators were incorporated into the leading edge of the front bumper. At the rear, there was a new panel below the bumper which had reversing lights set into it.

USA Legal Boxers
(or federalization as it is sometimes called)

There are currently no federalization companies for Boxers. Since January 1990, it has been illegal to import any Ferrari for which there is not a comparable USA-specification model. This is federal law.

The only exception to this law is automobiles that are 25 years old or older. This is calculated to the month, so in July 2007 the cut-off is cars manufactured before July 1982. These cars do not require modification to meet DOT/EPA standards. This means that no Ferrari less than 25 years old for which there was not a comparable USA version produced can be imported and legalized.

Richard F. Merritt, who has owned and written about Ferraris, is the recommended contact at the U.S. Department of Transportation. His contact details are listed below. But he will only repeat what is stated above. If the car is already in the United States, he can determine whether it's here legally or whether it might be subject to seizure because it is in the country illegally.

There are procedures to follow to get an illegal gray market car legalized if it can be proven that the car was in the United States prior to January 1990 and if the current owner was not the importer. It is called the innocent third party rule. But it requires patience and money. This information was correct at the time of printing, but for more information please check the following:

Dick Merritt
Voice: 202-366-5300
Fax: 202-366-1024
Department of Transportation
Office of Vehicle Safety (NEF 32)
Washington, D.C. 20590

Web sites:

http://www.nhtsa.dot.gov/cars.rules/import/

**http://www.cbp.gov/linkhandler/cgov/toolbox/publications/travel/
importexportcar.ctt/importingacar.doc**

(Author's note: Thanks to Gerald Roush of the Ferrari Market Letter for providing the above information.)

BB512i –
Press Reaction

CAR magazine's Steve Cropley got his hands on a BB512i in time for its May 1982 issue, and using the byline BB King, (one of the world's great blues guitarists) said, "In Ferrari's beautiful BB512i, the 'world's best engine' has been made better, an already-brilliant chassis has been hugely improved, and the car is now crafted to standards which seem fully 50 percent higher." Is it any wonder that Cropley loved the new Boxer? Of course not! CAR recorded performance figures of 0-60 mph in 5.8 seconds and 0-100 mph in 13.4 seconds. But the magazine was disappointed about the top speed. "Perhaps only top speed suffers -- because of the designer's greater

Ian Dawson

BB KING!

In Ferrari's beautiful BB512i, the 'world's best engine' has been made better, an already-brilliant chassis has been hugely improved, and the car is now crafted to standards which seem fully 50percent higher. Is it any wonder that Steve Cropley loved the new Boxer?

SPD 657X

concentration these days on low-end power. Whereas our carburetor 512 ran to 170 mph after a lengthy wind-up, we could not get the latest red car past 160 mph true - - in fact we'd have to say that these days, Boxers are 'sluggish beyond 160 mph.'" The magazine did at least estimate that the BB had a theoretical top speed of 174 mph at 6,500 rpm. It did, though, like the legendary exhaust sound, "The noise, that rasp that becomes a howl, then a wail, then a scream, is enough to make your scalp prickle.....this 5.0-liter at 6,500 rpm is quite the finest exhaust sound I know."

MotorSport magazine also got its hands on the same BB512i that CAR tested. MotorSport's tester started off with negatives: "It has a gear change which only a totally biased Ferrari enthusiast could describe as anything better than 'acceptable' ("it's better than acceptable" - author); "It's seats, while comfortable, are only adequate in terms of hip-hugging support; there is no room for any luggage of consequence... but, in the context of high performance motoring, they are probably not very relevant...Having said that, the car is a sheer, total joy to anybody who loves serious motoring." MotorSport's conclusion? "A purely objective assessment of the Ferrari BB512i would obviously come to the inescapable conclusion that it is one of the world's great high performance cars...I would defy none but the totally cynical to be less than enthralled with this, the fastest road-going Ferrari currently available."

BB512i –
Contemporary Competitors

With the introduction of the BB512i Ferrari upped the ante. Not surprisingly the competition reacted by upgrading some old favourites or even bringing out new models. The following were serious contenders for the Ferrari buyer's money.

Aston Martin V-8 'Vantage' -- Aston Martin continued to push forward with the specification of the top-of-the-range 'Vantage.' This genuine, 170+ mph coupe was still a prodigious performer, although the traditional front engine/rear wheel drive layout was viewed by some as outdated for an '80s supercar. Then again, others reveled in its traditional values.

De Tomaso Pantera -- This one seemed to run and run. It had more facelifts than a Hollywood actress. In 1981, a U.S. certified car was available that enabled American enthusiasts to obtain Panteras with 300/350 legal horsepower and thus regain lost performance.

Lamborghini Countach -- Not to be outdone by the BB512i, Lamborghini launched the LP500S Countach in 1982. Engine displacement was lifted from 4 liters to 4.7, although claimed power output remained static at 375 bhp. The Countach was claimed to have a slightly higher maximum speed than the Ferrari and was certainly more outrageous looking, but the BB usually received the accolade of being the better car overall. *Autocar* magazine in October 1982 recorded a 0-60 mph time of 5.6 seconds and 0-100 in 12.9. That's no slouch!

Lotus Esprit Turbo -- Not sure if this one should really belong here, but it just about made the 150 mph mark, and I like it! The power unit was a 2.2-liter turbocharged four-cylinder that delivered 210 bhp. Although the power output was way down compared to that of the Berlinetta Boxer, the Esprit only had to move about two-thirds of the weight, so performance was still good. Not only was it quick, it looked good as well.

1982 Lotus Esprit Turbo
Italian styling and British engineering looked pretty good. It also went well.
(Neill Bruce: neillb@brucephoto.co.uk)

Maserati Khamsin -- With a 4.9 liter V-8 producing some 320 bhp, the Khamsin was good for up to 160 mph depending on transmission and engine tune. When the Khamsin first went into production in 1974, the company was owned by Citroen, and the Khamsin incorporated some of the French concern's well-known quirky engineering. Some drivers found the power-assisted steering and brakes took some getting used to, but the handling was well liked. It was never a popular car with just more than 400 examples being built in its eight-year production run.

Porsche Turbo Carrera -- Introduced in 1975, the 911 Turbo was serious opposition for the Boxer because it was competitive on acceleration if not on top speed. Its main virtues seemed to be price and reliability. Porsche owners gleefully reminded Boxer owners that they'd been able to buy a car for the wife with the change and that they didn't have to stop every 3,000 miles to tighten the camshaft belts. Ferrari owners retorted that 'real sports cars' had the engine in the middle, not hanging out the back like Volkswagens!

Porsche 928S -- As if to confuse matters, Porsche also brought the 928 into the picture. If it hadn't been for the conservative styling (and a roof), this 4-litre V-8, front-engined/rear-wheel-drive machine could have been the Cobra of the '80s. As it was, the single camshaft per cylinder, Bosch fuel injected engine was only lightly stressed being designed to meet the stringent U.S. emission laws rather than for outright power. Nevertheless, the 928 could still perform and gave Porsche another contender in the 150+ mph club.

1984 Porsche 928 S2
An acquired taste? Probably, but a GT in the grand tradition. (Neill Bruce: neillb@brucephoto.co.uk)

One Man's Passion –

The Story of Don Steenkamp and his 365GT4/BB

Ever since I can remember, I have fantasized about owning a 12-cylinder Ferrari but never thought it would become a reality. My first car was a MG TC. After that I progressed to an XK140 Jaguar, a Morgan and a couple of Jaguar E-Types, one of which was prepared during a period of nine years to being possibly the best E-Type roadster in the world. The sale of this car helped make the ownership of the ultimate Ferrari -- in my opinion -- a dream come true.

My right-hand drive 365GT4/BB was originally ordered on May 2, 1973, by Maranello Concessionaires Ltd., as "Order No. 663 - Portman". The car, serial number 17793, was subsequently delivered to the United Kingdom on April 26, 1974. As the vehicle was first registered in South Africa in 1976, it is presumed it was shipped out in late 1975 or early 1976. I purchased the car at the beginning of 1987 at a time when prices were still regarded as being reasonable.

The condition of 17793 at the time of purchase left a great deal to be desired. The overall impression was one of neglect, yet mechanically she seemed sound as the engine pulled strongly and had good oil pressure. However, the rest of the Berlinetta Boxer, with the exception of the engine and gearbox, needed urgent attention. The interior looked shabby. Front suspension bushes were making odd sounds due to rust developing in them. The shocks were worn, and the tires were worn. But worst of all, the dreaded rust cancer had started to come through the outer sills as well as left and right pillar linings.

Initially, I intended to restore the Boxer in stages and still enjoy using the car, and during the months proceeding Easter 1987, I decided that the front suspension would be the first to receive my attention. Taking the car up to 260 kmph with worn Michelins, worn Koni shocks and odd-sounding noises did not seem in keeping with being a Ferrari owner! Halfway through that Easter weekend I realized that my initial plan of doing the restoration piecemeal was just not going to work. The more I dismantled, the more convinced I became that I would not be happy with the car until a thorough restoration had been completed.

By July 1987, I had totally stripped the car of every last nut and bolt, including removing the full wiring harness. Purpose-made mobile stands were fabricated and attached to the lower wishbone mounting points on the chassis to enable the body to be moved in and out of my garage and also to facilitate easy spray-painting at a later date.

The next hurdle was to remove all previous paint from every conceivable place, including the interior. By this time I had also removed the G.R.P. (Glass Reinforced Plastic) front bulkhead, together with the G.R.P. floor which is a complete molding with the rear bulkhead. Apart from the rust already mentioned, the bare body shell appeared sound except for some poorly executed panel beating to the offside engine cover -- obviously the legacy of a minor ding sometime. I am not in favour of sandblasting to remove paint, so all the stripping was completed by the application of Nitromors and hours and hours of hand scraping. Between April and November, approximately 1,000 hours were spent on preparing the shell for professional panel-beating/spray-painting. This entailed working every weekday evening from 6 p.m. to 1 a.m., all day Saturday and in many cases most of Sunday as well.

At the time I became more and more convinced that, ideally, the shell should be immersed in a huge bath, in the way that new car bodies are handled. An appointment was made with BMW in Rosslyn, Pretoria, to discuss this possibility. The paint shop supervisor kindly took me through its fully automated e-coating plant and explained the process. Basically, the body shell is fully submerged in a degreasing tank, and then passes to a second tank that has the various resins, paints and preservatives in it which, by way of an electrolytic action, bind themselves to the bare metal.

BMW has sufficient confidence in this process to provide a six-year guarantee against rust. The paint shop supervisor indicated that I should put my request in writing to the technical director, who would decide whether its system could cope with a Boxer body shell. A letter was duly sent off, and within a few weeks came back a reply indicating that my request was to be considered! Within another week, I received a phone call from the German paint expert who wanted to see the Boxer body shell and take some measurements.

An appointment was set up at my home where the gentleman became enthusiastic about e-coating the Boxer and confident that the automated system of hangers could cope with the size of the BB. Then came the shock. I would have to drill a number of holes in various parts of the chassis in order to drain the e-coating once the submerged body was lifted from the tank. I spent many weeks evaluating this and eventually decided that, apart from interfering with the originality of the car, I could even end up weakening certain stress sections and thus decided not to pursue the e-coating route. BMW even went as far as getting its facilities department to draw up an official measurement plan of where the hangers would engage the body shell for tank immersion.

To many persons, 1,000 hours for dismantling a car may seem ludicrous, but it must be stressed the extent to which this was done. At all stages, photographs were taken of sections of the vehicle, detailed notes about various parts were made, drawings were made and importantly, measurements were taken of all shims and spacers for setting up the front and rear suspensions. The wiring harness was carefully marked before removal, all parts were cleaned, and then glass bead blasted, then either painted or plated in white or yellow Cadmium, and then carefully wrapped in plastic and finally boxed. All boxes were numbered and a detailed list made of their contents. At the same time a separate list was compiled detailing all the parts that needed to be replaced.

As I had recently purchased a G.R.P. manufacturing company in partnership with my brother, money was just not available to purchase the spares or attend to the spray painting of the body at that time. It was not until July 1988 that the body shell was taken in for painting. About that time I also contacted the local Ferrari importer to obtain the prices for various spares that were needed. After near heart failure, I faxed Maranello Concessionaires in England to compare prices. I decided to fly to the United Kingdom in October 1988 and purchase the bulk of my requirements. This turned out to be a three-week holiday for my wife and me, touring Devon, Cornwall and south Wales. The cost of the spares and the holiday did not amount to what the locals would charge.

I replaced every single suspension bush and rubber, Koni shock, gas strut (for bonnet and engine cover), header tank, exhaust gaskets and seals, pedal rubbers, door rubbers, plug harnesses, timing belts, water pump kit, clutch, pressure plate, thrust bearing, fly wheel, tires and the front screen.

The complete interior was retrimmed, including the dash. The original suede type vinyl was substituted with imported leather as fitted to the late 365s and the 512 Boxer. As I could not obtain the vinyl strips for the seats (Daytona style), these were made up in red leather, embossed around the holes with a special tool, made up and inserted in a heated press. As the seats are in black, they look superb with red Daytona inserts.

I decided to go for a single colour for the body (red) and not incorporate the black lower body sections, as I prefer the look of a Boxer in one colour.

Originality is certainly important in the overall presentation, and in some cases I went to unbelievable lengths to adhere to originality. For example, the silicone tubing through which the starter cable runs across the engine cannot be bought anywhere. I eventually commissioned a medical supply company in Johannesburg to make up the correct diameter tubing, but the catch was that I had to take 10 meters! The same company also supplied the silicone tubing for the rear bumper harness to run through.

Another example is the aluminum mesh found inside the air vents just behind the rear quarter windows. All the resprayed Boxers I know in South Africa end up with this mesh the same colour as the exterior as there is no access to paint it in the correct black. I decided to remove my old mesh. It can be pulled out via the small plate which has the engine lights attached to it and is pop riveted to the rear bulkhead section behind the air vents. The only problem was that mine were so corroded that they broke whilst being extracted, and I was faced with having to replace them. I was unable to locate the correct pattern aluminum mesh and eventually found a company who set up its machine to match the original pattern, but again I had to purchase a sheet 8 feet by 6 feet.

The accelerator pedal is yet another example of the lengths sometimes necessary to maintain originality. The original pedal had a black nylon covering, but the nylon had worn through to show the metal of the pedal. I completely dismantled the accelerator pedal, which has two sets of roller bearings, and found a supplier to recoat the pedal in black nylon.

Hundreds and hundreds of hours were spent on stripping individual components and spray painting them at home using two pack paints. Each part was stripped back to bare metal and then wiped down using a solution of phosphoric acid and thinners etch primed; rubbed down with 600 water paper and finally painted in satin black. My garage had hundreds of hooks driven into the rafters, from which parts were hung until needed to be fitted to the car.

In many ways, I have over-restored the Boxer, but I was determined that every single component, every nut and bolt, would have the best possible finish so as to preserve the finish for as long as possible. I cannot see the point of spending all the hours on stripping the various components and then taking shortcuts to the finish. Far too often I have seen friends do that and finish up with a car requiring further work a few months later.

The most frustrating part of any restoration is, without doubt, the running around obtaining parts, buying paint, delivering parts for bead blasting, for Cadmium plating, for powder coating and then picking the whole lot up again. I would estimate that for every 100 hours labor, approximately 30 hours were wasted. This aspect of restoration is generally not appreciated by car lovers who have not undertaken restoration themselves.

Approximately 4,000 hours were spent on my Boxer, resulting in a stunning car which drives as new, smells like new and creates unbelievable impact wherever it goes.

The Specials

Unbelievably the BB wasn't fast enough for some people, so it wasn't long before the 'tuners' started showing what they could do. One of the first was a one-time sports car driver, and famous Ferrari modifier, Herr Willy Koenig. As one of Koenig's early brochures stated "Koenig-Ferrari has succeeded with unbeatable taste to make the most fascinating car of the world even more fascinating". Koenig's 'fascinating' creations are now almost legendary, and usually modified to such an extent that Ferrari insisted that if one of their cars was 'Koenigised' then the Prancing Horse badge must be removed.

Koenig offered a number of options for cars such as Mercedes, Jaguar, Lamborghini as well as Ferrari. One could purchase the specially produced high performance parts, or one could have Koenig do the job for you. Koenig would also re-trim the interior to the customer's specification or have his own designers do the work. So the end result was that one could have a standard performing car with Koenig bodywork, or a high performance car with standard bodywork or a combination of the two.

The story is that Willy Koenig bought a 365BB in 1974 for his own use and was disappointed. As an ex-racing driver in cars such as the Ford GT40 and Lola T70 he wanted more performance and so modified the BB primarily for his own use. Participation at various Ferrari events resulted in others hearing of the alterations that had been carried out, and asking Koenig to do the same for them.

Koenig began 'improving' Ferraris with factory parts and products "directly derived or copied from Ferrari racing cars". The obvious modifications were to the bodywork with extended wheel-arches, new air-dam and rear spoiler or rear wing. But Koenig also supplied wider wheels and tyres, uprated shocks and springs, a three plate clutch and high performance exhaust, as well as all the usual engine improvement parts.

The early Koenig cars were not as wild as later cars but the rear wings were still prominent as can be seen in this 1982 photo. (Massini)

Koenig's first BB was mildly modified with a rather uninspiring air-dam and almost crude looking tacked on rear wheel-arch extensions, but Koenig built on this base and eventually offered the carburettor flat-twelve in three different tuning options: the 370bhp version with high performance exhausts; the 400bhp version with high performance exhausts and camshafts, or the 450bhp version with all of the foregoing and special pistons, modified cylinder heads and rejetted carbs. The 450bhp version could reach 60mph from a standing start in just 4.5secs.

And so onto what is probably the ultimate road-going BB, the amazing, the incredible, the unbelievable Koenig Turbo. The aforementioned high-performance modifications were augmented by two Rajay-Albert turbos, two Albert-Wac bypass valves and two intercoolers to produce an incredible 620bhp. The package also included modified suspension, 9inch wide front wheels; 13inch wide rear wheels and up-rated brakes. To finish it off there were new body panels for every section except the roof and the upper front bodywork. The result, according to Koenig, was a tyre ripping 0-60mph time of 3.9secs and a top speed of 206mph: this despite a rear wing the size of a front door! I guess Koenig must also be quite some magician as one of his brochures features a side-on shot of the Koenig Turbo at speed, and yet there's no driver in it. Some trick hey?

The Koenig Boxer looks aggressive from any angle. (Koenig)

The affluent German economy of the '70s/'80s encouraged a number of companies to play around with cars such as the BB, and another who joined in the game was Lorenz & Rankl of Wolfratshausen (try saying that after a few drinks). Their speciality was individually constructed cars, armoured cars and V8 Mercedes-Benz engined Cobra replicas. Where the BB was concerned their efforts were quite modest and usually involved chopping the roof off and adding an electrically powered canvas convertible top. Mind you, this type of alteration is a lot more involved than it might seem at first glance. L & R start by stripping the BB completely of the interior and all the trim - then the chassis is reinforced, and then a most ingenious roll-over bar is fitted. The roll-over bar imparts rigidity to the chassis but it is electrically operated so that it pivots into the horizontal position when the hood is down and stands in the vertical position when the hood is raised. From the doors back there is all new bodywork. The tail is shortened and a new lower rear deck with raised clear perspex plenum chamber covers is fitted. With structural reinforcements in no less than twenty six different points Lorenz claimed that their convertible was actually more rigid than the coupe.

L & R said that their conversion was "Most likely the fastest open sportscar in the world." Certainly one that would blow your wig off, at least!

Lorenz & Rankl flyer for their BB spyder

The German company Zender made a styling kit for the BB. It was more subdued than most featuring a new lower nose panel, redesigned sills, and a very low boundary layer rear wing. [Ch. 24317] (Massini)

Another German company who would swap your hard earned Deutschmarks for a facelift were a Mülheim-Kärlich based outfit called Zender. Their modified BB512i was imaginatively called the Imola 1. Zender's modifications were mainly cosmetic and rather more subtle than some, although the narrow running boards and low rear wing instantly caught one's eye. They would also supply wider wheels and tyres and retrim the interior too, if you so desired.

Another company that chose the turbo route for the BB was the American company BAE of Torrance, California. As this was in late 1980/early 1981 chief engineer and President Bob McClure had to adopt the suck it and see (should that be 'blow it and see'?) technique. At that time turbo-charging was still a bit of a black art, and on top of that McClure also had to contend with designing and fitting a fuel injection system, before the factory made theirs available. Again, twin Rajay turbos were chosen and after numerous problems BAE succeeded in building an engine that produced a claimed 650hp and also passed both the federal and California emission standards. The result was a car that was astonishingly tractable and yet would rev to 8200rpm, and turn the standing ¼mile in 12.5secs at 123mph.

But perhaps the weirdest BB special was that known as the Anliker Ferrari. Whoever it was that designed and built this creation succeeded, that is succeeded in making a Pininfarina design look like a VW based kit-car. The grossly enlarged wheel arches were joined by wide angled running boards; the engine was given a slatted cover that looked like a poor imitation of the Lamborghini Miura's rear window, and a full-width rear wing was mounted on dog-leg shaped supports. The whole thing was finished in a garish red and white colour scheme with white wheels. Yuk!

Apart from the above noted examples there were various other companies that dabbled with the BB. Stateside there were specialists such as Straman and Chinetti who chopped tops off and otherwise changed things about. Over in England Modena Engineering produced a Targa topped BB for one customer and in Europe and Japan various owners carried out modifications, usually to their own designs and with varying degrees of success.

Over in the U.S.A. Straman were also chopping the BB. The Targa modification is less radical than most but still allows the open-air option. (Massini)

Another Straman Targa was this black version.

Open air motoring at 170+mph? Only if you don't wear a toupee! Check out the clear Perspex engine covers. [PS This is 31643] (Massini)

This BB features some unusual body modifications. The nose resembles those used on the 1978 Le Mans cars, but the engine cover treatment is unlike any other BB. Notice also the new sill treatment. (Bluemel)

21513 was photographed at Mugello in 1988. Modifications include widened wheel-arches and a rear spoiler. (Bluemel)

Nigel Builds a Better BB

Dramatic sky/dramatic cars. The Nigel Hudson modified BB (30311) looks little different from standard, only the subtly widened rear wheel arches giving any hint of the impressive performance available. Even the 250GTO owner looks envious! (NB Colln)

Now, before you get the wrong idea, the Germans weren't the only ones working on the BBs. Emblem Sports Cars in Dorset turned out one or two amazing conversions. Design engineer Nigel Hudson, (later with Nigel Mansell Sportscars) had the backing of director John Woodfield in building a couple of BBs. One involved raising the engine to Le Mans spec and the other involved two turbo-chargers.

The Le Mans spec engine was stripped and then reassembled using lightweight Mahle pistons, new bearings, valves and camshafts reprofiled to Nigel's design. The upper engine was adjusted accordingly with particular attention being paid to the carburettor set-up. A competition clutch was fitted and the suspension adjusted to get the best out of the wider than standard Pirelli P7s. But what was probably most outstanding about this particular modification was that apart from the slightly wider rear wheelarches the rest of the bodywork was left as standard! The ultimate 'Q car'?

Your author had the opportunity to ride in and then drive a similar, but later, Nigel Hudson conversion. With the experienced Nigel at the wheel the BB was soon showing a genuine 155mph on the clock and with cornering ability beyond anything that I had experienced before. Nigel very kindly took a friend of mine out in the BB for a drive that he will never ever forget. On climbing out, white faced, he looked at Nigel and asked "Does God know you drive like that?"

When I drove the Hudson BB I was stunned. My previous experience of driving a BB consisted of the owner continually admonishing me "watch the clutch, don't slip the clutch", and yet Nigel's BB with 460bhp didn't elicit a single word. Sure, I stalled it the first time I tried to move off, but still no complaint. The second time I moved it out with a few more revs and no problem. The acceleration was absolutely stunning! Unfortunately I didn't have it long enough to explore the full limits of performance yet I knew that the owner wouldn't have to worry about the clutch on this BB. The term that came to mind was 'bullet-proof'. Absolutely! If I had a BB then I'd ship it straight off to Nigel Hudson.

Regrettably, I didn't have the opportunity to try Nigel's twin-turbo version but I'm assured that with 650hp on tap the performance was adequate! Obviously the engine was completely rebuilt, but with twin Rajay Turbos and twin intercoolers plumbed in to produce the extra oomph. But again, one has to comment on the body restyling which was kept as near standard as possible and not tricked-up just to make it look good. Mind you Emblem could have done that if the customer had asked; they produced a twin turbo 308 that outshone even Koenig's extravagant creations.

The Berlinetta Boxer in Competition 1975–1985

1975

With Ferrari's history, it was inevitable that the Berlinetta Boxer would be seen in competition. That debut came in 1975 at Daytona, where a BB, serial number 18139, was entered, not by Ferrari, but by Luigi Chinetti's North American Racing Team (NART). The factory usually looked after the sports prototypes while entrusting the Grand Tourers to private teams. Foremost among these was NART. The long-time relationship between Enzo Ferrari and Luigi Chinetti usually resulted in NART being the first private team to enter any new Ferrari GT in competition.

In fact, at this point, it would seem that the factory had scant interest in seeing the Boxer race, as this appears to have been purely a private effort. The car was delivered to Chinetti's in November 1974, as a normal street car, and the NART mechanics took it apart and comprehensively rebuilt it for racing.

The first racing BB was NART's highly modified road car (18139). This is Milt Minter in action at Lime Rock. (Bill Oursler photo)

The first step was to remove all non-racing essentials and lighten the car as much as possible. By the time the team had finished, the weight of the Boxer had been cut by a considerable amount, even with a roll-cage and other racing parts added.

An almost entirely new center section was fabricated from aluminum, including the cockpit floor and front and rear bulkheads. Even a new dashboard was built to house the minimum necessary instrumentation, including a 10,000-rpm tachometer. The passenger seat was removed, and a large capacity fuel tank put in its place.

Nearly every part of the original Boxer was either modified or replaced. The brakes and suspension were changed (often using bits from the now redundant 512/712 sports racers that Chinetti owned), wider wheels fitted, new body panels fabricated and fitted with quick-release fasteners for rapid removal and replacement in the event of a race crash. The engine cover was hinged at the roof and opened in the opposite direction to the standard car. The front bodywork had new headlight housings built to replace the standard pop-up units, and both front and rear body pieces were widened to accommodate the racing wheels and tires.

The engine was virtually standard with some carburetor modifications and a fabricated exhaust system being the main changes made to extract a bit more power. The electrical wiring and hydraulic hoses were replaced with competition specification parts and a fire extinguisher system fitted.

Luigi Chinetti entrusted the BBs competition debut to Milt Minter (at the wheel) and Claude Ballot–Lena. (Fred Lewis photo – www.fredlewisphotos.com)

A fabulous photo of Milt Minter hurrying 18139 through Turn 5 at Atlanta. (NOTE: many BB/ LM references incorrectly show this event as 6/7/1975 and car as #5) (Fred Lewis photo – www. fredlewisphotos.com)

Another great shot of 18139. This time as the brake lights come on and the nose dips. (Fred Lewis photo –www.fredlewisphotos.com)

Less than two months after its arrival as a standard road car, 18139 made its competition debut on Jan. 22, 1975, at Daytona for the annual 24-hour race. The quick turnaround was some achievement for a private team with no factory assistance and limited resources.

Unfortunately, the debut was inauspicious. A hub carrier broke in practice due to the loading caused by the wider tires and the extra stresses of the infamous Daytona banking. The Boxer made the start but retired on the first lap.

But the team was not deterred and just a few weeks later turned out for the Sebring 12 Hours. Despite a multitude of problems, including three lost clutches during practice, a failed alternator and a pit fire during the race, the Boxer finished a credible sixth overall.

This car competed in two more stateside events during 1975, recording a 'did not start' at Road Atlanta in Georgia due to a broken hub carrier again, and a 'did not finish' at Lime Rock in Connecticut.

Interestingly, by the time the car appeared at Lime Rock the factory had produced (and sold to NART) a set of competition camshafts and pistons. Unfortunately, the engine failed during the race due to a broken connecting rod.

Another different Boxer, serial number 18095, almost made its competition debut in 1975 as well. This, again, was a NART project, converted from a road car, but not as radical as the first effort. In fact, the appearance was almost standard, with a quick release fuel filler cap, riveted-on wheel arch extensions and a small rear spoiler being the only visual changes.

Having just been unloaded NARTs competition prepared BB (18095) awaits its racing numbers. The only apparent changes from standard are the enlarged wheel arches and the 'Monza' filler cap. (NB Colln photo)

Mechanical changes revolved around those necessitated by the safety regulations, plus a deeper oil pan and the removal of the standard exhaust system. This is the car that turned up for the Le Mans 24 Hours.

In fact, NART had an interesting mixed bag of Ferraris entered for Le Mans 1975. Apart from the Boxer, NART also had a 308GT4; a Daytona rebodied by Michelotti and a normal Group 1V competition Daytona.

In qualifying, 18095 was the second-fastest of the NART entries with a time of 4 minutes and 30 seconds, which would have put it 40th on the grid out of 55 starters. Regrettably, neither the drivers nor the spectators had the chance to see how it would perform as the whole team was withdrawn before the race started. Chinetti had a disagreement with the race organizers over the 308GT4. The organizers insisted that it be placed in Group V with the outright sports racing cars such as the Gulf GR8 and Porsche 908/2s. Chinetti wanted it placed in the GT class (Group 1V) with the Porsche 911s and the Daytonas. The organizers stuck to their decision, so just hours before the race Chinetti withdrew all four cars. The first Boxer to run at Le Mans wasn't the first to race at Le Mans. That would have to wait until 1977.

1977

As mentioned earlier, the factory had shown scant interest in racing the Boxers apart from supplying the few engine parts to NART in 1975, and when the NART racing program was suspended there was no one to race the Boxers in 1976.

In the meantime, the original race-prepared Boxer had passed from Chinetti to Howard O'Flynn of Banker's Discount in New York. Although owned by O'Flynn, the car was entered by NART for the 1977 Le Mans epic. Francois Migault and Lucien Guitteny were the two drivers and they qualified with a time of 4 minutes and 27.9 seconds, although the fastest race lap was even better at 4 minutes and 23.8 seconds, or more than six seconds faster than the almost standard Boxer of 1975. A top speed of 166 mph was recorded along the Mulsanne.

Things went fairly well during the race except for an oil leak and minor problems with the clutch and gearbox. From the 10th hour on, the Boxer started picking up places regularly and from 48th on the starting grid finished a creditable 16th overall and 5th in the IMSA class.

NART's Boxer (18139) sweeps through the Esses on its way to 16th place at Le Mans 1977. (Keith Bluemel photo)

1978

After just a single competition appearance in 1977, things started looking better in 1978. NART continued to compete with the original Boxer, and following a visit to Maranello by Howard O'Flynn after Le Mans 1977, the factory promised a competition 5-liter engine in time for the Daytona 24 Hours. As it turned out, the competition engine that arrived was an almost standard 512 unit, but this was fitted in time to run at Daytona. Drivers Migault and Guitteny were joined for this event by Gregg Young, and the Boxer qualified a respectable 17th. After numerous electrical problems, it finished 22nd overall, although after six hours it had been running eighth.

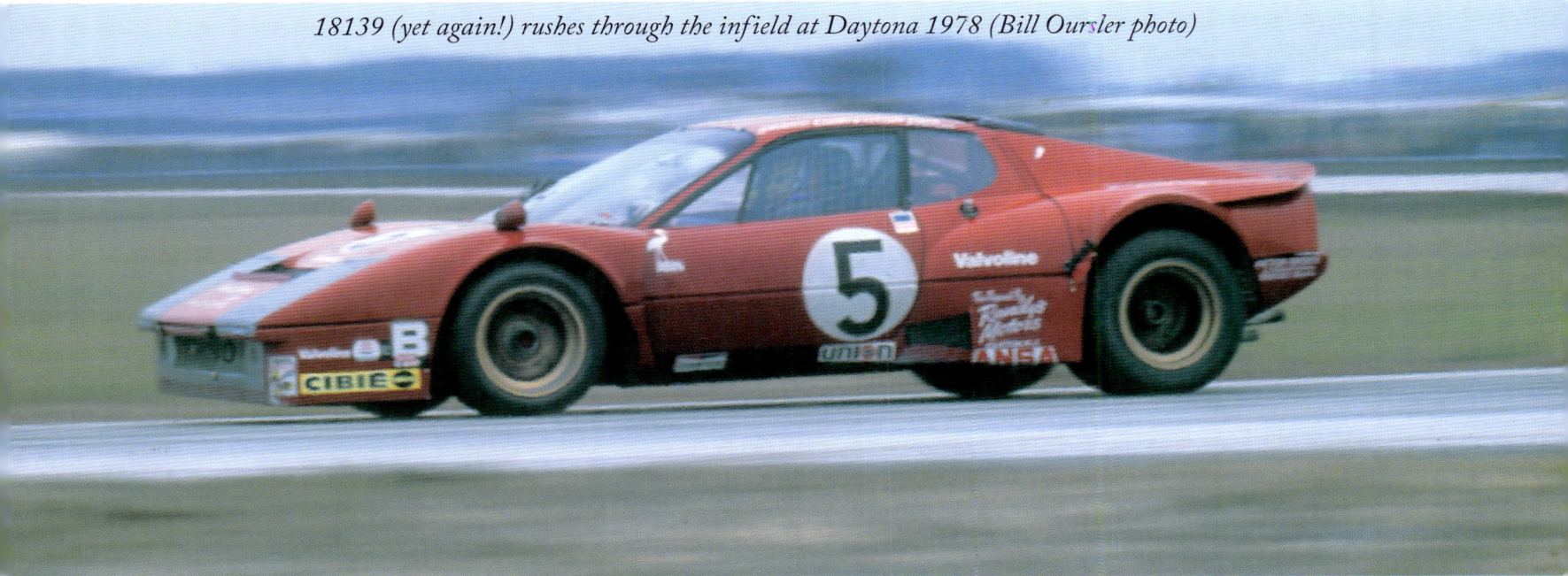

18139 (yet again!) rushes through the infield at Daytona 1978 (Bill Oursler photo)

Francois Migault hurries 18139 to 21st place finish at Road Atlanta 1978. Notice the width of the rear wheel arches and tyres. (Bill Oursler photo)

The Boxer next turned out at Road Atlanta, but the Boxer was an endurance racer and not ideally suited to this 40-lap sprint. Poor Francois Migault probably spent most of his time looking in the rear-view mirror as he was lapped five times on his way to a 21st-place finish.

The next competition appearance for O'Flynn's 'old faithful' was at Le Mans where it was joined by four other Boxers. Yes, from just the single car of previous years competition Boxers were sprouting up all over the place. The main reason for this was that the Ferrari factory had decided that perhaps there was potential in the Boxer after all. So for Le Mans 1978 the factory built three competition BBs. Two of these, serial numbers 24127 and 24129 were entered by the French Ferrari importer Charles Pozzi, and the third, serial number 24131, was entered by NART.

NARTs BB (18139) at Le Mans 1978 (Keith Bluemel photo)

In early 1978, a modified Boxer had been seen at Ferrari's Fiorano test track with Italian driver Elio de Angelis at the wheel. It would appear that Ferrari was beginning to take the Boxer a bit more seriously, and even the well-known Formula One engineer Mauro Forghieri spent some time working on improvements to the suspension and the aerodynamics. The most obvious change involved a large wing that hung out over the rear of the car and was rumored to have started life as the front wing of the contemporary 312 T3 Grand Prix Ferrari. At the front there was an optional removable piece of bodywork that recalled the nose treatment of the 1963 330 LMBs, having an oval grille with spotlights mounted on either side. NART ran the long nose bodywork, while Pozzi ran one car with it and the other without.

The Thomson sponsored BB (24129) looked stunning in red and white. This photo shows the optional extended aerodynamic nose-piece (with rather un-aerodynamic spotlights bolted on (John Allen)

According to Ferrari, the 5-liter engine featured modified pistons, racing camshafts and carburetors. The power output was said to be about 400 bhp. Mounted above the engine were two large air-scoops that opened just in front of the roof-mounted spoiler and sucked air into the carburetors.

The use of aluminum and fiberglass for the bodywork, along with other weight saving measures, reduced the total weight from approximately 1,400 kilograms of the standard car to a race ready average of 1,210 kilograms.

The fifth Boxer, serial number 22715, was entered by the Belgian driver 'Beurlys' (Jean Blaton) and had been entirely built at Garage Francorchamps under the direction of Jacques Swaters. Jean Pierre Uri had designed a large rear wing mounted on the engine cover and a distinctive 'snowplow' air dam below the nose. This was the heaviest of the five Boxers, weighing in at 1,333 kilograms.

Meanwhile, development continued on the O'Flynn car, which was now even lighter, with new front and rear bodywork. In fact, the rear panel looked like a giant cheese grater with no less than 79 holes drilled in it. This attention to detail obviously worked as it was the lightest Boxer at 1,166 kilograms. What it didn't have though was some of the factory modifications such as tuned exhaust headers and larger gear cases.

In practice, the fastest Boxer was the Pozzi car of Claude Ballot-Lena and Jean Louis Lafosse with a lap in 4 minutes and 7.1 seconds, but even our old friend, with Migault and Guitteny sharing the driving, had trimmed its time to 4 minutes and 15.9 seconds. Interestingly, the O'Flynn car at 188.275 mph was fastest on the Mulsanne

Ecurie Francorchamps self-built competition Boxer (22715) featured a large snow-plough air-dam and F1 derived rear wing (John Allen)

Straight although the slowest qualifier of the five. It was 1.6 seconds quicker in the race than during practice, so maybe the drivers weren't trying that hard in qualifying, doing just enough to make sure that they started.

There again, the race doesn't always go to the swift, and guess who came out best of the Boxers after 24 hours? Yes, despite dropping to 50th place at the end of the third hour, thanks to a 49-minute stop to repair the gearbox, the oldest of the Boxers climbed back through the field to finish 16th overall, and third in class, at 4 o'clock on Sunday afternoon.

Of the other Boxers, the Belgian car retired first after nearly three hours due to transmission problems, and the factory-built cars all succumbed to various ailments, although the Pozzi car of Jean Claude Andruet/Spartaco Dini had been running 11th just before Sunday lunch.

Although the results might not have been as good as hoped for, the Boxers showed that they had potential as endurance racers. They didn't have the outright speed to match the turbo-charged Porsche 935s that also ran in their class, but during a full race distance they could be competitive.

A Boxer appeared in competition once more in 1978 at Watkins Glen for the Six Hours race. The car, serial number 18139, had minimal preparation after Le Mans, and yet still managed 11th. This was to be the last racing appearance of 'old faithful,' at least until 1984, but more of that later.

18139, in its last race, is about to lap some old BMW. Here at the Glen it finished 11th. (NB Colln photo)

In the meantime, interesting developments were afoot. Ferrari was actually getting seriously interested in developing the Boxer for racing. Photographs published in the motoring press in winter of 1978 showed a rebodied Boxer being tested at a snow-cleared Fiorano. Details were a bit sketchy, but the photos showed an aerodynamic looking body that had an obviously extended tail and a raised rear wing.

Ferrari had called in Pininfarina to design the new bodywork, and this had been developed in their wind tunnel at Grugliasco, Turin. The end result was a Boxer that was 15.6 inches longer than the 1978 car and 5.9 inches wider. Front wheels were 1 inch wider at 10 inches, and the rear wheels were 2 inches wider at 13 inches. All this upped the weight by some 30 kilograms. In recognition of Pininfarina's assistance, its name was featured prominently on the windscreen sun-strip.

Although the new car weighed more, the addition of Lucas mechanical fuel injection upped the power output to about 475 bhp to 480 bhp. The fuel feed was modified and was now fed by two Turolla pumps. The gearbox had also been strengthened and the cooling system enlarged. The suspension had been modified to take advantage of the new Michelin TR-Xs. These tires, mounted on special rims, were expected to improve the handling, especially going into the corners and accelerating out of them.

Major changes were also made to the brakes, which now had new discs, calipers and dual pumps. The new 512BB/LM was expected to go faster and stop quicker. According to reports, the car had been timed at 212.66 mph when tested at Fiat's Nardo test track in southern Italy. Considering that the Boxer didn't quite make 200 mph even at Le Mans, it would seem that this claim was suspect.

The development and production of the new Boxer was carried out at Ferrari's Assistenza Clienti department under the direction of Giuseppe Girotti and Gaetano Florini. Much of the track testing was entrusted to veteran Ferrari driver Enrico Giorgio.

According to the factory, nine of these cars were built in total, with three of them due to turn up at Daytona for the 1979 24 Hours.

1979

In January, the three Boxers arrived by transport plane at Kennedy Airport, two for Pozzi, serial numbers 26681 and 26685, and the other for the NART team, serial number 26683. Ferrari was obviously interested in the Boxers doing well because it sent Giuseppe Girotti from the Assistenza Tecnica department with the cars to help set them up.

Journalist and race driver Patrick Bedard was one of the drivers entered to share the NART car at Daytona. His account of events at the 24 Hours is reproduced here with the kind permission of *Cavallino* magazine.

NART's new BB/LM (26683) showing off its Pininfarina designed streamlined bodywork on the Daytona banking. Later all three BB/LMs would be retired due to tyre problems caused by the forces generated by the banked part of the track. (Bill Oursler photo)

Ready and waiting – the Pozzi BB/LMs (26681 and 26685) are prepared for the 1979 Daytona 24Hrs. (Daytona International Speedway photo)

"One night early in January I met Luigi Chinetti Jr. for dinner. We had both seen photos in the European racing papers of the new 512BB his father was bringing over for Daytona. It was so unexpectedly beautiful that we had to get together like a couple of schoolgirls and talk about it.

But we didn't really have enough info to fuel a proper fantasy. Yes, it had done 336 kph (208 mph) in testing, thanks to much work in the Pininfarina wind tunnel; and it had a fuel-injected five-liter engine; and the tires were Michelin radials. Moreover, preparation was being done by the factory. But somehow, all this background stuff wasn't truly convertible into exactly how neat it was going to be.

Pininfarina's super-smooth new bodywork transformed the look of the Boxer. Their involvement is acknowledged on the sunscreen. (26681) (Daytona International Speedway photo)

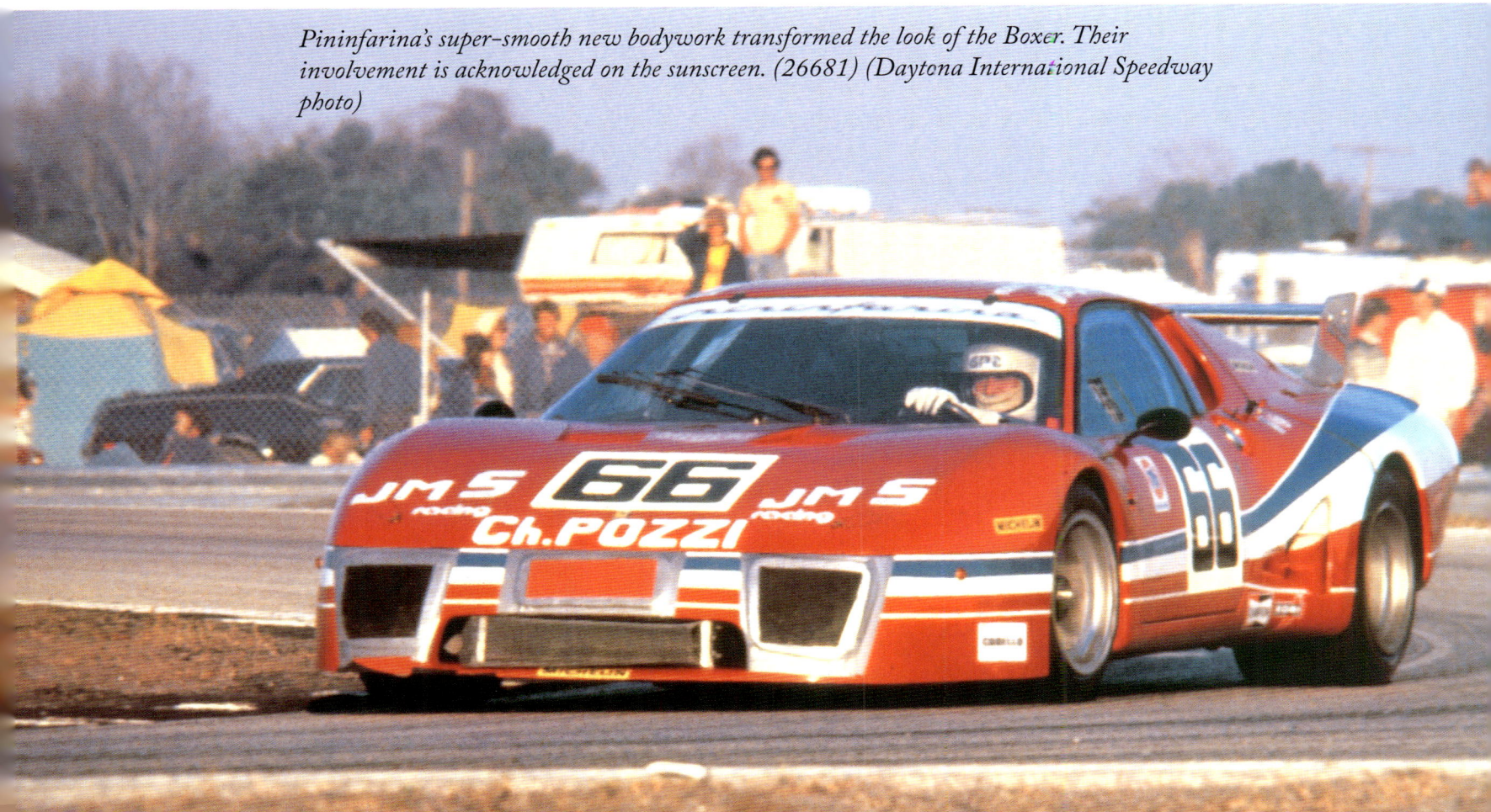

'I hope you'll be able to see the horse,' he said during one of the contemplative lulls in the conversation. 'When you're driving and you can see the horse, you feel really good.'

A few weeks later we met again, this time at Kennedy Airport, as the official welcoming party for the three 512BBs, one of which was entered by NART and the other two by Ch. Pozzi, the Ferrari importer for France. It was a terrible day, a cold rain slanting down from the east, but that didn't stop us from climbing up on the steel unloading platform where we could, after months of anticipation, actually touch the cars.

They were still strapped to pallets, their fenders cavernous over the narrow shipping wheels. Perhaps because of this, the bodywork appeared even longer and wider than in the photos. The headlights were faired in, the body had very few scoops and vents, and the rear wing was tiny by today's standards. They were very deliberate cars; streamliners; speedway bullets. That familiar cold feeling came into my stomach again, just as it always does when I confront a racing car that promises so much it borders on a threat. What if I can't keep up with it?

Somebody had the driver's door open. I could hear talk about the roll cage, how it was neatly hidden behind a layer of upholstery. As a driver, I knew I should be concerned about the protective systems. Certainly today's professionals would check that out. But when I stuck my head into the cockpit, my eyes immediately began searching for the horse. It wasn't on the console, and it wasn't on the dash. What a bummer. Then I spotted it, right in the middle of the steering wheel, as black and as challenging as that region beyond human experience. Later I remembered that I never did look for the roll cage.

It wasn't until Daytona that I actually saw the BB all together, sitting at design height on proper wheels and tires. It seemed much too beautiful to be risked on the track.

Usually it was Giuseppe Girotti, Assistenza Tecnica straight from Modena, who drove the racer from the garage area to the pits and back again for practice - the drivers walk, affecting great nonchalance. But I wasn't very good at this part; I kept turning back, hoping to catch a glimpse of the machine as its nose poked through the parting crowd. I probably lost style points for this, but the BB's beauty was such that I couldn't help myself. Once, as I resumed my forward progress, I caught the stoic Mr. Tullius looking back. No one was immune to that car.

When my turn came to drive, Girotti let me finish the ritual with helmet, gloves and belts, and then leaned in through the passenger side to explain the controls. The 11 switches and four warning lights were painstakingly labeled in Italian, which would do me no good even if I understood the language because there is no time for reading in a racing car. Everything must be learned by position and feel. Since it was broad daylight I swallowed *abbaglianti* and *cambio luci* knowing that I would have time before night practice to dig out the precise difference between the two. But I thought I was hearing things when he mentioned the turn signals and rear fog lights.

By contrast, the mechanical instructions were quite simple; stay under 7000 rpm, be a little easy on the synchros, and remember to turn off the *pompa benzina* when I leave the pits because it's only necessary for starting.

Naturally I forgot that part. This invariably happens on my first trip around in a fuel-injected car, probably because I'm concentrating so hard on all the other inputs.

Daytona 1979 and a relaxed Claude Ballot-Lena awaits the start of practice. (26685)
(Daytona International Speedway photo)

But since the checkered flag came out at the end of my first lap, I think we can assume the pump was spared any damage. In the meantime, my concentration was rewarded with a flood of new perceptions. This BB is a very refined racer. The cockpit is quiet; no engine noise to speak of and no exhaust shriek, although this engine wasn't given to that sort of expression anyway. At full throttle on the oval, the transfer gears were the loudest sound. No rattles anywhere. And no breeze inside. I've been in draftier closets.

Later Girotti explained that except for the aerodynamic nose and tail, these cars were not much different from the production BB. Frame and chassis were essentially the same and the engine still used stock crank, rods, pistons and two-valve head. Output was just under 500 hp. Weight was 2550 lb including water and oil but not fuel. That it clocked 208 mph in testing was testimony to its excellent penetration, he thought.

With three drivers - Jean-Pierre Delaunay of France and of course the Steve Canyon look-alike, Mr. Tullius, were the others - no one gets much practice time. On Thursday I did my longest uninterrupted stint, six full laps including warm-up and cool-off. Never has the oval's back straight been shorter. It felt like somebody had cut about quarter of a mile out of it since the last time I raced there. So that I would give Mr. Chinetti no reason to doubt his judgment in putting me into his car in the first place, I elected to avoid all heroics. That was pretty easy to do in front of the pits anyway because six laps was no enough to get used to the way the car would squirm when the brakes go hard at what must surely be 180 mph. I was, however, very impressed with the way it would pull off the turns. Opening the throttle too quickly would bog the engine so it was necessary to get the chassis settled early, and then slowly squeeze on the power. When the job was done right, that beauty would enter the straights with a most satisfying rush.

At the end of my six laps I thought the car was just wonderful, but the other two drivers were used to a little finer standard of comfort. There was a low frequency aerodynamic buffeting in the nose at certain speeds on the oval, which they wanted to fix under warranty. One of the Pozzi cars had it too. Both, it turned out, were brand new, supposedly built to the same specification as the other Pozzi car that was the prototype. It had never experienced any buffeting in testing and it didn't at Daytona either so the mechanics set to work on the puzzle.

I must say the NART crew is a skilful bunch. Mr. Chinetti has raced very little in the last several years, but he has assembled a cadre of loyal craftsmen that can handle anything. When one of the Pozzi cars suffered a flat right-rear tire on the banking and went into the wall, it was Wayne Sparling, a NART crewman, who stepped into the breach and fabricated a new body section out of nothing but flat aluminum and pure genius.

He and Francois Sicard set out to eliminate the buffeting with the same determination. This is inevitably trial-and-error work. Various combinations of front suspension height, reinforcing inside the nose section and small leading-edge lips to increase down force were tested in the space of three days. At one point they managed to trade small vertical buffets for lateral darts of heart-stopping proportions, and I think it was this one session that gave rise to so much speculation amongst outsiders about the BB's instability on the banking. In any case, by race time they had everything in good order.

Mr. Chinetti's long experience of endurance racing allowed him to establish a pace for the early going which was conservative and yet, considering the final outcome, would have had us in second place. The plan was to hold this pace until morning, or until the plot of the race became clear, then speed up or slow down as necessary. Tullius started, then Delaunay. The car was easily holding a position in the top ten. We were ready for the next stop - the gas hose was out and I was over the wall waiting - when the car didn't come round.

In just a few minutes Delaunay came into the pits on foot. A right rear tire had failed on the banking, putting the beautiful Boxer into the wall. The damage was too great even for the NART crew to repair.

In the midst of my disappointment I thought of Mr. Chinetti. It was, after all, his car; he went to Italy to shepherd it through its final preparation, and it appeared at Daytona through force of his own perseverance. Yet he showed no regret and spoke none. I think, in less time than it takes to say this, he had postponed his psychic payday for another five months - from Daytona to Le Mans."

What might have been! The Boxers had, in fact, qualified quite well in 13th, 15th and 16th positions, with nearly all the other quicker qualifiers being Porsche Turbos. In the race, this trio was faster than anything except the top Porsches. All three were running easily in the top 10 after just two hours when the tire went. This was on the banking just where a tire had also gone in practice. With the NART car already out, Jean Marc Smajda withdrew the two remaining Pozzi cars due to the possibility of the tremendous G-forces causing more Michelin failures."

The next time the BB/LMs appeared was at Le Mans in June. Pozzi had the two Daytona cars painted up in a colourful and unusual red and gray colour scheme. Modelers and BB/LM fans know these as the 'clouds' cars. NART also brought its Daytona car, and these three were joined by a new 1979 car, serial number 27577 entered by 'Beurlys' (Jean Blaton), and prepared by Garage Francorchamps. Joining 'Beurlys' were Bernard de Dryver, Nick Faure and the manager of the Pink Floyd rock group, Steve O'Rourke.

Pozzi's 1979 Le Mans entries were generally regarded as the most colourful of all the BB/LMs. The pale blue and red colour scheme punctuated by flying birds was very pop artish. (26685 and 26681 below) (NB Colln photo)

At Le Mans in 1979, 27577 was the last Ferrari to be entered by Garage Francorchamps in serious competition. The Belgian Ferrari importer was a serious private entrant having started with a 500F2 single-seater in 1952, and over a 27 year period had nearly 600 racing entries. (Blumlein photo)

In qualifying, the fastest of the BB/LMs was the Pozzi 3M-sponsored car, in which Frenchman Michel Leclere just failed to break the 4-minute barrier by 0.78 seconds, but during the race he actually knocked about 1 second off that time to break the 4-minute mark.

The race itself brought mixed fortunes for the various Ferraris, as Le Mans tends to do. First of the BB/LMs to retire was the NART car, which Preston Henn comprehensively restyled by stuffing it into barriers down in the esses, just before the 4-hour mark. It was officially retired in the sixth hour.

In the meantime, the Pozzi cars were going well. The 3M BB/LM had worked its way up to a fine 10th spot until Leclere got tangled up with one of the 2-liter Chevrons at the end of the Mulsanne Straight. Scratch BB/LM number two. Meanwhile, the second Pozzi car was going great guns. At 2 a.m., the rains set in and the Andruet/Dini car was lying 20th. For the next four hours, Jean-Claude Andruet drove like a hero -- in one two-hour stint not one other car, and bear in mind that there were outright sports-racing cars in this race, overtook him. In the four hours he pulled back five laps on the class-leading Porsches, and when he handed over to Dini at 6.06 a.m. the car was up to 10th. But more was to come. Before engine failure caused their retirement just four hours from the finish, this dynamic duo had been as high as fifth. A great achievement that deserved a better result.

While all this excitement was going on, the 'Beurlys' BB/LM was making steady progress. The only real problems came during the night when water kept getting into the distributor, which obviously caused longer than normal pit stops while the mechanics tried to dry it out. Nevertheless, they plugged on until the end and were rewarded with 12th place overall.

1980

Daytona was, by now, becoming the traditional first annual appearance of the BB/LM as there always seemed to be at least one team willing to try its hand for the 24 hours, and 1980 was no different. This time, the willing entrant was Preston Henn who had the car that NART had run at Daytona and Le Mans the previous year. Also making an appearance was a competition Daytona, which could perhaps be considered as old and past it, or alternatively as fully developed. The Boxer qualified 23rd in 1 minute 59.403 seconds, and the Daytona qualified 29th, just 2.1 seconds slower. By early Sunday morning the Boxer had retired with, of all things, a leaking fuel tank, having been as high as 11th at the 7-hour mark. The old Daytona meanwhile was going great, and after 20 hours was lying fourth! Unfortunately, it broke the left rear axle not much later and slipped down to 14th by the end of the 24 hours.

Daytona 1980 and 26683 waits to have its Le Mans numbers replaced. Notice the super-narrow slave tyres used when moving the car around the preparation shop. (Daytona International Speedway photo)

Bellancauto's first BB/LM, (28601) seen here at Monza in 1980 was almost standard - only the louvres atop the front arches and the wider NACA duct being noticeably different. (NB Colln photo)

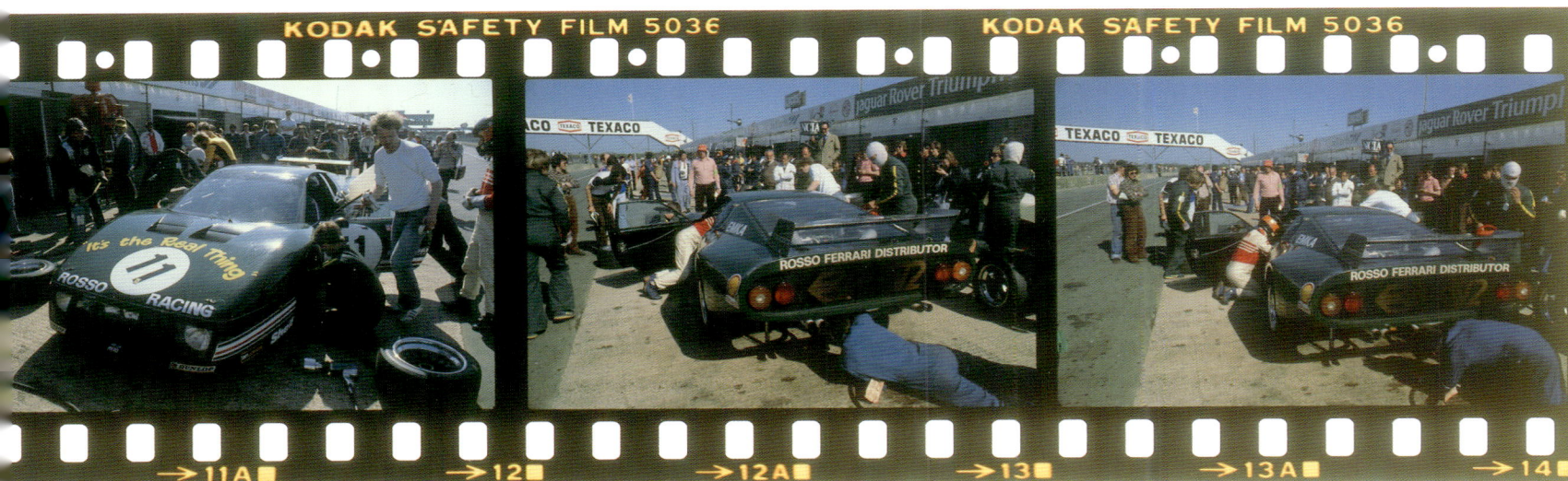

"It's the Real thing" – well it's a real pit stop at least. The O'Rourke BB (27577) makes a pit stop on its way to 7th place in the 1980 Silverstone 6 Hours (NB Colln photo)

The next appearance of a BB/LM went virtually unnoticed at the time, but at the Monza 1,000 kilometers a new Boxer made its debut. This was serial number 28601, which had been built by the factory and delivered to Scuderia Bellancauto in October 1979. It was obvious that in the six months between delivery and its appearance the Italian team had been doing some tinkering. Louvers had been let into the bodywork above the front wheels. The rearview mirrors had been faired in, and the ducts in front of the rear wheels on either side had been enlarged. Sadly, these modifications didn't make it any more reliable -- it retired.

One BB/LM turned up for round five of the World Championship for Makes, the Silverstone Six Hours, which at that time was billed -- and quite rightly -- as "Britain's Le Mans Preview." Steve O'Rourke entered serial number 27577 for himself, Chris Craft and Vic Norman. This was the ex-Francorchamps car now repainted British Racing Green (or at least a 1980 version of the colour), with the words 'It's the real thing' painted boldly across the bonnet. In practice, the Group 6 Lancia Beta Monte Carlos and the Group 5 Porsche K3s set the pace, but De Cadenet won in his Cosworth-powered car, much to the delight of the home crowd. The BB/LM qualified 18th, about 13 seconds slower than pole position, but finished a credible seventh overall.

At Le Mans, Ferrari enthusiasts were treated to the sight of six Boxers competing for the 56 grid slots, although only five would actually start. An unusual new rule, introduced in 1980, was responsible for sidelining the brand-new NART car, serial number 30599, even though it had qualified and was fit to run. The rule was, in actual fact, aimed at the mass of Porsches dominating sports car racing. Unhappily, the Ferrari was the only car that it affected.

Porsche mechanics, aided by the rear location of the Porsche engine, had succeeded in getting the time for a complete engine swap down to about 30 minutes, and some

A rare photo of the NART Boxer (30559) at Le Mans 1980. Because of the regulations the NART car only appeared in practice and did not start the 24hrs. (Keith Bluemel photo)

teams had even changed broken engines during the longer races. To counteract this trend and to give the Cosworth engined, but French built, Rondeaus a chance of victory, the race organizers had brought in a new rule that effectively banned engine swaps. This rule stated that each car had to begin the race with the same engine that it used in practice. The NART car broke its engine in practice and so was not allowed to start the race on a technicality.

It was a pity that the NART car wasn't able to start because it was one of three brand new Boxers. These were easily identified by their new "ground-effect" look bodywork. Whereas the sills on the 1979 cars rolled under the car, the sills on the new car went straight down to the ground. Also the ducts in front of the rear wheels were enlarged with a couple of fins added. The new car was also about 100 kilograms, or 9 percent, lighter thanks to the use of fiberglass for the doors, front and rear panels, the sill extensions, and a new lighter chassis made in KMO steel.

The other two new cars, serial numbers 31589 and 32129, were entered by Charles Pozzi, who also had one of the 1979 cars, serial number 26685, running. All three Pozzi cars were painted dark blue with yellow lettering and yellow wheels. But this eye-catching colour scheme was not all that they had in common. All three cars featured the words 'European University' prominently displayed on the windscreen sun strip and over the rear wheel arches. This apparently was the result of a novel sponsorship idea instigated as a work project by 12 students at the European University of Antwerp, Belgium. The idea was to raise the money to run a Belgian team at Le Mans, and in so doing the students would get an insight into the many different aspects of business finance and publicity. The result was a three-car Franco-Belge effort that even had the time and resources to test privately at the Paul Ricard circuit.

The other two Boxers were O'Rourke's car that Beurlys ran at Le Mans in 1979, and Bellancauto's modified #79 car.

Bellancauto's first Boxer (28601) appeared at Le Mans in 1980. It was going well until Spartaco Dini stuffed it into the Armco (Keith Bluemel photo)

The advantage of the newer cars was shown conclusively in practice, as the two Pozzi BB/LM80s were the fastest of the six BB/LMs. The Ballot-Lena/Andruet car qualified on the ninth row, fourth fastest of the IMSA cars but behind three Porsche 935K3s. The other 1980 car was 22nd. The third Pozzi car was 36th; the Bellancauto Boxer was 41st. And that was it.

Well, not quite. In what some cynics have said was an attempt by the organizers to favour a French victory, certain new regulations were introduced. As already mentioned, one of these prohibited engine swaps once practice had begun. In other words, whichever engine a team started practice with could not be changed and therefore had to run all through practice and do the 24-hour race as well. One can well imagine the ulcers this caused among the team managers.

Another regulation limited the amount of fuel to 120 liters and also slowed down the flow rate at refueling, so that to refill a full tank took a mind-numbing two minutes. Furthermore, turbocharged cars would only be allowed to change one turbocharger during the race. The Daytona 24 Hour winning Porsche had changed between four and seven depending on which account one reads. The upshot of this was that the faster, thirstier Porsches would have to go hard to keep pace with the Ford-Cosworth engined DFV cars, the quickest and most numerous of which just happened to be the locally built Rondeaus. And the Porsches' half-hour engine changes were also out.

Therefore, when the final starting lineup was posted a number of teams were definitely unhappy. As qualifying was the based on the average times of all the nominated drivers per car, some teams had to drop their slowest driver in order to qualify. Other teams, finding that they were outside their class qualifying times, had to sit back and watch slower cars from slower classes line up on the grid in their place. And if that wasn't enough the organizers also allowed a number of 'discretionary' entries on the back of the grid, although they weren't officially qualified. This resulted in such anomalies as a 4 minute and 37 seconds Porsche starting the race, but a 4 minute De Cadenet being packed off home. Some teams were even threatening legal action against the organizing Automobile Club de l'Ouest.

Le Mans 1980 was wet and miserable (I know, I was there) but Dieudonne and co. splashed through the rain that blighted most of the 24hrs. Their reward was a fine 10th place. (32129) (Keith Bluemel photo)

As far as the Boxers were concerned, these regulations worked both for and against them. The NART team was the one to suffer when their engine blew in practice, so they were out. Amazingly, this then allowed O'Rourke's EMKA-sponsored BB/LM in as a replacement in the IMSA class.

The 1980 Le Mans began on a soaking wet track, as the heavens having dropped what seemed like a million gallons of fresh water only minutes before the start. Despite the weather, thousands of damp spectators were considerably brightened by the performance of the 21st-place starter, a certain Hans Stuck in a BMW M1. Stuck was absolutely brilliant, making up 14 places on the first lap alone. For two hours he put on a virtuoso performance, the Day-Glo red and white M1 would come glowing through the darkness, slipping and sliding, and almost seeming to accelerate into the corners, hovering on the edge of disaster, and holding down second place.

Ballot-Lena and Andruet shared Pozzi's car (31589) at Le Mans in 1980 but this time the electrics let the pair down (NB Colln photo)

Further back the Boxers were enjoying mixed fortunes. Ballot-Lena, in 31589, lost 17 minutes in the first hour trying to dry out the electrics and dropped back to 50th position. He then spent the next two hours emulating Hans Stuck, throwing the big Boxer round the soaking Sarthe circuit and making up 26 places in the process. With Andruet's assistance, the car was up to 15th place before retiring in the 11th hour with electrical problems.

The horrendous conditions cause problems for all but one of the Ferraris in the first hour or so as they stopped to have bits dried out and plastic bags fitted over various susceptible bits -- very high-tech this motor racing). Only the Bellancauto Boxer was unaffected, but as Dini stuffed it fairly comprehensively with just more than an hour passed, it probably wasn't around long enough to suffer from the weather.

Pozzi's 26685 was the next to go when Gerard Bleynie abandoned it out on the track with just more than four hours gone.

This left just the remaining Pozzi car, 32129, and the English BB/LM, 27577, to uphold Italian honor. Out of the two, the Pozzi car did the best coming in finally 10th overall and third in the IMSA class. The biggest problem was a half-hour lost just

Despite this nose-bending spin #76 (32129) went on to finish 10th in the wet 1980 race (NB Colln photo)

before midnight with a leak in the petrol tank, but the worst moment was a spin in the race's third downpour less than two hours before the finish.

But the most amazing was the EMKA car, which somehow seemed to survive all efforts to sink or break it. Or maybe the team managed to survive all the cars' effort to do the same. Apart from losing time with water in the electrics, the race was only 2 hours old when O'Rourke dropped it in the Ford corners. A few minutes spent with the duct tape saw the Boxer on its way again, but a number of niggling stops were needed to fix the engine cover. This problem, though, was resolved in a dramatic way, and again it was O'Rourke who suffered. About 11 p.m., a rear tire let go on the Mulsanne Straight and the troublesome engine cover was dispatched into the French countryside. The team then did a deal with the Bellancauto team to graft its spare onto the already beat-up British car. After one hour in the pits, the now green and red duct tape special rejoined to continue the battle against the odds, the weather and other assorted ailments. No doubt the whole team, and especially the mechanics, were greatly relieved when the whole 24-hour thing was over. They finished 23rd overall, a mere 76 laps behind the winner's 338 laps.

After a 1hr 35m stop to replace the rear bodywork, and repair accident damage the O'Rourke BB rejoined the race and ploughed on through the puddles to an eventual 23rd place finish. (NB Colln photo)

The Rosso team was determined to finish despite writing off the tail section of 27577. So they did a deal with Bellancauto for their spare tail section; hence the bizarre two tone colour scheme. (NB Colln photo)

1981

The 1981 Daytona 24 Hour event promised to be an exciting one for Ferrari fans. Ron Spangler's Prancing Horse Farm had its new BB/LM, serial number 34445, there was a 365GTB4 Daytona with Al Unser Jr. sharing the driving, and the amazing Carma 308 GTB bi-turbo of Carlo Facetti and Martino Finotto was also entered, making quite a mixed bunch.

The 308 was an awesome device, with its twin-turbo engine reckoned to produce more than 800 bhp. It was certainly fast and naturally outqualified the other two Ferraris to take sixth place on the grid; the BB/LM was 23rd, and the Daytona 45th.

Comparison of the lap times is interesting as it shows how much faster the BB/LM was than the Daytona, but how much potential was in the 308 bi-turbo:

308GTB bi-turbo	1 minute 46.914 seconds
512BB/LM	1 minute 57.664 seconds
365GTB/4 Daytona	2 minutes 06.344 seconds

Sadly, the race performances were not as good as practice. The first two retirements were the 308 on lap four with a burst radiator, after setting the fastest lap of the race, and the Daytona on lap nine when a fuel line fractured and started a fire.

Meanwhile, the BB/LM was going great. Just before half-distance, at about 3 a.m., the Spangler team was in second place. The car was running well, and a strong finish was a distinct possibility when disaster struck. Gianpero Moretti in his Porsche 935 had a tire blow out on the banking, and who should get caught up in the resulting incident? The unfortunate Prancing Horse Farm boys. It was a sad end to what had promised to be most rewarding. (For a more detailed insight into the BB/LM's involvement in this race see page 170 – Chassis 34445).

The Mugello Six Hours was the third round of the 1981 World Endurance Championship for Drivers, in which the only entrants of any significance were the Martini-sponsored 1.4- liter Lancia Beta Turbos, although Finotto and Facetti had their turbo-charged 308 entered. Our story, though, concentrates on the BB/LMs and only Giovanni Del Buono had his car there to be shared with Govoni. The race was actually won by a 2-liter Osella BMW with the 308 retiring after 20 laps and the BB/LM finishing ninth having completed 155 laps to the winners 177.

Round Two of the World Manufacturer's Championship (Note: 'The World Endurance Championship for Drivers' and 'The world Manufacturers Championship' were separate championships at this time, and not all endurance events counted for both championships) was the Monza 1,000 Kilometers, where a single BB/LM was entered, this time Bellancauto's re-modelled 35529. This was a totally unique looking BB/LM as the bodywork forward of the windscreen had been totally redesigned. The bonnet took one long swoop from the windscreen to the ground, with the radiator inlet being set back lobster-claw fashion between the wings and head-lights. (Look at the photos – it'll make sense then)

This race marked the debut of the Lola T600, and our Italian friends again had the rapid but fragile 308 bi-turbo. In fact, they wrapped up pole position in 1 minute 46.49 seconds – more than 1.5 seconds faster than any other car. The Bellancauto team suffered a burst radiator and missed most of the dry practice session, but was still able to line up a respectable 16th and fastest in the IMSA class at 1 minute 59.99 seconds. Despite appalling weather conditions, the Bellancauto team had a good start and the

This great shot of O'Rourke's BB (27577), now back in yellow, shows just how bad the conditions were at Silverstone for the 1981 race. (NB Colln)

former Formula Two ace Maurizio Flammini soon had the Boxer up to 12th. Sadly, the team were plagued by overheating and excessive fuel consumption and eventually finished 15th and last, some 46 laps behind the winning Porsche.

At the Silverstone Six Hours, British Ferrari fans were in for a rare treat as two BB/LMs were entered -- O'Rourke's car for Bobby Bell, Steve Griswold and Richard Bond; and Simon Phillips' car for himself, veteran Mike Salmon and American Historic race organizer Steve Earle.

It's interesting to compare the qualifying times of the two BB/LMs. Mike Salmon's 1 minute 36.24 seconds put Phillip's newer car on 25th starting spot, while Bond's 1 minute 39.20 seconds was good enough for 31st. Bell seemed content just to get to know the car and allow Bond to set the qualifying mark. The race, as those who were there will no doubt remember, started off in appalling weather. It wasn't long before the O'Rourke car was in the pits having the electrics sprayed and plastic bags wrapped round the distributors in an effort to keep the essential bits dry. Despite these problems, the hardy trio spluttered and splashed their way around Silverstone until the transmission gave out at about the three-and-a-half hour mark.

The Phillip's boys lasted longer, and despite a stop to change a driveshaft and brake disc were on their way to a reasonable finish when with just 40 minutes left the Boxer stopped out at Becketts Corner and was unable to restart. The team was naturally disappointed as a top 10 finish had been a possibility.

By mid-1981, Ferrari had built 23 BB/LMs, of which 11 were of the LM80 type. As all of these had gone into private ownership, the arrival of five for the Le Mans 24 Hours was most noteworthy. Two were entered by American teams and one each from Italy, France and England. One would hate to think that the NART team was favoured in any way, but their BB/LM, delivered direct to Le Mans from the factory, was more than 30 kilograms lighter than any of the others.

Bellancauto's second BB/LM (35529) made its debut with special swoopy bodywork at Monza in 1981, prior to Le Mans. The unusual shape of the elongated nose shows in this shot. (Collezione Maranello Rosso photo)

So the five cars were:

No. 45, S/N 35529 - Bellancauto's special bodied "BBB"car for Flammini/Violati/Truffo;

No. 46, S/N 35525 - Bob Donner's Rennod Racing car for Xhenceval/Dieudonne/Libert;

No. 47, S/N 31589 - Pozzi's car for Ballot-Lena/Andruet/Regout;

No. 48, S/N 35523 - Simon Phillip's car for himself/Salmon/Earle;

No. 49, S/N 35527 - NART's car for Morton/Cudini/Gurdjian;

Final preparation is carried out on NART's BB/LM (35527) prior to the start at Le Mans in 1981 (NB Colln photo)

Unsurprisingly, the fastest Boxer qualifier, with the assistance of Goodyear Formula One tires, was the NART car in 3 minutes 52.60 seconds, which was 29th overall and fourth fastest in the IMSA class; 6.38 seconds slower than Henn's K3 Porsche.

The other BBs lined up as follows:
34th No. 45   3 minutes 55.66 seconds;
36th No. 46   3 minutes 56.72 seconds;
37th No. 47   3 minutes 56.89 seconds;
40th No. 48   3 minutes 59.98 seconds.

As one would expect, the race brought differing results, but overall the Boxers put up a good showing. The NART car was particularly strong and was up to a magnificent fourth after four hours. But at 9:12 a.m. Sunday morning, while running sixth, the French production car driver Phillipe Gurdjian slipped off the track, and the Boxer was unable to return to the pits and so had to retire.

Le Mans 1981 and the travel stained NART car (35527) proudly bears its allegiance to Luigi Chinetti's late wife, Marion. (Blumlein photo)

Meanwhile, the Pozzi car ran at a slightly more relaxed pace, moving into the top 10 after five hours, with only a 17-minute stop just before half-distance to give the team any worries. A delighted Jean-Claud Andruet took the Boxer across the finish in an excellent fifth place and first in the IMSA class.

The experienced pairing of Andruet and Ballot-Lena took Pozzi's car (31589) to a best ever-5th place at Le Mans 1981 (NB Colln)

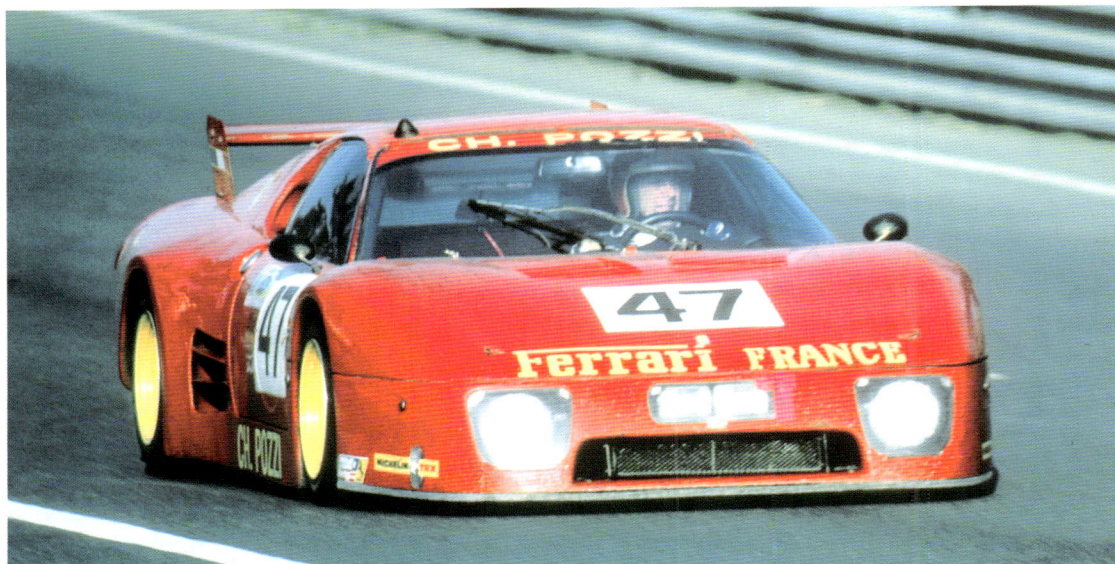

Le Mans 1981 and Bob Donner's European University sponsored car (35525) heads for 9th place. (NB Colln)

The red European University-sponsored Rennod Racing Boxer started steadily and worked slowly onto the leader board. Pierre Dieudonne's illness during the race hampered the team's effort, with Jean Xhenceval and Jean Paul Libert having to cover the second half of the 24 hours by themselves.

Despite this setback, the team ran as high as sixth and finished a credible ninth overall, having covered 323 laps.

The other two Boxers both had slow starts. With only 42 minutes gone, the Simon Phillips car was back in the pits for a 23-minute stop to replace the radiator. The team fixed this but by 2 a.m. the car was retired with transfer gear failure.

The Bellancauto team's BBB had numerous problems, with three separate stops each more than 20 minutes long before stopping at 2:10 a.m. with transmission problems.

So ended a good race for the BB/LMs. In the five years that the BBs had participated at Le Mans the results had gradually improved from 16th and 16th again to 12th to 10th and now fifth. Would 1982 be even better?

The 1981 Enna-Pergusa Six Hours on June 28 was Round Nine of the WEC for Dirvers. The entry list featured the Lola T600, the Carma 308 twin-turbo and further

Simon Phillips car (35523) carried allegiance to his wife(NB Colln)

down the page the Bellancauto Supercar BBB. The 308 sat on pole, but again when the race was underway it was struck by gremlins, retiring on lap three when the back of the car caught fire. This left the Lola to score its maiden victory, and the Supercar boys persevered to finish a valiant fifth.

The 1981 Silverstone Relay was a BB/LM's final competition appearance for the year. The Silverstone Relay is one of those peculiarly eccentric English traditions where teams of sometimes diverse and seemingly unrelated machines take each other on over a six-hour handicap race. You know, the type of thing that might have started at Brooklands. One might find a team of Porsches against a team of Morgans against of team of pre-war Aston Martins, etc. So now you're thinking: "I know, a team of Ferraris! Hence the BB/LM connection." Wrong! This was Simon Phillip's team, and all the cars were owned by Simon. So the BB/LM was teamed with a 1938 BMW 328, a 1951 Frazer-Nash, a 250 GT SWB Berlinetta, a Porsche RSR and a Chevron B16. A mixed bag indeed, and an event that would be unremarkable if it weren't for the presence of serial number 35523 and the biggest race shunt ever to involve a BB/LM. The unfortunate recipient of the "Biggest Race Shunt Ever in a BB/LM" award goes to veteran racer Mike Salmon. As a picture is worth a thousand words, I'll save a few thousand here by suggesting that you refer to the series of photos that adequately illustrate how to flip a 512BB/LM.

Probably the most spectacular crash involving a BB/LM was at its least significant event. The Silverstone Six Hour Relay was an end of season event for amateur drivers to enjoy. Mike Salmon clipped the rear of another competitor's car whilst lapping it and flipped Simon Phillips immaculate BB (35523) into a complete 360° barrel roll. (John Gaisford photo courtesy Simon Phillips Colln)

The importance of this event can be gauged by the packed grandstands! On the left Mike Salmon is being helped away from a comprehensively bent car. (Simon Phillips Colln)

1982

The next racing year began, as usual, with the Daytona 24 Hours. Bob Rapp was there and his 'inside story' is reproduced with the kind permission of *Prancing Horse* magazine.

"To me, one of the exciting things I have experienced during the 15 or so years I have been traveling to Daytona to watch the great 24 hour spectacle is the anticipation I always have en route, and finding the official entry list for the race and quickly scanning it to count the number of Ferraris entered. This year I had been led to believe from informed reports that there would only be one Ferrari 512BB/LM there, but imagine my amazement when I picked up a copy of the entry list! There they were! four (count them) Ferrari 512BB/LMs.

The No. 6 car listed Bob Wollek, Edgar Doeren and Randy Lanier as drivers. The No. 47 car showed Skip Scott and Tom Davis. The No. 48 car showed Claud Ballot-Lena and Jean-Claud Andruet (both of Paris, France) as the pilots. The No. 65 car, which we were to be associated with, was owned by Ron and Patti Spangler of Bel Air, Maryland and was to be driven by Carson Baird, Rick Knoop and Tom Pumpelly. After arriving at the track we saw No. 48 on a trailer and heard a report that it had been sold and would not enter the race, so that left the effort at three. As I scanned the list more thoroughly this time in search of a Ferrari Daytona I was disappointed to find none there, and that's the first time since 1969 that one has not been entered. 'Pace Requium Daytona.'

The entry list also showed a Who's Who in racing as to former Ferrari drivers now driving something else. There was John Morton, Milt Minter, Preston Henn, David Hobbs, Derek Bell, Eppie Wietzes, Jim Adams and in addition to the listed drivers we saw the great Brian Redman (recently retired - maybe) and Jackie Ickx (also retired) and there were perhaps others we overlooked.

Another item in the local Daytona paper was the list of former 24-hour winners and I immediately scanned that for past Ferrari victories. The first listed Pedro Rodriguez in 1963 and in 1964 Pedro Rodriguez and Phil Hill. The next victory was in 1967, which perhaps was the most historic of all for Ferraris, when the first three places went to Ferrari 330P4 prototypes, the winning car having been driven by Lorenzo Bandini and Chris Amon. Victory eluded Ferrari then until 1972 when Mario Andretti and Jackie Ickx drove a Ferrari 312PB to victory. After that every race has been won by a Porsche including this year's. Incidentally, one of the reasons Porsche has won so many of these races, in addition to having fielded a very fast car, is the sheer number that have been in the race. This year I counted 30 Porsche entries out of a total of 70 spots. That kind of clout has got to produce results.

The No. 6 Thunderbird Swap-Shop Ferrari, which carried a NART entry, was the fastest qualifier at 1:54, which placed it 15th on the grid for the nearly four mile course. The No. 47 car entered by Tide Racing time was 2:08, and the No. 65 car run in Patti Spangler's Prancing Horse Farm entry was the 18th fastest. It, along with the Tide Racing entry, ran a special qualifying race Friday because they had not posted a time within 110% of the fastest car in their class. They finished the qualification event first and third but started 51st and 53rd.

The sights around the garage area took us back to many years ago during the era of the prototypes, which always were the most exciting cars, to me, anyway. There were the Rondeaus, the previous winners of Le Mans, as well as the Cooke Lola T-600 and

At Daytona in 1982 the TIDE Racing BB/LM (31589) was allowed to use its 1981 Le Mans race number. (Daytona International Raceway photo)

Preston Henn wasn't afraid to spend money to get the right drivers and at Daytona 1982 'Brilliant' Bob Wollek shared this BB (30559) with Edgar Doren and Randy Lanier even though an outright victory was hardly a possibility. (Daytona International Speedway photo)

besides that the BMW-March - all immaculately prepared. There were several BMW M1s around as well as a very ugly Mazda Chevron that proved to be as slow as it was unattractive.

The starting line-up showed the Chevrolet March entered by Garretson Enterprises in the pole position with a time of approximately 1:43.9 followed by David Hobbs, Hurley Haywood, Bill Whittington, John Paul, Preston Henn, and Bob Akin, all in Porsche turbos. Next in line were the Chevrolet-Lola of Eppie Wietzes and Jim Adams, followed by two more Porsches, a BMW, a Porsche turbo, two Rondeaus and then the No. 6 Ferrari belonging to Preston Henn.

The next Ferrari was the 51st place Prancing Horse Farm entry No. 65 followed by the Tide Ferrari No. 47 starting in 53rd place. It's interesting to note that the car starting in 50th place, which was a Porsche 911, had qualified at 2:12. Had it not been for the 110% rule referred to above we would have started in 18th spot, but outside of the prestige of starting near the front, obviously, position is not too important in this type of marathon race. Probably the most interesting thing for those lucky enough to be in the pits (which seems to be the majority of the people at the race) is the hoopla on pit road preceding the start. This is your chance to look at the drivers as they suit up, to get a final look at the beautifully prepared machines and to chat with those in the crew who may have a moment to talk. The air of excitement has to be experienced to be believed. Our own car, the No. 65 Prancing Horse Farm Racing car, was immaculately prepared and was easily the class of the field. It was the same car, which had been knocked out of third position during the 1981 race by a Porsche and would probably have finished third or second had not that incident happened.

Early Sunday morning at Daytona 1982 and the PHF BB (34445) makes a smoky exit. (NB Colln photo)

The race started uneventfully with the Porsches, Rondeaus, March-BMW and Lola all making flying laps in the area of 1:46. After one lap the No. 47 Tide Racing Ferrari was gone with fuel injection problems but the No. 6 and 65 cars began moving up through the pack doing lap times of 1:50 and 2:00. At the end of the first hour the standing sheets showed No. 6 in sixth position and No. 65 in 11th position. End of second hour showed No. 65 in eighth and No. 6 in ninth and this position held through the seventh hour. At the end of the eighth hour (11:30 p.m.) the lighted leader board now showed No. 6 in fourth position and No. 65 in fifth position! We were all ecstatic! And would you believe at the end of the 11th hour No. 6 was in third place and No. 65 in fourth? At the end of the 14th hour No. 65 had dropped out of the race having retired after 377 laps and of all things, although the engine, drivers, and team were going strong, it was the gearbox that gave up. A bushing hadn't been secured, which left the shift linkage in disarray and made the car jump out of gear. The Preston Henn Thunderbird Swap-Shop entry was now in third place but early Sunday morning it too gave up with gearbox problems after one of the drivers had spun it in the dirt and evidently fouled up something in that area. That ended the effort for the Ferraris but even more interesting was the behind-the-scenes preparation and the incredible number of people who contributed to this volunteer effort. Ron Spangler is quite an organizer along with Patti and the preparation for the race started many months prior to it.

Ron sent out a preparation brochure which listed practically everything that one could have thought of. The table of contents on this list included sponsors and patrons, preparation items, race items, crew and expenses, pass lists, hotel, track and restaurant information, rooms, travel to and from Daytona, race jacket lists and sizes, financial analysis, final checklist items, and participants names and addresses. Incidentally the scene of some thirty Ferrari enthusiasts all wearing Prancing Horse Farm jackets was one of the most exciting scenes I have ever seen in racing, and probably the some 50,000 people who witnessed us pushing the car onto the grid were similarly impressed.

If you are interested just in the cost of such an effort the budget showed about $60,000 not including the car or parts. In addition, it didn't include meals or hotel or travel expenses for the majority of the people who were there, as they paid their own ways. With some thirty people having come to the race in support of car No65, and considering the car and parts in excess off $150,000, I figured the effort was at least $250,000 without counting anything for the free time of the volunteers. And do you know what you get should you end up in first place as prize money? $15,000 That's what!

And had we finished in fourth place we would have received all of $3,250. The site of Patti Spangler stirring a kettle of soup in the motor home for the drivers made me realize just how much it takes in detailed planning to get an effort like this on the road. And there were hundreds of small examples of pure devotion to the effort on an unpaid basis by literally hundreds of people, most of who were not even at Daytona. Congratulations to Ron and Patti, to the drivers and the crew and to all who participated. The Ferrari Club of America should be proud of this effort and we hope that next year more of you can participate. Forza Ferrari."

The entry for the Sebring 12 Hours was down to three BB/LMs, including Henn's car for an all-woman team consisting of his daughter Bonnie, Formula One racer Desire Wilson and American Janet Guthrie. The Prancing Horse car with Chip Mead replacing Rick Knoop in the three driver line-up, and the Tom Davis car, which did not start, completed the Boxer entries. The two starting BB/LMs had a less-than-average event, qualifying 17th and 12th respectively, but with neither of them running at the end.

Monza was the setting for Round One of the 1982 WEC and featured a mix of Group C cars, with Group 6 and Group 5 cars to make up the numbers. Ricardo Patrese and Michele Alboreto shared the leading Group 6 Lancia and put it on pole in 1 minute 39.91 seconds. At the other end of the grid, in 29th place, was the BB/LM of Del Buono/Govoni in 2 minutes 03.16 seconds. The five-and-a-half hour race was actually won by a Rondeau, and the Boxer was a good eigth overall out of 11 classified finishers, recording a time of 5 hours, 35 minutes and 43.6 seconds for 151 laps, some 22 laps behind the winner.

Simon Phillips again had serial number 35523 at Silverstone to share with Steve Earle and Richard Jones. Earle was the quickest of the trio in practice and recorded the fastest lap ever for a BB/LM at Silverstone with a 1 minute 35.62 seconds. Sponsorship for this race was obtained from Algarve Beach Villas, but Simon felt that there wasn't enough money to warrant repainting the Boxer so it appeared in a light brown undercoat. Some spectators thought that the unusual sand-like colour was to fit in with the sponsor, but it was just an unusual coincidence.

Del Buono's 34157 only ran in two events. It's shown here at Monza in 1982 where it finished 8th. (NB COLLN photo)

Del Buono's 34157 again at Monza. (NB COLLN photo)

Simon started the race, and all three drivers enjoyed a reliable, trouble-free run through the six hours. Simon took the wheel with 48 minutes left to take his own car across the line in 17th place and 199 laps completed.

The year was to be the BB/LMs last major effort at Le Mans. Four cars were entered. Spangler and his Prancing Horse Farm team had its well-prepared car with the experienced Pierre Dieudonne sharing the driving; Charles Pozzi's car sported Pioneer sponsorship and looked superb in blue and white. NART had its 1981 car but were looking for a better result, and finally Preston Henn had his Daytona and Sebring car.

Pozzi's 41263 sported one of the smartest looking colour schemes seen on a BB (NB Colln)

Practice went according to form with the NART boys being the fastest of the four to be 37th on the grid. The PHF and Pozzi cars were 40th and 41st, respectively, with the Henn boys, seemingly content merely to qualify, 51st.

The laurels were divided evenly with the Henn and Pozzi cars both retiring in the sixth hour with engine problems, while the PHF and NART teams went onto to finish sixth and ninth, respectively.

The immaculately prepared PHF car (38179) finished a deserved 6th (NB Colln)

NART's BB (35527) heads into the setting sun and a 9th place finish at Le Mans 1982 (NB Colln)

30559 stretches its legs down the Mulsanne (NB Colln)

Despite having the experienced Jean-Claud Andruet and Claude Ballot-Lena in the driver line-up 41263 still failed to finish the 1982 Le Mans 24hrs (NB Colln photo)

Truffo and Violati ran Bellancauto's second car (35529) with special bodywork into 10th place in the 1982 Mugello 1000kms. (Collezione Maranello Rossa photo)

A 23-minute stop at midnight probably cost the PHF team one place, and the NART car was on its way to a possible fourth when gearbox gremlins struck.

The Bellancauto team made only one race appearance in 1982, at the Mugello 1,000 kilometers on Sept. 19. Despite being a round of the WEC, the entry list was poor with only the three works-entered Group 6 Lancias having a hope of victory. The BBB qualified 14th out of 19 starters. Truffo's time was 2 minutes 04.88 seconds compared to the pole time of 1 minute 45.29 seconds. The race took 6 hours18 minutes for the winning Lancia, and the Boxer eventually finished 10th, having completed 148 laps to the winner's 191.

The final event on the WEC calendar took place in Japan. The following is an eyewitness report of the race at Mount Fuji by Ferrari enthusiast Michitake Isobe and is reproduced with his kind permission.

"With the inception of the World Endurance Championship, Fuji Speedway hosted the 7th round of the 1982 WEC Drivers Championship: The Fuji 6 Hours on Oct 3rd.

Among the ten overseas entries was Preston Henn's 512BB/LM entered in the IMSA-GTX class. IMSA cars were encouraged to enter by the organisers for fear that the new Group C cars would not come all the way to Japan, the Manufacturers Championship have already been decided.

It was the only Ferrari in the race, but it had been a several years since a Ferrari had come to Japan to race. The chassis No was 30559, engine type F102BOO, and race No12. The drivers were Preston Henn and his daughter Bonnie.

While most eyes were on the works Porsche 956 entries driven by Icxk, Bell etc. the Ferrari was not totally forgotten. A well-known mechanic in Japanese racing circles came to observe closely the BB in between his own work. So, the BB was interesting to those who knew!

Practice was cold and wet and the BB needed constant attention by its two Swap Shop mechanics. Preston Henn said jokingly to the writer, "I should have brought my Porsche!" The BB qualified 16th on the 40 car grid with a time of 1m27.07s, (avg. 180.227kmh) which was some 14s slower than the pole-sitting Lancia of Alboreto/ Ghinzani. It was surrounded on the grid by the IMSA-GTX Mazda RX7s and was seventh fastest among the overseas entries.

It was Preston Henn, and not daughter Bonnie, who turned the BB (30559) into scrap. (Isobe photo)

Race day Sunday turned out to be dry and sunny with no sign of rain. The BB held its position for the first few laps but soon began to slip back. On lap 10, after the leaders had passed by and gone down the main straight I caught sight of a red flash out of the corner of my eye. It was the BB spinning out on the high-speed corner just before the start/finish line - it came to stop against the outside retaining wall.

When the BB reappeared the front and rear body panels were heavily damaged. The BB came out to the middle of the track and slowly headed for the pits. After a short inspection it was decided to retire. A contemporary race report states the BB was the fifth retirement of the race; 18 cars finished.

Losing interest in the race your writer decided to go into the paddock for one last look at the BB. 30995 already had the damaged panels removed and a disgruntled Preston Henn was explaining to a mechanic what had happened.

After a few laps the gearbox had started to give problems, and on the final lap the BB had come out of the hairpin curve but would not go into second or third gear at all. Preston Henn had fought to find a gear, but the BB got away from him in the last corner.

Fuji Speedway is a very high-speed circuit and after the hairpin curve the track is more or less a long, high speed, right handed sweep, and missing a gear is trouble.

Unfortunately Bonnie Henn never had the chance to drive in the race; but there is an interesting anecdote that bears repeating here.

Some members of the team along with their Japanese friends played a practical joke on her. Some Japanese words were written on the driver's side of the car just above the door and next to the driver's names. Translated into English it reads "A dangerous woman driver, but don't tell her!"

Unfortunately, someone did! When Bonnie Henn found out she was not very pleased, to put it mildly. It was rumored in the paddock that communication between the co-driver and the team staff became non-existent for an afternoon. But on race day a determined Bonnie was seen in appropriate racing attire walking towards the pits - peace had returned to the team."

The Japanese writing above the door refers to Bonnie Henn. It translates as "A dangerous woman driver, but don't tell her!" (Isobe photo)

1983

For 1983 the PHF team picked up sponsorship from Electrolux and NTW Tires. (34445) (Daytona International Speedway)

The 512BB/LM teams experienced a lean year in 1983. After the reasonable success of 1982, it was disappointing to see only two events involving the Berlinetta Boxer in 1983. Both of these were single entries and both in U.S. events. The success of Group C and the regulations for Group B really excluded the 512BB/LM, except in America where it was still IMSA-eligible. The Prancing Horse Farm team turned out with serial number 34445 for its third Daytona 24 hours.

In 1982, the team ran in the qualification race to make the grid, but this year its 1 minute 55.925 seconds was quick enough for an excellent 19th place on the grid. By the sixth hour, the Prancing Horse Farm boys must have been in seventh heaven. Who was leading the race? Yes, there they were, officially listed as race leaders from laps 168-171. Race leaders! They were ahead of the Porsches and the Jaguars and the Aston Martin Nimrods.

Sadly, it was not to last, as the team were to retire with engine failure having completed 294 laps. And this really is one of those 'what if' stories. Much of the second half of the race was run under the yellow flag with no overtaking due to torrential rain, and in fact at 11:15 Sunday morning the race was suspended for an hour, so if the BB/LM could have stayed out then even a rostrum spot could have been a possibility.

At Daytona, no less than Derek Bell had tested Preston Henn's 512BB/LM, although it didn't race. Was this to impress a potential purchaser? Who knows, but Henn's serial number 30559 turned up at Sebring for the 12 hours in the hands of the Shelton brothers from Florida. They qualified a reasonable 29th but retired just after half distance with transmission problems.

The Prancing Horse Farm car makes a nighttime pit stop during the Daytona 24Hrs. (34445) (Daytona International Speedway)

1984

The only BB/LM at Daytona in 1984 was 30559 shared by the Shelton Brothers, and shown leading the #21 Pontiac Firebird. (Daytona International Speedway photo)

There was just a single Ferrari entry for this year's Daytona 24 Hour event. The Shelton brothers were giving it another go in Henn's serial number 30559. The team actually hired Bob Wollek and Claude Ballot-Lena to qualify the car, with Wollek reputedly being paid $500 for just five laps. Their 2 minutes 05.875 seconds practice time was good enough for the 27th starting position, but again they did not finish this time due to an oil leak.

Nighttime at Daytona (Daytona International Speedway photo)

For the annual 12 Hours at Sebring, the Shelton brothers' again entered Henn's serial number 30559 and were joined on the entry list by serial number 31589, entered by Tom Davis, who invited Ballot-Lena and Andruet to share the driving chores. Andruet declined in order to do a round of the French Rally Championship, and Ballot-Lena found himself Ferrari-less when the engine blew in practice. Ballot-Lena was then co-opted into the Hurley Haywood/Al Holbert Porsche 935, but when that retired during the race he did a stint in the remaining BB/LM. He was a busy man!

The Sheltons got to start 67th with no qualifying time officially listed. They battled through various problems, including bodywork loosened by a rough racetrack and a brush with the wall when Sarel Van de Merwe forced his March-Porsche past. Undeterred, they plugged on to a 23rd-place finish, 52 laps behind the winner.

Our attention now switches to the west coast and the *Los Angeles Times* six-hour event at Riverside. Here we find another BB/LM entered, but this unbelievably is old friend serial number 18139, which last raced nearly six years earlier! The old warhorse was the first ever racing Boxer, having started its competitive life in the 1975 Daytona 24 Hours. In late 1983, it was purchased by Mike Sheehan, who prepared it to the latest IMSA specifications and updated it. Frankly it was no longer competitive, qualifying 37th out of 52 entries but retiring after 76 laps.

From Riverside we now move to Lime Rock Park in Connecticut for the Coca-Cola 500, which despite the name was only a 1-hour race, hardly long enough for a BB/LM to get warmed up one would think. And whereas the previous event had seen the oldest BB/LM reappear, this event saw the appearance of another early BB/LM, but this one was to make its race debut. This was John Gelles' serial number 29511, which had been prepared by engineer Lee Dykstra. Driver Steve Cohen hustled round the 1.53-mile track in 58.593 seconds for 13th and penultimate place on the grid. To put this in perspective, the pole lap was Randy Lanier's 48.328 seconds in a March 84G-Chevy. The car finished 13th overall, completing 44 laps to the winner's 56.

Bellancauto's second BB/LM (35529) with its second bodywork. Car ran legendary no27; the same number as the Formula One team's Number One driver. (Collezione Maranello Rosso photo)

And so to the final competitive appearance of the BB/LM at Le Mans. Sadly, the scene of some of the Boxers better results was down to just a single, but nevertheless fascinating, entry. After a three-year absence, the Bellancauto team was back and had again rebodied its already radical 512 BB/LM. Both the nose and tail were shorter than previous, with the weight going down from 1,102 kilograms to 970 kilograms. Despite all the effort, the car could only qualify 41st in 4 minutes 00.20 seconds. Still worse was to come. The engine blew up during the Saturday morning warm-up, and the team only just managed to change the engine – the rules had once again been changed to allow this -- in time to make the starting line-up.

They probably wondered why they bothered at all. The car never got higher than 32nd and retired before quarter distance when the gearbox packed up.

The quaintly named Camel Double 3-Hour at Watkins Glen saw the next appearance of the Gelles Ferrari. Despite starting 33rd, a steady run found the team in a final 17th position out of 57 starters.

One hundred and twenty-five laps of the 4-mile long Road America circuit adds up to 500 miles and takes the fast boys a bit less than five hours to complete. For this event, the Shelton brothers' car was back but in the hands of new owner, Warren Mosler. John McComb was retained on the team and was joined by Fred Fiala and

Bellancauto's (35529) was the only BB to run at Le Mans 1984 (Keith Bluemel photo)

one-time Corvette man Rick Mancuso. Although qualifying a lowly 40th out of 60 entrants, the team achieved a reasonably good 15th-place finish.

Meanwhile, across the other side of the pond the Bellancauto team was giving the BBB one final opportunity to redeem itself. After qualifying 23rd out of 28 for the Imola 1,000 kilometers, it gave up at about half distance and was quietly retired to a museum.

The final BB/LM event for 1984 was at Watkins Glen for the New York 500 kilometers on Sept. 30 when the Gelles brothers again turned out. The result for the team was similar to that of the first visit to The Glen. The car qualified 35th and finished 20th, but at least it avoided the dreaded DNF.

1985

And so we arrive at the final season of serious competition for the BB/LMs. Amazingly, two teams were still willing to campaign what were by now basically five-year-old cars. The Equipco team had the revamped serial number 29511, and the Florida based Mosler team had serial number 30559 as well as a modified 308 GTB (serial number 18905 for the chassis number buffs out there). Both 512BB/LM's qualified about the same -- the Mosler car 34th and the older car 36th. The Mosler car retired with 171 laps completed, but the Equipco team went on to complete 567 laps (136 behind the winning Porsche 962) and finished 16th. By the way, the 308 started 69th and retired after 219 laps.

Surprise, surprise. At Sebring, the two teams were still willing to give the BB/LMs a chance. The Gelles car actually performed quite well in practice with a time of 2 minutes 41.480 seconds being good enough for 24th place, while the Mosler car was back in 35th. Regrettably both cars retired. The Gelles car completing 54 laps to the Mosler car's 88.

So, to that sad but inevitable event -- the BB/LM's final competitive appearance -- or maybe that should be last appearance in competition. Mid Ohio IMSA ran a separate race for the GTO/GTU classes, but even so the Boxer was up against factory-backed Ford Mustangs and the like. Also, the race was virtually a sprint in Boxer terms, being only two hours long. But the Mosler team qualified 17th and finished 13th out of 37 starters. That was probably about as good as could be expected.

Thus ended the ten-year career of the racing Boxers. It was a career with flashes of brilliance interrupted with spells of unreliability. But it should be remembered that with one notable exception, little or no development was put into the Boxers, and each one was run by private teams -- individuals who supported the racing out of their own pockets and usually with little to show at the end of it, certainly not financially anyway. Without these enthusiasts, there would have been no Ferrari involvement in sports car racing as the factory concentrated on Formula One since 1973.

This is a shame because sports car racing is where Ferrari made its name. Ask an enthusiast who won the Mille Miglia or Targa Florio or Le Mans or Daytona in a certain year, and more than likely the reply will center on the make of car. Ask him who won a particular Formula One championship, and the answer will inevitably be the name of a driver.

The Gelles BB/LM (29511), here leading a Corvette, thunders round the banking on its way to a creditable 16th place at Daytona in 1985. (NB Colln photo)

And leans through an infield corner (NB Colln photo)

BB/LM Performance Comparison - Le Mans 1975 - 1984

Year	No.	Kgs.	Practice	Race	Top Speed
Track length 13.640kms					
1975	99	1351	4'30.0	n/a	n/a
1977	75	1233	4'27.9	4'23.8	166.53
1978	85	1333	4'10.9	4'14.0	178.33
	86	1166	4'15.9	4'14.3	188.28
	87	1221	4'07.9	4'13.6	182.68
	88	1210	4'07.3	4'07.0	180.82
	89	1204	4'07.1	4'07.9	185.17

Porsche Curves added in 1979 – Track length 13.626kms

Year	No.	Kgs.	Practice	Race	Top Speed
1979	61	1198	4'11.98	4'12.5	186.41 r
	62	1258	4'02.42	3'58.6	192.00 r
	63	1227	4'00.78	3'59.2	194.49 r
	64	1187	4'06.30	4'10.7	193.87 p
1980	74	1066	n/a	n/a	n/a
	75	1211	4'06.8	4'10.6	178.95 r
	76	1093	4'00.3	3'58.0	197.60 r
	77	1096	3'57.9	3'57.6	188.90 r
	78	1196	3'57.9	4'10.4	193.25 r
	79	1148	4'00.0	4'27.1	188.90 r
1981	45	1102	3'55.66	4'02.7	188.90 r
	46	1130	3'56.72	3'59.6	195.11 r
	47	1102	3'56.89	3'59.3	193.87 r
	48	1107	3'59.98	4'02.6	197.59 r
	49	1070	3'52.60	3'56.2	197.59 r
1982	70	1115	3'56.52	3'59.7	196.97 r
	71	1058	3'56.80	3'56.4	196.97 r
	72	1084	3'54.07	3'55.5	194.49 r
	73	1098	4'07.32	4'01.2	198.83 r
1984	27	970	4'00.02	4'04.5	190.76 r

BB/LM Race Results

DATE	EVENT	#	Ch. #	Driver	Driver	Driver	Result
1975							
2/1/1975	Daytona 24hrs	1	18139	Ballot-Lena	Cudini	Minter	DNF
3/21/1975	Sebring 12hrs	111	18139	Minter	Wietzes		6
4/20/1975	Road Atlanta	111	18139	Minter			DNS
5/26/1975	Lime Rock	111	18139	Minter			DNF
6/14/1975	Le Mans 24hrs	99	18095	Guitteny	Haran	Bucknum	DNS
1977							
6/10/1977	Le Mans 24hrs	75	18139	Migault	Guitteny		16
1978							
2/4/1978	Daytona 24hrs	5	18139	Migault	Guitteny	Young	22
4/16/1978	Road Atlanta	5	18139	Migault			21
6/10/1978	Le Mans 24hrs	85	22715	Pilette	Beurlys	Tourol	DNF
6/10/1978	Le Mans 24hrs	86	18139	Migault	Guitteny		16
6/10/1978	Le Mans 24hrs	87	24131	Delaunay	Guerin	Young	DNF
6/10/1978	Le Mans 24hrs	88	24127	Andruet	Dini		DNF
6/10/1978	Le Mans 24hrs	89	24129	Ballot-Lena	Lafosse		DNF
7/8/1978	Watkins Glen 6hrs	25	18139	Migault	Guitteny		11
1979							
2/3/1979	Daytona 24hrs	66	26681	Andruet	Dini	(Ballot-Lena)	DNF
2/3/1979	Daytona 24hrs	67	26685	Ballot-Lena	Leclere	(Andruet)	DNF
2/3/1979	Daytona 24hrs	68	26683	Tullius	Delaunay	Bedard	DNF
6/9/1979	Le Mans 24hrs	61	27577	Beurlys O'Rourke	Faure	De Dryver	12
6/9/1979	Le Mans 24hrs	62	26681	Andruet	Dini		DNF
6/9/1979	Le Mans 24hrs	63	26685	Ballot-Lena	Leclere	Gregg	DNF
6/9/1979	Le Mans 24hrs	64	26683	Delaunay	Grandet	Henn P	DNF
1980							
2/2/1980	Daytona 24hrs	69	26683	Dieudonne	Henn P		DNF
4/27/1980	Monza 6hrs	31	28601	Dini	Violati		DNF
5/11/1980	Silverstone 6hrs	11	27577	O'Rourke	Norman	Craft	7
6/14/1980	Le Mans 24hrs	74	30559	Delaunay	Henn P		DNS
6/14/1980	Le Mans 24hrs	75	26685	Guitteny	Bleynie	Libert	DNF
6/14/1980	Le Mans 24hrs	76	32129	Dieudonne	Xhenceval	Regout	10
6/14/1980	Le Mans 24hrs	77	31589	Ballot-Lena	Andruet		DNF
6/14/1980	Le Mans 24hrs	78	27577	O'Rourke	Down	Phillips	23
6/14/1980	Le Mans 24hrs	79	28601	Dini	Violati	Micangeli	DNF
1981							
1/31/1981	Daytona 24hrs	65	34445	Adamowicz	Knoop		DNF
3/21/1981	Sebring 12hrs	91	30559	Henn P	Gunn	Belcher	DNS
4/12/1981	Mugello 6hrs	29	34157	Del Buono	Govoni		9
4/26/1981	Monza 1000kms	15	35529	Flammini	Dini	Violati	15
5/10/1981	Silverstone 6hrs	41	35523	Earle	Phillips	Salmon	DNF
5/10/1981	Silverstone 6hrs	42	27577	Bond	Bell	Griswold	DNF
6/13/1981	Le Mans 24hrs	45	35529	Violati	Flammini	Truffo	DNF

DATE	EVENT	#	Ch. #	Driver	Driver	Driver	Result
6/13/1981	Le Mans 24hrs	46	35525	Xhenceval	Libert	Dieudonne	9
6/13/1981	Le Mans 24hrs	47	31589	Ballot-Lena	Andruet		5
6/13/1981	Le Mans 24hrs	48	35523	Earle	Phillips	Salmon	DNF
6/13/1981	Le Mans 24hrs	49	35527	Cudini	Morton	Gurdjian	DNF
6/28/1981	Enna 6hrs	5	35529	Violati	Truffo		5
10/18/1981	Silverstone Relay	5F	35523	Phillips	Salmon		DNF

1982

DATE	EVENT	#	Ch. #	Driver	Driver	Driver	Result
1/29/1982	Daytona Prelim 13 laps	65	34445	Knoop			1
1/29/1982	Daytona Prelim 13 laps	47	31589	De Dryver			3
1/30/1982	Daytona 24hrs	6	30559	Wollek	Doren	Lanier	DNF
1/30/1982	Daytona 24hrs	47	31589	De Dryver	Davis		DNF
1/30/1982	Daytona 24hrs	65	34445	Knoop	Pumpelly	Baird	DNF
3/20/1982	Sebring 12hrs	47	31589	Rubino	Davis		DNS
3/20/1982	Sebring 12hrs	6	30559	Guthrie	Wilson	Henn B	DNF
3/20/1982	Sebring 12hrs	65	34445	Baird	Pumpelly	Mead	DNF
4/18/1982	Monza 1000kms	98	34157	Del Buono	Govoni		8
5/16/1982	Silverstone 6hrs	80	35523	Jones	Phillips	Earle	17
6/19/1982	Le Mans 24hrs	70	38179	Dieudonne	Libert	Baird	6
6/19/1982	Le Mans 24hrs	71	41263	Ballot-Lena	Andruet	Regout	DNF
6/19/1982	Le Mans 24hrs	72	35527	Cudini	Morton	Paul	9
6/19/1982	Le Mans 24hrs	73	30559	Henn P	Lanier	Morin	DNF
9/19/1982	Mugello 1000kms	5	35529	Violati	Truffo		10
10/3/1982	Mount Fuji 6hrs	12	30559	Henn P	Henn B		DNF

1983

DATE	EVENT	#	Ch. #	Driver	Driver	Driver	Result
2/5/1983	Daytona 24hrs	65	34445	Baird	Pumpelly	Mead	DNF
3/19/1983	Sebring 12hrs	8	30559	Shelton S	Shelton T		DNF

1984

DATE	EVENT	#	Ch. #	Driver	Driver	Driver	Result
2/4/1984	Daytona 24hrs	97	30559	Shelton S	Shelton T		DNF
3/24/1984	Sebring 12hrs	96	31589	Ballot-Lena			DNS
3/24/1984	Sebring 12hrs	97	30559	Shelton S Ballot-Lena	Shelton T	McComb	23
4/29/1984	Riverside	75	18139	Schwarz	Christian	Smart	DNF
5/28/1984	Lime Rock	21	29511	Cohen			13
6/16/1984	Le Mans 24hrs	27	35529	Micangeli	Marazzi	Lacaud	DNF
7/8/1984	Watkins Glen	21	29511	Cohen	Gelles	De Pasquale	17
7/8/1984	Road America	97	30559	McComb	Mancuso	Fiala	15
9/16/1984	Imola 1000kms	27	35529	Micangeli	Micangeli	Del Balzo	DNF
9/30/1984	Watkins Glen	21	29511	Cohen	Gelles	De Pasquale	20

1985

DATE	EVENT	#	Ch. #	Driver	Driver	Driver	Result
2/2/1985	Daytona 24hrs	21	29511	Cohen	Gelles	Walker	16
2/2/1985	Daytona 24hrs	51	30559	McComb	Mancuso	Fiala	DNF
3/23/1985	Sebring 12hrs	21	29511	Cohen	Gelles		DNF
3/23/1985	Sebring 12hrs	51	30559	McComb	Mancuso	Fiala	DNF
6/8/1985	Mid Ohio	51	30559	McComb	Mancuso		13

"BB's Blues" This superb Nick Watts' painting shows the Pozzi Boxer swimming its way to 10th place in its only competition appearance at Le Mans in 1980. (NB Colln)

Individual Chassis Histories

L. to R. – # 29507, # 32131, # 18139 & # 26683 (Keith Bluemel)

17577

If ever a race car had a strange history then it might be this one. Would you believe a race car paid for by a bank?

17577 was a road-going 365BB imported into the US from Belgium in 1980. The BB, along with other property, was put up as collateral with the United California Bank, who seized it for non-payment of the debt. The car was put into store, but unfortunately for the bank the car had not been US legalized, and did not meet the necessary 'Department of Transport' and' Environmental Protection Agency' requirements. US Customs were

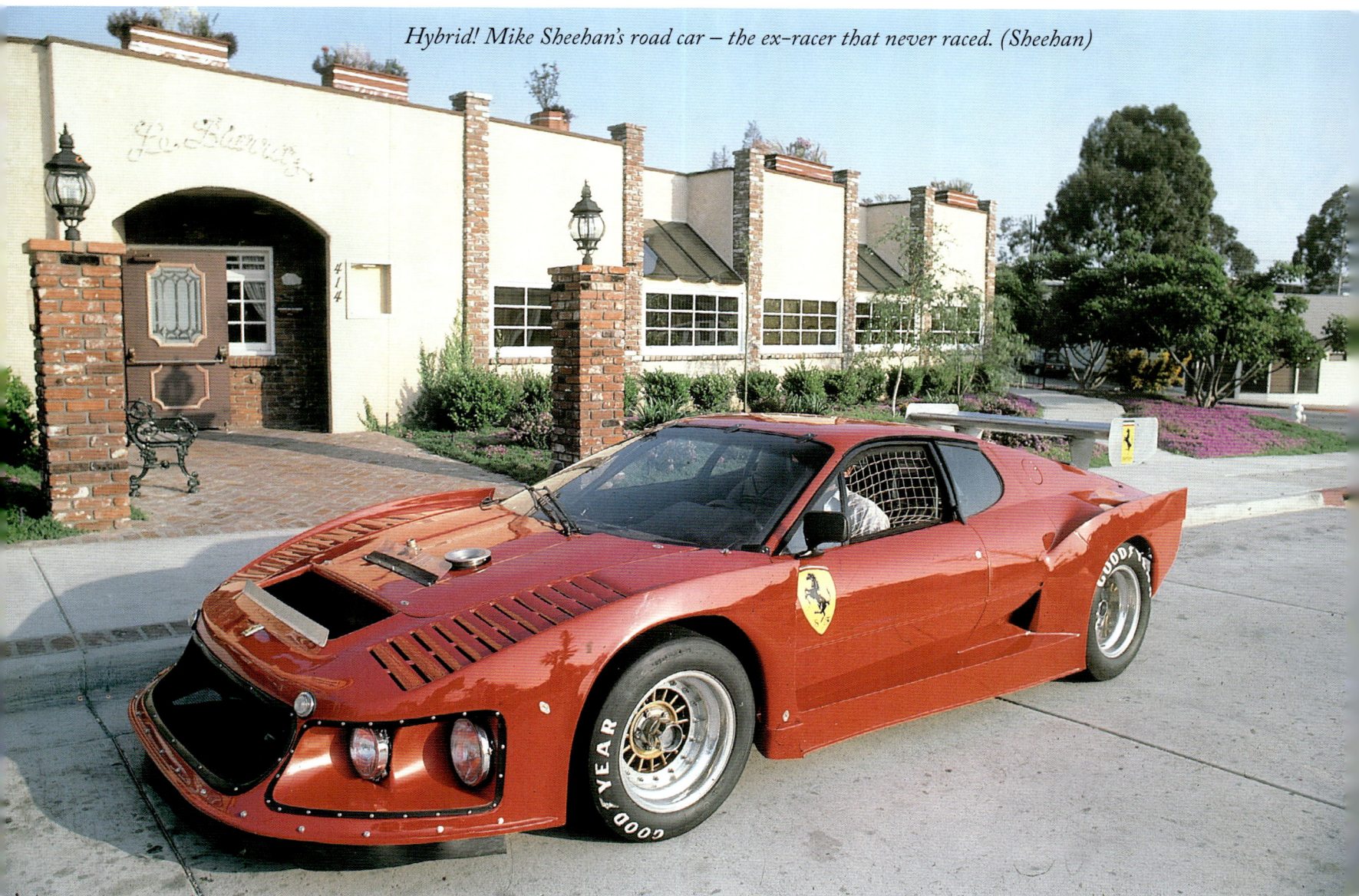

Hybrid! Mike Sheehan's road car – the ex-racer that never raced. (Sheehan)

17577 displays its Porsche K3 rear and large rear wing. (Sheehan)

responsible for seeing that all imports are 'federalised' within 90 days of arrival, and any cars that were not converted were recalled to be crushed. So the UC Bank duly received notice to give up the BB to be crushed on Sept 27th 1980.

The problem was that the Bank had less than a week in which to convert the car, and thus save their money. It seemed as if the only way out was to turn the BB into a race car, and thus take advantage of one of the US Customs exemption laws. This option would be less expensive to the Bank than trashing the Ferrari.

So on Sept 23rd three days of frantic activity began in order to beat the dead-line and turn the BB into a racer. The car was shipped to John Mason and all the road going equipment such as air-conditioning, heater, door panels and trim was ripped out. Door window glass was removed, NASCAR style netting added, a roll-cage built in, and even the suspension was lowered. Bruno Borri of Modena Sports Cars was also called in to do some mechanical work.

On Sept 26th Borri submitted a full report to the Customs people explaining all the modifications that had already been made, those that were still to be made, and why this particular car could never be converted back to a road car. He also had to prove his own credentials as a race car preparer, and the intention to enter the 1981 Daytona 24Hrs.

Other modifications included the fitting of Girling disk brakes, an engine rebuilt with higher compression pistons and racing camshafts, conversion to dry sump system, and the addition of a megaphone exhaust system.

Apparently all this work persuaded the Customs authorities that the BB was now a race car, and that the bank could keep their racer. So the UC Bank became the only bank to commission and own a Ferrari race car.

But the story doesn't end here. Well it does for the bank, but not for the BB. The bank, being a bank, decided that they would rather have the money than own a race car, and sold the BB to Paul Lewis and Ray Sylvain of Los Angeles. They decided to modify the BB even further, and in so doing made this story even weirder.

Because what they eventually created was a car with a BB centre section, but Porsche 935K3 style front and rear body panels, and a high mounted rear wing.

The 'Porrari'(?), the 'Ferrorsche'(?), didn't actually make Daytona, but did eventually appear during practice at Riverside in April. As the engine blew up during qualifying the BB was listed as a Did Not Start.

Owner Paul Lewis did a few SCCA races in 1981 but I have been unable to obtain any further details about these events.

The BB was then purchased by Mike Sheehan of European Auto Restoration in Costa Mesa, California. Mike, bravely, used the BB as a road car until the attention of the local law enforcement officers persuaded him that something a little less obvious would be an advantage.

18095

This was the second BB to be race prepared by Chinetti, but this one was under the control of Luigi Snr. who felt that Chinetti Jnr. had gone over the top with 18139. 18095 started life as regular street car, red paint finish, and black interior. It was prepared for Le Mans 1975 by the NART team under the direction of Nereo Iori.

Only minor modifications were made to make the BB race ready, and reference to photos shows a virtually standard looking BB on the track. The obvious changes were flared out wheel arches to cover the wider than standard wheels, these being 8 inch at the front and 11 inch at the rear. Also noticeable was a small tacked on rear spoiler, and a quick-fill fuel cap just in front of the driver's side rear wheel. The rest of the car was

18095 was the first BB to run at Le Mans although it didn't actually start the 24hrs. (NB Colln)

substantially standard, even down to the driver's seat. Naturally certain safety features such as a roll-bar, seat-belt and fire extinguisher had to be added, but other items that were usually modified such as the engine, suspension and transmission were left untouched. The exception being a 1inch spacer inserted between the oil pan and transaxle housing to increase the oil capacity, and the removal of the standard exhaust system.

So off to Le Mans! And Chinetti turned up with a real mixed bag. Each of the four NART cars entered were different. There was a normal competition Daytona, a Michelotti bodied Daytona, the BB and a 308GT4. The BB qualified quite well (40th/55; 4m30.0), although more than 12secs slower than the Daytona, but the cause of all the trouble was the 308GT4. The race organisers, the ACO, decided that if the 308GT4 was going to compete it had to be in the Gp5 class. In other words, as far as they were concerned it was the same as a Porsche 908 or a DFV engined Gulf GR8. Chinetti, not surprisingly, found this to be unacceptable and when the organisers were not prepared to assign the 308 to another class Chinetti withdrew the whole team.

This particular BB never raced and after Le Mans was returned to the United States where it was used by the Revlon Cosmetic Company for a TV commercial. During filming it was crashed, injuring a cameraman.

It was rebuilt as a street car and repainted in metallic green with black lower body panels. It was 'legalized' by Dick Fritz's Amerispec Corporation and then given to J.G. Walker Jr. who was one of the Chinetti team sponsors.

As if it hadn't suffered enough it was later badly damaged in a garage fire, and after having a number of owners, it eventually finished up with Mike Sheehan in California. Mike restored it back to its 1975 Le Mans spec.

| 14/6/75 | Le Mans 24 Hrs | 99 | NART Guitteny/Haran | DNS |

18139

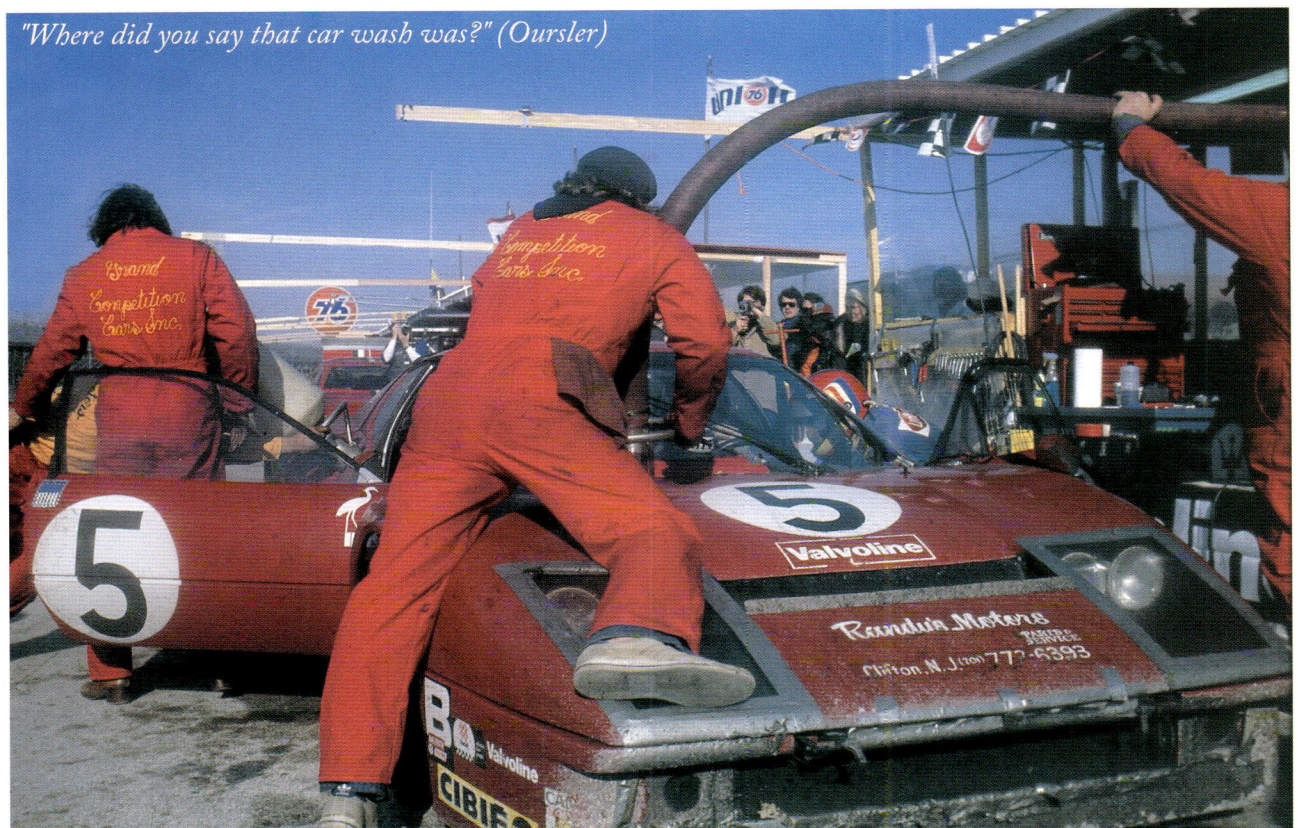

"Where did you say that car wash was?" (Oursler)

A rare photo of the 365BB racing engine (Fred Lewis – www.fredlewisphotos.com)

Race preparation allows the enthusiast a rare glimpse of the interior of a racing BB. Here with the door removed the fabricated fuel tank and even the front of the engine are visible. (Fred Lewis – www.fredlewisphotos.com)

From behind the extended bodywork of 18139 is obvious. (Fred Lewis – www.fredlewisphotos.com)

Photos of this car at Daytona 1975 are so rare, and even more so in colour. 18139 retired on the first lap so the best we can hope for are photos taken during practice. During practice the hub carrier broke and here the team have stripped out the suspension in order to effect repairs. (Fred Lewis – www.fredlewisphotos.com)

1977 and 18139 is pushed to the Le Mans start. 24hours later they would finish in 16th position (John Allen)

This was the first BB built for competition. Its development as a race car is described in the section 'The BB In Competition'. The BB had cost Chinetti $25,000 to purchase and another $50,000 to develop, a not insubstantial sum in 1975!

After the four races in 1975 the BB sat out the 1976 season, ostensibly waiting for a new 5 litre racing engine. In the meantime 18139 had been put up as collateral by Chinetti, and when the loan was not repaid the BB went into the ownership of Howard O'Flynn of Bankers Discount of New York. Although owned by O'Flynn it was entered for Le Mans 1977 by NART.

O'Flynn decided to race the car again in 1978, and a 5 litre engine was purchased from the factory in time for the Daytona 24hrs where it finished 22nd. It also ran at Road Atlanta and then Le Mans.

For Le Mans the factory made a competition prepared 450bhp 512 engine available. Francois Migault drove over to Maranello in his Renault van, collected the engine, and delivered it to Le Mans in time to be fitted for the twenty four hours. His reward was 16th overall and 3rd. in the IMSA class.

Although the team were more than a little upset to find out that despite purchasing a factory engine they had not been supplied with other modified parts such as the tuned exhaust headers and larger transfer gear cases. A protest was put in to the factory representative, Sig. Florini, but it was too late to do much.

At Road Atlanta (1978) Francois Migault brought 18139 into 21st place. (NB Colln)

By now the BB was outclassed in the IMSA series and ran just once more, at Watkins Glen, before going into lengthy retirement.

In 1980 it was sold to Homer Rader of Texas who allowed his mechanic, Bob Norwood, to run it in a few historic and Ferrari Club events.

In September 1983 it went to Mike Sheehan who ran it in SCCA. SCCA races were generally the equivalent of U.K. 'club' races, which usually meant that the cars serious competitive career was over; but not so in the case of 18139. Mike Sheehan felt that as more than 1000 BBs had been built he had a very good chance of qualifying the BB in IMSA's GTO category, instead of the GTP (GT Prototypes) class. It was obviously not a contender for outright victory as it would be up against Porsche 962s and the like, but in the GTO class it could put up a good show against the Corvettes and Camaros. A phone call to John Bishop of IMSA confirmed that the BB would be classed as a GTO car, and so over the winter of '83/84 Mike began preparation for a season of IMSA racing.

Quite a lot of work was put into updating the BB. Modifications included the following......

new roll cage fitted;
new modular wheel allowing larger 12inch disc brakes with Dunlop calipers to be fitted;
a rebuilt cockpit with new dash and wiring system;
new fuel cells;
new extinguisher system;
air jacks fitted to speed up tyre changes;
suspension, engine and transaxle overhauled;
body stripped and repainted;

Obviously a tremendous amount of work went into preparing what was by now a nearly ten year old race car.

On December 15th 1983 IMSA dropped their bombshell on Sheehan. Because of the width of the rear wheels and rear tyres the BB would have to run in the GTP class after all.

Having put so much work into preparing the car Mike decided to enter it in competition anyway. At Riverside, on April 29th the BB turned up for the Los Angeles Times/Nissan Grand Prix of Endurance - a six hour race. The BB qualified 37th out of 52 entries but retired after 76 laps when the transfer gear stubs pulled loose from the bell housing

Driver Ed Swart reported quite favourably on the performance of the BB, only bemoaning the lack of power compared to the opposition.

Owner Mike Sheehan, ever the optimist, decided to rebuild the engine incorporating special high compression pistons, larger valves and special cylinder heads, in an effort to obtain more power; approx. 480 bhp was achieved. Sadly, Mike came to the realisation that the BB's days were numbered, at least as far as serious competition was concerned, and 18139 was sold to an enthusiast in Europe.

In what Mike has described as "a fit of nostalgia" he then bought 18139 back, and ran it in occasional club and historic races; which I reckon is a fitting end for an 'old trooper'.

2/1/75	Daytona 24 HRS	1	NART	Ballot-Lena/Cudini/Minter	DNF
22/3/75	Sebring 12 Hrs	111	NART	Minter	6
20/4/75	Road Atlanta	111	NART	Minter	DNS
26/5/75	Lime Rock Race 1	111	NART	Minter	DNF
26/5/75	Lime Rock Race 2	111	NART	Minter	DNF
10/6/77	Le Mans 24 Hrs	75	NART	Migault/Guitteny	16
4/2/78	Daytona 24 Hrs	5	NART	Migault/Guitteny/Young	22
16/4/78	Road Atlanta	5	NART	Migault	21
10/6/78	Le Mans 24 Hrs	86	GCC	Migault/Guitteny	16
8/7/78	Watkins Glen 6Hr	25	NART	Migault/Guitteny	11
29/4/84	Riverside	75	Sh'n	Schwarz/Christian/Swart	38

22715

22715 (sometimes listed incorrectly as 22175, which is a 308GTB) made its debut, and only race appearance at Le Mans 1978. The Belgian driver Jean Blaton (Beurlys) had a road going BB converted to competition specification by Jacques Swaters at Garage Francorchamps. It was noticeably different from any other competition BB thanks to the sno-plow air-dam and large adjustable rear wing designed by Jean-Pierre Uri. Not surprisingly, it was the heaviest of the five BBs, and at 178.33mph was the slowest down the Mulsanne by almost 10mph.

The 24 hours got under way at the traditional start time of 4 o'clock but within three hours Teddy Pilette had brought it in to be retired with transmission problems. It never raced again.

This unique BB/LM recently resurfaced, and is now in Germany. On finding the car the new owner reported; "Interestingly the car is "as is" when it left LeMans 1978: All chips in the paint, LM race stickers and even the tyres from that year. Must be one the most untouched cars I've seen in a long time. Restoration will focus on complete mechanical overhaul, sans engine. Body will remain untouched, but we are fabricating another body for racing (would be a shame to damage the original body in a race). Nice detail: The Spoilers were done in cooperation with BMW Motorsport - recognize the similarity of the rear wing and front spoiler with M1 cars of that era?"

| 10/6/78 | Le Mans 24 Hrs | 85 | Beurlys | Beurlys/Pilette/Tourol | DNF |

22715 made it's only competition appearance at Le Mans 1978. This photo shows the unique air-dam, and the unusual clear headlamp protectors (LAT)

24127

24127 was the first of a batch of three BBs specially built by the factory for competition. Over the winter of 1977/78 a modified BB was seen running around Ferrari's Fiorano test track. It was obviously more than an ordinary Boxer, as was borne out by the new nose with pronounced air-dam, widened rear wheel arches, and prominent rear wing. The rear wing was actually the front wing off Ferrari's then current grand prix car, the 312T3.

The BB underwent a considerable weight saving exercise, thanks to the extensive use of glass-fibre and aluminium for the bodywork. This loss of weight, added to an increase in power output (now about 400bhp) resulted in a considerably quicker Boxer.

For Le Mans Ferrari had provided an alternative nose section, which was reminiscent of the 1963 330LMBs. The BBs could run with or without it fitted; the BB with the nose fitted picked up an extra 200rpm on the Mulsanne but as all three cars qualified within 0.8 secs of each other the long nose didn't seem to offer any

24127 pictured here in 1982 at the Pierre Bardinon's private Mas du Clos circuit. (Bluemel)

The air-boxes were a unique feature of the Series 1 BB/LMs. The rear wing was a variation of the Ferrari 312B3 front wing. (John Allen)

noticeable advantage. Pozzi chose to leave it off this car, but mounted two large spot-lights in the middle of the grille instead.

No.88, in 34th place, was the second quickest BB in qualifying It's time of 4m07.3s putting it only 0.2s behind the other Pozzi car and 6th fastest qualifier in the IMSA class.

Andruet was entrusted with the first couple of stints before handing over to Dini, and by the third hour they were in a respectable 15th. overall, but just before the four hour mark Dini had to pit to have the clutch bearings changed, and the 40 minute delay immediately dropped 88 down to 37th. Despite losing even more time with a 15 min. stop to replace the fuel pump, and another 14 min. stop to change the bell housing Andruet and Dini battled on valiantly. Finally, with more than twenty hours passed, and having worked back up to 11th they were thwarted when the transmission gave out. Poor reward for their hard work.

Le Mans 1978 was the only competition appearance for 24127 which was later owned by 'Uderzo', the creator of the cartoon character 'Asterix The Gaul'.

| 10/6/78 | Le Mans 24 Hrs | 88 | NART | Andruet/Dini | DNF |

24129

This was the second of Pozzi's new cars, (for details see 24127) and was entered for the experienced Claud Ballot-Lena and Jean-Louis Lafosse. It ran with the pointed nose, and was the fastest qualifier of the five BB/LMs, Ballot-Lena doing the business with a 4m07.1s.

The Pozzi BB/LM ran just the one time – at Le Mans 1978 where it retired. (NB Colln)

Unhappily, the good results of practice were not to carry over into the race, and after only 1hr. 25mins. Ballot-Lena came in for a 36min stop to replace the alternator and fix the clutch. However Ballot-Lena and Lafosse continued, and despite a further 28min stop just after mid-night to adjust the alternator belt they were back up to twelfth when a broken transmission caused their retirement about 9am Sunday.

After Le Mans 24129 was returned to the factory to be rebuilt, and then was purchased by Ferrari enthusiast Mark Tippetts. This was after an agreement between Gaetano Florini of Ferrari and Daniel Marin of Pozzi, that Mark should have the BB after it had done Le Mans. The story of Mark's acquisition of the BB/LM actually goes back to 1974 - Mark had an agreement to purchase the last competition Daytona. If the factory built a competition Boxer for Pozzi to run at Le Mans 1975 then Mark would get the Daytona immediately; if not, then Pozzi would run the Daytona and Mark would get it after the race, and after it had been rebuilt at the factory.

As things turned out Pozzi didn't get a BB in 1975, and also decided not to run the Daytona so Mark took delivery of a brand new unraced 1975 spec competition Daytona. Mark was so impressed with the Daytona that he asked for, and obtained, a similar deal on one of the first BB/LMs - in other words after the race the car would become his.

In fact the only time Mark ever went in the car was when Claude Ballot-Lena drove him round a private race track in the pouring rain. Mark confesses that being in the BB with no passenger seat, no seat belt, and Ballot-Lena throwing it around like a rally car on a soaking wet track was 'a terrifying experience' which probably put him off the BB somewhat.

So 24129 went into storage in Geneva until it was sold in 1984 to a Swiss collector. Later believed to be in USA.

| 10/6/78 | Le Mans 24 Hrs | 89 | Pozzi | Ballot-Lena/Lafosse | DNF |

24131

24131 was the third and last of the first batch of factory built competition cars. The NART team opted for the long nose version (LAT)

As you've probably guessed by now, this was the third and last of the first batch of factory built competition cars.

This one went to NART and also made its competition debut at Le Mans 1978. In practice the best recorded time by one of the nominated drivers was 4m16.3s by Daniel Guerin, which was nearly 10s slower than the two Pozzi cars managed. Whether this BBs lack of speed was down to its pilots' inexperience or a deliberate decision by the team to take it easy during practice is unsure. In fact its grid position was actually down to Jean-Claud Andruet who managed to qualify it with a 4m07.9s lap, less than 1s slower than his fastest lap in his own BB. The fact that the other two BBs managed to turn in race laps in the 4m 07s range, as compared to this cars 4m13.6s might indicate that the chosen drivers needed a bit more experience either with the car, or with the circuit.

Maybe their slower speed was instrumental in ensuring that, of the three cars, this BB spent the least amount of time in the pits during the race. Even so it was only up to 11th when it retired just after 9am Sunday morning with a broken transmission.

Was at one time believed to be owned by Walter Medlin (USA)

10/6/78   Le Mans 24 Hrs   87   NART   Delaunay/Guerin/Young   DNF

26681

This was the first of a new batch of three modified, so-called 'silhouette' BB/LMs. Over the winter of '78/79 Ferrari had updated the BB/LM specifications and had enlisted the help of Pininfarina to design a new aerodynamic body. (For further details see the 1979 Daytona race report.)

The fabulous 'clouds' colour scheme was created by Thieery Fougerol, a Parisian artist for Charles Pozzi. (Blumlein)

All three cars appeared at Daytona for the annual 24hr. race. Two for Pozzi and the third for NART. No.66 qualified in 15th spot, amongst the slower Porsche turbos. Within 2 1/2hrs all three BB/LMs were in the top ten, and looked to be heading for some extremely good results. However, things don't always work out how they should, and within a short while all three cars were out of the race. The NART car had a tyre burst whilst at full chat on the banking which almost destroyed the car although driver Delaunay was, thankfully, unhurt. As a similar incident had occurred in practice Team manager Jean Marc Smajda (who, incidentally was the same JMS whose initials often appeared on the side of Pozzi's cars) decided to withdraw the two remaining cars before someone was injured. It was believed that the problem was caused by the tremendous force exerted on the cars by the banking.

The next outing for 26681 was at Le Mans in June, where both Pozzi cars featured a distinctive 'clouds' colour scheme by Jean Fougerol who also designed the paint schemes for the JMS Porsche in 1977. At 2773lbs. this was the heaviest of the four BB/LMs. Andruet qualified second quickest of the BB/LMs in 4m02.42s, but this was more than 12s slower than Stommelen's class leading Porsche 935. Top speed was 186.411mph on the Mulsanne, about 6mph faster than the 1978 car. Not surprisingly, as most middle order runners don't thrash their cars in practice, the race times were a bit quicker, as Dini did a 3m58.6, and upped the top speed to 192.0004mph.

26681 had a pretty tough time in the fist seven hours, spending more than an hour in the pits altogether having different problems fixed. Even the floor needed refitting! But from then on it motored like a train, and from resuming in 31st. place climbed as high as 6th before finally retiring with a broken engine with less than 5 hours to go.

| 3/2/79 | Daytona 24 HRS | 66 | Pozzi | Andruet/Dini/Ballot-Lena | DNF |
| 9/6/79 | Le Mans 24 Hrs | 62 | Pozzi | Andruet/Dini | DNF |

26683   Engine 001

This was the second of the three BB/LM79s, and was delivered to NART in time for the 1979 Daytona 24hrs. It qualified in 16th place but on lap 73 a tyre let go on the banking causing its retirement. Because of this incident and a similar one during practice the two remaining BBs were retired on safety grounds.

The first factory built BB/LMs made quite an impact with their aerodynamic Pininfarina designed bodywork (Oursler)

The mighty 5litre BB/LM engine in the back of NARTs 1979 Daytona car
(Fred Lewis – www.fredlewisphotos.com)

The next outing for 26683 was at Le Mans in early June. Delaunay qualified third fastest of the BBs and 8th in the IMSA class with a time of 4m06.30, despite being quicker on the Mulsanne (193.868mph) than any of the other IMSA cars, including the Porsche 935Ts. Obviously the sleek Pininfarina-designed body slipped through the air very effectively, but the BB/LM79s still couldn't overcome the 250/300lb weight advantage of the Porsches.

A Ferrari stalwart – Luigi Chinetti (in glasses) walks behind his NART entered BB/LM
(Fred Lewis – www.fredlewisphotos.com)

From its 36th starting spot No64 was up to 20th by the 4th hour and was running reliably with no problems. Then Preston Henn managed to hit the barrier at Tetre Rouge and put an end to what had looked like a promising race.

26683 made its third and final competition appearance back at Daytona in 1980. Sharing the driving with Preston Henn was experienced Frenchman Pierre Dieudonne. They qualified 23rd out of a massive field of 73 runners, and retired after 341 laps, due to a leaking fuel tank, although officially listed in 36th place.

3/2/79	Daytona 24 HRS	68	NART	Tullius/Delaunay/Bedard	DNF
9/6/79	Le Mans 24 Hrs	64	NART	Delaunay/Grandet/Henn	DNF
2/2/80	Daytona 24 HRS	69	HENN	Dieudonne/Henn	DNF

26685

This was the third of the new Pininfarina bodied '79 cars that appeared at Daytona for the 24hrs. Qualified 13th but was withdrawn after 101 laps due to tyre problems.

The Pozzi team prepare 26685 for practice at Daytona 1979. (NB Colln)

Just admire the body-makers art as repairs are made to the damage caused by the right rear tyre blow out. (Fred Lewis – www.fredlewisphotos.com)

At Le Mans this Pozzi entered car had the same colourful 'clouds' colour scheme as its team mate but with major sponsorship by 3M instead of ISO. It was the fastest of the BBs in practice with Leclere being just .78s outside the 4min barrier.

At half distance the BB was holding a solid 10th place and looking good for a top ten finish but disaster struck at 8:15am when Leclere collided with the No33 Chevron 2-litre at the bottom of the Mulsanne. Maybe the torrential rain that flooded the track in parts had something to do with the collision.

Le Mans 1979 and the two Pozzi team cars head down towards the Esses. The famous Dunlop bridge can be seen at the top of the hill in the background. (NB Colln)

26685s final race appearance was at Le Mans in 1980. It featured the same distinctive blue and yellow colour scheme, and European University sponsorship of its two newer team mates. As the oldest BB at Le Mans in 1980 it was also the heaviest at 1211kgs. Nevertheless, Guitteny qualified it 36th with a time of 4m06.8 which was still quicker than a couple of the other BBs.

Le Mans 1980 began on a soaking wet track, as less than half an hour before the start the heavens had opened in a torrential downpour. I remember it well; I was there at the time. Everybody tiptoed round the warm-up lap, and then the field came power-boating down into the Esses in a ball of spray. Despite the horrendous conditions the spectators were enthralled by the performance of Hans Stuck in a BMW M1 who was in a good second place at the end of the first hour. Alas our Ferrari didn't do any where near as well and lingered around thirtieth place, give or take a few spots, before being abandoned out on the course after 4 hours.

26685 shoots through The Esses at Le Mans 1980 (NB Colln)

26685 disappeared for a few years, then was bought and given a ground up restoration by Nigel Chiltern-Hunt.

3/2/79	Daytona 24 Hrs	67	Pozzi	Ballot-Lena/Leclere/Andruet	DNF
9/6/79	Le Mans 24 Hrs	63	Pozzi	Ballot-Lena/Leclere/Gregg	DNF
14/6/80	Le Mans 24 Hrs	75	Pozzi	Guitteny/Bleynie/Libert	DNF

27577

This was the fourth of the '79 spec cars built by Ferrari, although the final preparation was carried out by Garage Francorchamps. The car was actually owned by 'Beurlys', which was the pseudonym of Belgian driver Jean Blaton. The drivers were a mixed bunch including Bernard de Dryver, a Formula 2 driver at the time, and enthusiastic amateur Steve O'Rourke, who was better known as the manager of rock group Pink Floyd than as a racing driver. Both were making their first appearances at Le Mans. 'Beurlys' on the other hand was in only his 15th 24hr epic!

Nick Faure qualified the BB 45th overall and 10th in IMSA with a time of 4m11.98, and slowest of the four BBs entered. The other drivers were 15-25secs slower than Faure, but this may have been a deliberate strategy to send just one driver after the fastest lap.

Lights ablaze! The Francorchamps BB cuts through the murk at Le Mans 1979
(David Blumlein)

Despite breaking an engine in practice the BB ran a steady pace in the race being slightly delayed by clutch problems early on, and by water in the distributor from about 2 in the morning when it started to rain heavily. In this instance the tortoise finished 12th.

Steve O'Rourke had been one of four drivers who raced 27577 at Le Mans in 1979 when it was painted yellow. They had finished a fine 12th. After Le Mans O'Rourke brought the car and had it repainted in patriotic British racing green, as seen here at Silverstone 1980. Within 12 months it was back to yellow, and is now back to green (Bluemel)

27577 was then purchased by O'Rourke who had it repainted British Racing Green instead of the Belgian yellow that it carried at Le Mans. The next outing was at Silverstone in 1980. O'Rourke was joined for this event by Vic Norman, (the boss of Ferrari dealers Rosso Ltd.) and Chris Craft; an accomplished historic (no, he wasn't historic, his cars were!) and sportscar racer.

In fact it was Chris Craft who set the qualifying time of 1m35.21, quick enough for 18th spot on the grid, 13s slower than John Fitzpatrick's 1m22.09 pole position time in the Porsche 935K3/80. The BB ran well and reliably, and completed the 6hr event in 7th place. All augured well for the next event, the Le Mans 24hrs.

Regrettably Silverstone only flattered to deceive. In fact the EMKA team were fortunate to even make the race at all. The A.C.O. had brought in some new regulations which caused a certain amount of confusion. One said that the qualifying time would be the average time of all the drivers in each car; the other was that cars would qualify according to class. The result was that some of the slower cars in the fast classes were pushed out in favour of even slower cars because they were the fastest in the slower classes. (I hope you followed that!) So despite a qualifying time that would have put it about 50th on the grid (out of 56 starters) the BB was relegated to first reserve in the IMSA class. Nevertheless the third new regulation came to EMKA's rescue. This rule said that once qualifying started no team would be allowed to change engines. Unfortunately the No.74 NART BB/LM fell foul of this rule, and so the EMKA car was pushed onto 56th and last place on the grid. The team's relief at getting a start would soon change once the race got under way.

Early part of the race and 27577 looks superb (NB Photo)

The least experienced of the three drivers, car owner Steve O'Rourke decided to take the first stint, but a torrential thunderstorm on the pace lap probably made him wish he'd put one of the other guys in. But by dint of some steady driving the BB survived the worst of the weather and slowly moved up through the field, until just after midnight when a rear tyre blew out on the Mulsanne and demolished the rear bodywork. The EMKA team then did a deal with the already retired Bellancauto team to use the rear bodywork off their car, and after more than 1½ hrs in the pits the now bi-coloured BB rejoined the race. After this major drama anything else was an anti-climax, and apart from a couple of minor problems the team soldiered on to a well earned 23rd place finish, a mere 76 laps behind the winning Rondeau.

Later part of the race and 27577 looks less than superb, but still finished (NB colln)

27577 next appeared at Silverstone in 1981 for the annual 6hrs event where it appeared in yet another new colour scheme - pale yellow. This time O'Rourke elected not to drive, but brought in the vastly experienced Derek Bell.

Nick Mason has added 27577 to his collection, and it is now back in British Racing Green.

9/6/79	Le Mans 24 Hrs	61	Beurlys	Beurlys/Faure/de Dryver/O'Rourke	12
11/5/80	Silverstone 6 Hrs	11	EMKA	O'Rourke/Norman/Craft	7
14/6/80	Le Mans 24 Hrs	78	EMKA	O'Rourke/Down/Phillips	23
10/5/81	Silverstone 6 Hrs	42	EMKA	Bond/Bell/Griswold	DNF

27579

27579 was another '79 style factory built car. It was sold to Scuderia Samocar and was never raced.

Although never raced 27579 made a few appearances – see here at Mugello in 1992 (Marcel Massini)

28601

Bellancauto had two BB/LMs. The first one shown here at Le Mans in 1980 looked very near factory standard, although the grilles on top of the front wheel arches were team modifications. (NB Colln)

This is one of the more interesting BB/LMs. It was built by the factory, finished in Oct. 1979 and bought by Bellancauto. Scuderia Bellancauto was a restoration specialist founded by Signor Biasini who was the Talbot dealer in Rome. Historic racer Fabrizio Violati was also involved and when the BB appeared it showed signs of having been tested and modified.

Its first race appearance was at Monza for the 1980 6Hrs race. The team qualified a respectable 25th but retired on lap 108 with engine failure. This race was unusual as it was one of the few world championship races to be won by a woman driver – Desire Wilson who shared Alain de Cadenet's de Cadenet Lola Ford-Cosworth.

Having warmed up at Monza the team turned up at Le Mans in June for the 24hr. epic. In practice Spartaco Dini was the fastest of the team's three drivers with a lap in 4m dead, but as both the other two co-drivers were more than 20s slower they lined up a lowly 39th. If all three drivers had been able to turn comparable lap times then they could have started as high as 20th.

As things turned out, it didn't matter where they started from. Despite a streaming wet track Dini was off like a rat up a drain-pipe, and then he was just 'off'. The BB was wound up to 15th place when Dini comprehensively stuffed it into the Armco to become the first Ferrari to retire, and the fourth official retirement.

28601 was then retired from competition and became part of the Collezione Maranello Rosso, Fabrizio Violati's museum in San Marino. In recent years it has competed in Europe in the Ferrari Shell Historic Challenge Series.

| 27/4/80 | Monza 1000 Kms | 31 | Bellancauto | Dini/Violati | DNF |
| 14/6/80 | Le Mans 24 Hrs | 79 | Bellancauto | Dini/Violati/Micangeli | DNF |

29507   Engine 002

29507 was finished by Ferrari in October 1979 and its first owner was Albert Obrist. After the car was delivered it was modified by Bruno Wyss who fitted it with pneumatic jacks, air vents to duct air into the cockpit and a fire extinguisher system.

Obrist never used the car and within a few weeks sold it to Californian Ferrari collector Jon Masterson

It was never raced by Jon, but did appear at a number of American Ferrari Club events. It was sold in 1992 and again in 1999. The new owner entered it in a few Historic Challenge events.

29507 (Keith Bluemel)

29509

Bob Donner ran his new car to 2nd overall in the SCCA Regional Race at Pueblo Motorsports Park in 1980. Notice the tape round the NACA duct to protect the paint from stone chips. (Donner)

29509 was finished in November 1979 and was sold through Albert Pedretti's U.S. Ferrari dealership to gentleman racer Bob Donner. It has been reported that this car was unraced, yet Bob told me that he competed in a number of events run by the SCCA (Sports Car Club of America). These events were organized by the Colourado region of the SCCA in the A Sports Racing class - ASR. The BB was actually illegal under club rules because of having fuel injection fitted, but Bob was permitted to race 'as a favour' to give him some racing time and practice. Most of the competition was large engined carburettor equipped Lola and McClaren CanAm cars. In this company the BB/LM was naturally out-paced, but Bob did pick up a good 2nd, behind a Lola in a National Event at Continental Divide Raceway in 1980. For Bob it brought back memories of his first race at CDR way back in 1959 when he won in a Porsche RSK.

Bob also ran his car at various Ferrari club events, and also in the annual Virginia City hill-climb.

In 1981 it was advertised for sale at $125,000 and was sold to Claude Belenger in Canada; it then went to Joe Marchetti, a Ferrari dealer and organiser of the Chicago Historic Races. It was next heard of in 1985 when Walnut Creek Ferrari of California offered it for sale at $135,000. In view of the fact that it was sold at the Orion Auction at Monte Carlo in November 1989 for more than $1mill, the 1985 price seems to be quite a bargain. At the end of 1990 it was being offered for sale again by Dr. Herbert Gerl of Austria. It went to Japan and was last seen in the USA, where it raced in a few Historic Challenge events.

29511

29511 hurtles round the banking on its way to 16th place at Daytona 1985. (Daytona International Speedway)

29511 has an unusual story. It was finished in November 1979 according to the factory, and was sold through Pedretti to John Gelles of Scarsdale, New York. It was unraced for four years and then made its first appearance at an IMSA event at Lime Rock in 1984. Quite why it was four years before Gelles decided to race the car is uncertain, but when it did appear it was obviously a serious effort. Engineer Lee Dykstra redesigned the suspension and steering rack etc. and the modifications were carried out by Fabcar in Atlanta.

The Lime Rock event, despite being called the 'Coca-Cola 500' was in fact a short one hour sprint (in fact just 56 laps, or 86 miles). The BB qualified and finished 13th - at least it was consistent - and earned the grand total of $750 in prize money.

The next event was expected to suit the BB better. For the Watkins Glen Double 3-hour (i.e. 6 hours) Steve Cohen was joined by Eno DePasquale and John Gelles brother Bill. They qualified 33rd. and actually finished 17th. As the prize money for 17th, and 6 hours, was $800 they probably felt that they'd done a lot better financially at Lime Rock!

Nevertheless, undaunted they appeared again at Watkins Glen in September for The New York 500 (kms). This time the intrepid trio completed 80 laps to the winners 92, and finished 20th. Again earning $750 - not much when split three ways

The next appearance of 29511 was for the 1985 Daytona 24hrs. There they were joined by the newer Mosler Racing BB/LM which qualified just a couple of places ahead of them in 34th place. Whilst the Mosler team retired the Gelles car recorded the best ever finish for a BB/LM at Daytona - 16th overall. The team feel that they could have done even better but the car caught a rock in the fuel injection surge tank which meant that they were unable to fill the tank completely and lost 20-30mins running time on each fill-up. Even so the prize money this time was a more respectable $2200.

Finally, a two man team turned up at Sebring for the 12hrs. This time they qualified a quite respectable 24th overall (considering the age of the car and the opposition), and 2nd fastest in the GTO class but retired on the 54th lap.

28/5/84	Lime Rock	21	Equipco	Cohen	13
7/7/84	Watkins Glen	21	Equipco	Cohen/Gelles/De Pasquale	17
30/9/84	Watkins Glen ll	21	Equipco	Gelles/Cohen/De Pasquale	20
2/2/85	Daytona 24 HRS	21	Equipco	Gelles/Cohen/Walker	16
23/3/85	Sebring 12 Hrs	21	Equipco	Gelles/Cohen	DNF

30559   Engine 010

When I started researching this book I had no idea that this would turn out to be the most raced of all the BB/LMs, but over a five year period 30559 was entered in thirteen races. It was completed by the factory in April 1980, and was the first of the new lighter weight cars with the 'ground-effect' type bodywork. The first owner was Luigi Chinetti, and it was entered under the auspices of his NART team at Le Mans in June. During practice the team broke the engine and due to the rules prohibiting engine changes (which was really aimed at the Porsches) once qualifying had begun, they had no choice but to withdraw.

Now owned by Preston Henn who, despite the name, was no 'spring chicken'; the 49 year old from Pompona Beach, Florida had started sports car racing in 1977, and whilst he entered the BB/LM he was himself usually to be found racing his Porsche 935K3.

The T-Bird Swap Shop team swarm round Preston Henn's BB/LM making final preparations before the practice session begins (NB Colln)

The first appearance under Preston's ownership was Sebring 1981 where the car practised but didn't start. The team switched to the Porsche K3.

For Daytona 1982 Henn had drafted in the 'brilliant' Bob Wollek, Edgar Doeren and Randy Lanier (who would become IMSA Champion in 1984). They were fastest of the three BB/LMs entered in 1982 qualifying in 15th place with a time of 1m54s which compared well with the 1m43.9s of the pole position March Chevrolet. The race went really well for 18hrs, working its way up to 3rd. place overall, when gearbox problems caused its sad retirement. The team must have been extremely disappointed to have worked all through the night and then have to pull out.

For Sebring Henn brought in an all girl team to handle the BB. American Janet Guthrie was joined by Preston's daughter Bonnie, and one time Formula One racer Desire Wilson. They qualified 17th out of 67 runners and retired after 163 laps.

Preston Henn's 30559 was the only BB/LM to race in Japan. Here it is being wheeled out to the start. It came back in looking slightly different (Isobe)

Next event was Le Mans, where despite recording the highest top speed of the four BBs present (320kmh/198mph) they were the only BB to take more than 4mins (4m07.32 to be precise), and started from a lowly 51st. In the race things looked distinctly better despite Henn spinning only a few laps into the race. After three hours they were lying 21st with Morin at the wheel when they ran out of petrol. Really!

Henn's final race with this car was at Mount Fuji for the 6 Hours. (For the full story see the competition section under 1982).

30559 was then lent to the Shelton brothers (of Shelton Ferrari in Florida) who race prepared the car and entered it in the 1983 Sebring 12hrs. The two Shelton brothers qualified a good 29th out of 84, but retired after 120 laps with transmission damage – caused when Tom ran over a man-hole cover.

The next time they appeared was in 1984 at Daytona. where a practice lap in 2m05.87 put them 27th on the grid. They were just 15secs slower than the pole-sitting Porsche 962 of Mario and Michael Andretti. They retired at 242 laps with an oil leak.

At Sebring the team qualified a lowly 67th. They had a frustrating time in the race, mainly due to the front bodywork supports breaking up, (caused by the roughness of the Sebring track), and also because of damaged inflicted when Sarel Van der Merwe pushed his way past in his March Porsche (or when McComb ran into the back of the Porsche – depending on whose account you hear). For the latter part of the race they were joined by Claud Ballot-Lena whose Porsche 935 had retired, and between them managed to carry the BB to 23rd. place.

30559 was then sold to Warren Mosler and for its final event in '84, the IMSA event at Road America, was entered by Mosler Racing of West Palm Beach, Florida. This was a 500 mile race, expected to last about four hours. The new driving team was John McComb, who had raced Mustangs in Trans-Am; Porsches and the famous Group 44 Jags. He was also an instructor with the Skip Barber Racing School. The

Yet another set of sponsor's decals for Sebring 1983 (Fred Lewis – www.fredlewisphotos.com)

second driver was Rick Mancuso of Lake Forest Sportscars in Illinois, who had raced Corvettes for John Greenwood. The third member of the team was Fred Fiala, a three time SCCA National Champion. This experienced team qualified 40th and the BB ran reliably to finish 15th.

Mosler Racing ran three IMSA events in 1985, and the team felt that the change in IMSA regulations would help them. The BB/LM was now eligible for the GTO (GT cars over 3 litres) rather than the GTP class. Although still not a contender for outright honours the within-class competition would be more equal.

The campaign began at Daytona where the team qualified 34th, two spots ahead of 29511, the Equipco car, but retired after 171 laps.

Sebring was no better, and again the dreaded letters DNF were put on the balance sheet.

So the final event for 30559 was at Mid Ohio. The BB was able to run in a separate race solely for GTO/GTU cars. Even so this was not really an ideal event for the BB/LM being only 2hrs long, but at least they would have a chance of finishing, and they did. From 17th starting spot they finished 13th overall.

It was last heard of with a French collector.

14/6/80	Le Mans 24 Hrs	74	NART	Delaunay/P Henn	DNS
21/3/81	Sebring 12hrs	91	Henn	P Henn/Gunn/Belcher	DNS
30/1/82	Daytona 24 HRS	6	Henn	Wollek/Doeren/Lanier	DNF
30/3/82	Sebring 12 Hrs	6	Henn	Guthrie/Wilson/B.Henn	DNF
19/6/82	Le Mans 24 Hrs	73	Henn	Henn/Lanier/Morin	DNF
3/10/82	Fuji 6 Hrs	12	Henn	P.Henn/B.Henn	DNF
19/3/83	Sebring 12 Hrs	8	S'ton	S.Shelton/T.Shelton	DNF
4/2/84	Daytona 24 HRS	97	S'ton	S.Shelton/T.Shelton	DNF
4/3/84	Sebring 12 Hrs	97	S'ton	S.Shelton/T.Shelton/McComb	23
29/8/84	Road America	97	Mosler	McComb/Mancuso/Fiala	15
2/2/85	Daytona 24 HRS	51	Mosler	McComb/Mancuso/Fiala	DNF
23/3/85	Sebring 12 Hrs	51	Mosler	McComb/Mancuso/Fiala	DNF
8/6/85	Mid Ohio	51	Mosler	McComb/Mancuso	13

31589

31589 was completed in time to run at Le Mans in 1980, and appeared in the blue and yellow colour scheme of European University. It was the second of the '80 ground-effect style cars. The vastly experienced Claude Ballot-Lena and Jean-Claude Andruet both achieved practice laps of less than 4mins and qualified a superb 17th overall, and 4th fastest in the IMSA class, right in amongst the much more developed, and more powerful Porsche K3s.

After the promise of practice the race itself didn't go too well for the team. Within half-an-hour of the start they were in the pits for a 17min stop because of an ignition problem. So at the one-hour mark No77 was back in 50th position, but with Ballot-Lena at the wheel the BB was spectacular. Using his considerable talents the big car was slipping, sliding and fish-tailing its way through the field. In two hours the BB moved up 24 places, and climbed back as high as 15th before retiring just before half distance with electrical problems.

The 2nd Series BB/LMs featured rudimentary ground effects. The efficiency of the ground effects can be judged by comparing the amount of water on the track in front of the car with the considerably drier patch behind it. (NB Colln)

31589 returned to Le Mans in 1981 with the same driver team. Again both drivers were under 4mins in practice, but as the competition had grown stronger the BB was back to 35th and 9th in class. And yet, whereas last year promised much and didn't deliver, this year didn't seem very promising, and yet turned out to be the best ever result for a BB at Le Mans. Apart from a small hiccup just before half distance - a 17min stop caused by a petrol leak - the BB ran really strongly, and from the 5th hour was never out of the top ten. The final result was 5th overall, and 1st in the IMSA GTX class by one lap from the Cooke Woods Racing Porsche K3.

31589 was then sold to Thomas A Davis Jr. who entered it for Daytona 1982. Its best practice time was 2m07.47 but because the time was more than 110% of the fastest in class it had to run in a special qualifying race on the Friday. It finished 3rd. to claim the 51st. starting position.

Pozzi's 31589 rounds Mulsanne Corner (NB Colln)

As if to prove the vagaries of motor racing, the same car that had lasted twenty four hours in its previous race this time went out on lap 1! Yes, a fuel injection problem side-lined it immediately.

And then to really rub it in the very same car that finished 5th at Le Mans 1981 didn't even get to start in either of its last two races.

14/6/80	Le Mans 24 Hrs	77	Pozzi	Ballot-Lena/Andruet	DNF
13/6/81	Le Mans 24 Hrs	47	Pozzi	Ballot-Lena/Andruet	5
29/1/82	Daytona Prelim	47	Tide	de Dryver	3
30/1/82	Daytona 24Hrs	47	Tide	de Dryver/Davis	DNF
30/3/82	Sebring 12 Hrs	47	Tide	Rubino/Davis	DNS
24/3/84	Sebring 12 Hrs	96	Tide	Ballot-Lena/Andruet	DNS

32129

32129 was Pozzi's second '80 style car, and like the other two team cars was in the European University colours. Xhenceval did a 4m00.3 in practice, and the BB qualified 24th and 2nd fastest of the Ferraris. Yet despite losing more than an hour in total due to various stops to fix the ignition, repair a split petrol tank, and to patch up front bodywork damage the Pozzi entered car was 10th overall, 3rd. in class, and 1st Ferrari home.

1980 Le Mans was its only competition appearance and in 1982 it was purchased by Dr. Walter Aus Der Au of Switzerland, who ran it at various club events. In 1987 it was entered for auction at Christie's Motorfair sale - it was unsold at £140,000.

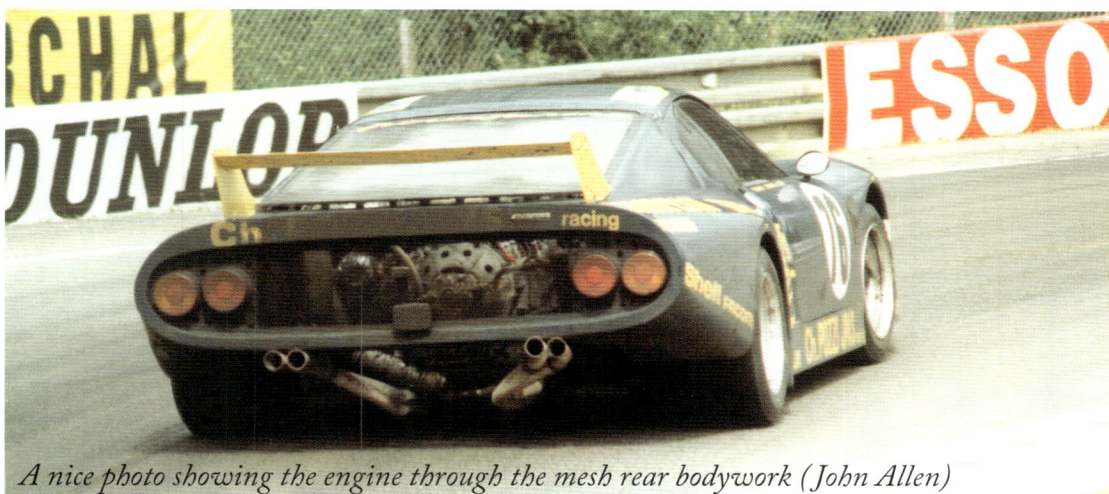

A nice photo showing the engine through the mesh rear bodywork (John Allen)

And this is the other end (NB Colln)

It re-appeared in recent years in the hands of Paul Knapfied, compet_ng in various rounds of the Shell Ferrari Historic Challenge series.

| 14/6/80 | Le Mans 24 Hrs | 76 | Pozzi | Dieudonne/Xhenceval/Regout | 10 |

32131

Was finished in July 1980, and purchased by Paul Pappalardo, who listed his occupation in the 1982 F.O.C. U.S.A. Membership directory as 'Squirrel Feeder'. It has no racing history, although it was used as a 'muletto' at Daytona 1981. (See history of 34445 for full story)

32131 (Keith Bluemel)

33647 – Engine 016

Was completed by the factory in October 1980. Went to Chinetti. Now in Holland.

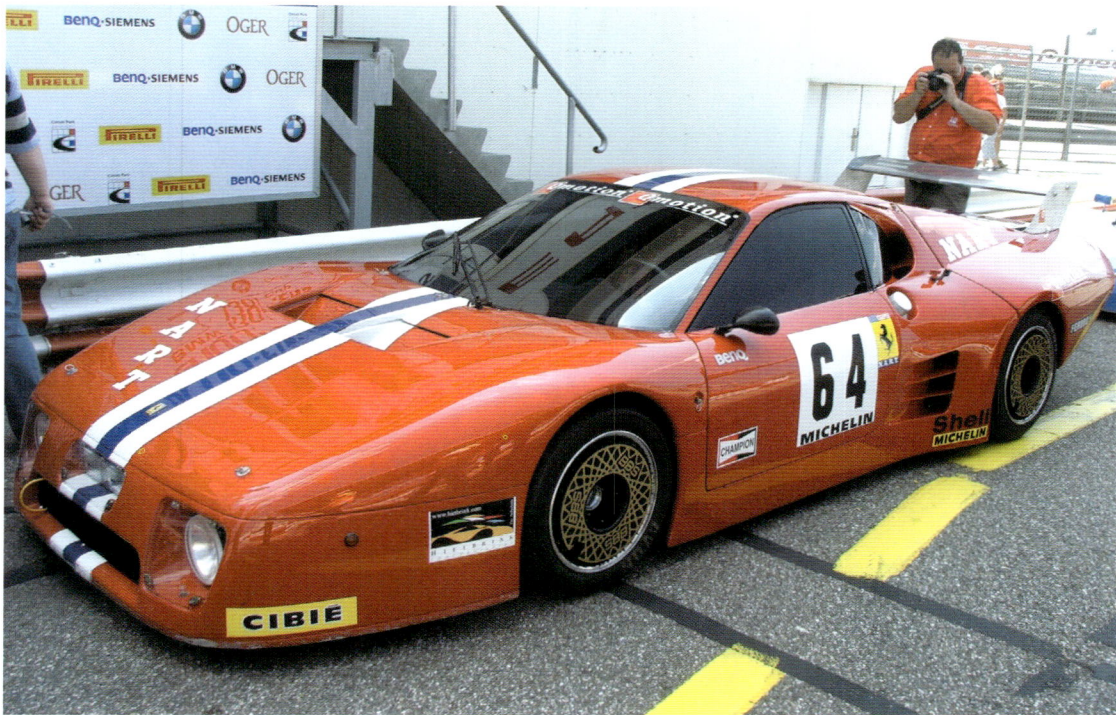

33647 was never raced. It was taken to Le Mans in 1980 as a spare car but didn't run. It is now in an a collection in Netherlands (Lammers)

34157

34157 was completed in November 1980 and was purchased by Del Buono in Italy. It ran reliably in the two events in which it was entered, finishing in the top ten both times.

| 12/4/81 | Mugello 6hrs | 29 | Sc. Guercino | Del Buono/Govoni | 10 |
| 18/4/82 | Monza 1000 kms | 98 | Sc. Guercino | Del Buono/Govoni | 8 |

After its short racing career 34157 was sold to the USA where it appeared at various track days. (NB Colln)

34445

34445 was completed in December 1980 and purchased by Ron Spangler's Prancing Horse Farm dealership. Spangler was determined to mount a serious challenge with the BB and with no factory backing he called in a number of Ferrari enthusiasts to assist in the running of the BB/LM. The full story of this effort is reproduced here courtesy of BOB DONNER and 'PRANCING HORSE' magazine.

"My 512BB/LM (29509) was delivered in February 1980. During the summer it was run in several SCCA regional and national races and in a few Club events. It was in these events that several mechanical and design faults were noted and efforts were made along the course of the season to correct them. It was a standing joke among my crew that the Ferrari had a 50/50 chance of finishing a 30 minute SCCA national - it was a case of racing the car to find out what would happen next! However, Elkhart Lake in July found the Boxer relatively debugged, we thought, and on Saturday the car was showing a good turn of speed on the 4 mile course when the fuel tank split. All night repairs by Jim Robinson and Ken Sindall at the local sprint car shop saw the car on the course bright and early Sunday morning. Serious lapping was producing a treacherous amount of brake fade at the bottom of the downhill back straight at Turn 3 and the car was eating up its rear tyres at an alarming rate. This later problem was due to too much negative camber in the rear wheels and the lack of adjustment to take it out. To correct these problem areas there were two solutions; fit larger brakes and redesign the rear suspension.

Since the BB/LM is primarily a long distance race car thoughts of Daytona in late January entered the minds of Paul Pappalardo, Ron Spangler, Alberto Pedretti and me. With the help of Alberto and Wide World of Cars, Ron was awaiting delivery of a 512 BB/LM in November and was willing to run it at Daytona and provide a major part of the expenses. This was an ideal situation and would easily give us time to make the technical changes and prepare the car for a 24 Hour Race. Our shop in Colorado Springs was chosen to do the work - Jim Robinson was ready to transport the car and Francois Sicard, whose knowledge of long distance racing at Le Mans, Daytona and Sebring would prove invaluable, agreed to join us in the task.

Spangler's 512BB/LM (34445) did not arrive in November, or by Thanksgiving, or by Christmas. We were about to scrub the effort when the car finally arrived by air on December 31st, and it was agreed to go ahead. With time so short, Paul very generously donated his garage for the needed preparation and, of all the garages in Greenwich, Conneticut, Paul's is The Garage for Ferrari aficionados. Jim joined Francois and work commenced in earnest. Lee Dykstra of Special Chassis Inc., (and also the designer of Group 44s fabulous Jaguar XJR-5 - author's note) of Grandville, Michigan, flew in to supervise the changes to the front and rear suspension. The major feature of the changes, besides allowing proper rear camber adjustment, would permit the installation of Goodyear 27.5 x 14.5-19" tires in place of the standard 15" size. These huge tires would run longer and are available in very soft, soft, medium and hard compound. Porsche use this size and it was quite honestly a case of 'if you can't beat 'em, you'd better join 'em.' The drawings and special machine work had already been accomplished using Paul's 512 as an example, and the larger brakes had been booked in November from Automotive Products for early January delivery. An expert with a heli-arc was kept busy for 5 days. Spare bodywork was fitted, wired and painted. Spare parts, enough to build another car with the exception of the frame, engine and transaxle, were inventoried and crated. Jim, Francois and Ron Clark worked hard and late. Paul was ecstatic and donated his 512 as a back-up car having pronounced that 'anything worth doing is worth over doing.'

Both cars were transported to Daytona a week before the start of the race. Bob Akin had kindly allowed us to test on the Saturday before the race when he had the track rented - for a slight fee, of course.

Tony Adamowicz and Rick Knoop were there as drivers - both experienced in distance racing and both known quantities. It was decided that Paul's 512 would be given to Tony and Rick for familiarization and so that the performance of a Boxer in standard trim could be compared to one which had been rather extensively modified. Paul was obviously a bit nervous about his 'baby' going out on the super-speedway and admonished Tony to observe a careful warm-up (since the oil cooler might burst), and to limit the revs to 7000 on the straight and no more than 5000 on the banking. With the short course gears (top speed at 7000 is 165mph) Tony went out for five laps, did the

It's Daytona 1983 and 34445 heads into the night, and into the lead! The only BB/LM to lead a major sports-car race. (Daytona International Speedway)

Rick Knoop certainly wrung everything out of the BB/LM. Here at Daytona 1982 he has the inside front wheel off the ground. (Fred Lewis – www.fredlewisphotos.com)

sixth at a fast 1:56 and brought the car in with most of the rubber chunked out of the inside of the right rear - just what we thought would happen to the highly loaded outside tire (15") under excess negative camber.

Paul desperately wanted to load up his car but 32131 was to do a few more laps. We fitted a new right rear tire and Rick took the wheel for a few laps of familiarization with strict instructions from Paul to limit the speed on the banking and to stay far away from the wall (and no 1:56 laps). He worked the car quite vigorously in the turns in the infield, brought the Boxer in after a few laps, and remarked that the car exhibited excessive oversteer in all the turns which Tony had also noticed. Tire temperatures were measured by Lee Dykstra and were very hot on the inside, about right in the middle and too cold on the outside.

Paul took his own Boxer out observing all the speed limits while the real Boxer for the race was pushed to the pit area. It was resplendent in No.65, the number of the Ferrari Daytona (16407) which had such a famous history at Daytona and is in Ron Spangler's collection at Prancing Horse Farm. Oh, it was so peaceful at the track with no rotary engines to rattle your brains, few people in sight and only the strong sound of Paul's Boxer and the turbo whoosh of a Porsche 935 as they ran the 3.8 mile course.

Paul offered me a few laps in his Boxer, and I immediately jumped into a suit and behind the wheel. It was great fun to see the course again from behind the wheel and the 31 degree banking still looks like a solid wall of asphalt as you approach it on the back straight at 150+ mph. I delivered the car back to Paul in one piece and the back up car was soon resting in the garage under wraps. The new rear tire was ready to blow out again.

Tony was first to try out Boxer No.65. It should be noted that the car had never, until this point, turned a lap on a race course, and with so many changes being made it was imperative to keep a watchful eye on it. Tony brought it in after some warming laps and the car was examined - tire temperatures, tire clearances, oil and water leaks, bodywork, brakes suspension etc. All was well except for some rubbing by the rear tires on the inner fender panels.

Tony went out again and appeared to be comfortably circulating in 1:58's and 1:57's. He came to the pits, made some suggestions to cure some minor oversteer and brake bias adjustments (more brake on the rear was needed) and these were promptly done by the crew and Lee Dykstra.

It was Rick's turn and after a few laps in the new car settled right in the groove with 1:57's and 1:58's. Both drivers were pleased with the car - its handling was superb, it was rock steady on the banking and more rear brake effect could be found later. Tony went out again with 0degrees on the rear wing, picked up 500rpm on the back straight and clipped off some laps in the low 1:56 range. We declared it a day and a superb test session. There were no mechanical problems, our modifications had worked, lessons were learned and the few remaining adjustments could be attended to during official practice. Although it had been a strenuous exercise on everyone's part, it was felt by all, including Tony and Rick who knew best, that a competitive Ferrari had been born and that 512BB/LM 34445 would make its mark on Daytona at the end of the 24 hours.

The weather report gave us temperatures in the 60's and 70's through the race weekend and down jackets and long underwear were left in the rooms. Sunday found the crew not on the beach or in the surf but in the garage and on the car. There are an unbelievable number of adjustments to be made on a well prepared race car and particularly on one that has to go 24 hours. Francois set to building new fender wells and Jim tackled a redesign of the brake and clutch fluid reservoirs which were leaking hydraulic fluid all over. Ron, Ken Sindall and Rick were busy bolting BBS wheels together to accept the Goodyear tyres. Radios, so kindly donated by Bobby Hillin of Longhorn Racing, had to be charged, checked out and installed. A smaller diameter steering wheel was installed courtesy Jon Masterson. Proper lighting (thanks to Cibie and SEV Corporation) had to be installed in the car and in the extra front bodywork and adjusted at the Cibie garage. Francois and my son, Bob, attended to the valve adjustment - not an easy task with the engine in the car. Did anyone check the cam belts? Who was the guy walking about doing car lettering? How about grinding the brake pads so they will slip in and out easily at 1300 degrees? Sandwiches, what sandwiches? And PAM made another run to town - go to the trim shop and pick up the resewn seat belts - Heimraths, too, since they needed the same. How about a special socket? Quick, get the car on the track - the photographer is here for publicity shots. What car? It's in pieces! Where's Tony? Fix the side mirrors as they were flying loose. Rick and Tony need a thermos for Gatorade (a soft drink - author). Check the radio installation - it works for as far as I can walk. Enclose the pits before night practice. A Mazda fired up in the garage and the sound was pure pain. Chris Cord came by to say hello and wish us luck. Remount the battery - the J.C. Penney 610 amp battery was loose and we were not about to have electrical problems! What if it rains? Talk to Francois about proper rain gear for the electrics. The new quick jack for the front is at the airport. Oh my God, in the midst of all the excitement the French on board fire extinguisher did just what it was supposed to do if a fire had been present. There are no more bottles and it can't be recharged. I called everywhere. Walt Medlin saved the day by driving to Orlando and supplying a US system. Steel mesh for the radiator opening. Change the quick-change from the middle to the lowest gear (we wanted a maximum of 7000) and try it in first practice. The master work list became shorter as the car became ready.

Opening practice Wednesday afternoon saw Tony take the car out - Rick took a turn at the wheel and a total of 24 laps were covered. Each tire was measured for temperature on the inside, middle and outside. From my notes you can see how the rear temperatures read:

Right rear 145 - 160 - 135   Left rear 124 - 143 - 118

The stressed right side tires ran medium compound - they made the tire wear more even from right to left side. The left wore soft compound.

Both Tony and Rick agreed with the gear change. Both also wanted more rear brake. However, what do you do when all the brake bias adjustment is used up? You take the .75" front master cylinder and use it on the rear and the .70" cylinder on the rear is switched to the front - then neutralize the bias adjustment. Those huge 10" rear Goodyears were doing a majority of the work under braking.

The car was qualified on Thursday in the 22nd spot with a 1:57.6 and was dropped one place to 23rd. by the end of qualifying. The point was to assure the car a start - the second place Porsche (Akin/Bell/Siebert) qualified 9th and the winners (Garretson/Rahal/Redman) qualified 17th

Night practice on Thursday went well as both drivers became accustomed to the car in the dark. The centre mounted Cibie driving lights needed to be spread out to pick out the corners more distinctly. Tony requested a 1 degree change in the left main beam. The Motorola radio was loud and clear. Radio contact is a must in this game - lap times and any problems with the car can be relayed immediately - and the driver doesn't feel alone driving his stint at the wheel.

Friday practice was used for running in our race tires and brake pads. temperature paint again verified our front and rear brake settings - different coloured paint stripes were painted on each rotor and burn off under operating conditions - indicated that the fronts were operating at 1000°. Temperature paint was also used on the quick change gear case - 250-275 degrees was the reading - the Valvoline rep told Paul and I that 280 was optimal with 400 the absolute maximum for the EP 90 lubricant. We thought we were safe but in the future a larger transmission oil cooler and positive displacement pump will be incorporated.

Ferrari use two Bendix fuel pumps (!) to pass hot transmission oil through a common 308 by-pass oil cooler - not exactly Mickey Mouse but Porsche mechanics were observed smiling when they examined the arrangement! Jim had machined a neat scavenger gear driven oil pump from a Formula Ford to bolt on the gear cluster of the quick change but its use could not be permitted since it had never been tested.

Race day finally arrived! It is almost an anti-climax compared to what had gone before. We skipped the warm up practice, did a final on the car and pushed it out to the pre-grid. It seemed like thousands of people were milling about and the 512BB/LM collected more than its share of onlookers. Vicki and Leslie had bedecked the car with yellow bows or ribbons in respect to the American hostages and there were many remarks on such a thoughtful gesture.

It is nearing 3:30pm and the start is almost upon us. The car has been warmed thoroughly by Francois and Jim and tension is prevalent everywhere. Some of the turbos are balky. Tony is behind the wheel to start the race and we all appreciate the difficult driving chore he faces - bring yourself and the car in running and well for your first scheduled stop amid 60 other drivers who are going like hell on a course which is becoming progressively more unpredictable. My headset is on and I attempt to relay a word or two of encouragement. It is difficult at best.

Off they go! It is a mad rush of cars, with a few early callers at the pits; the turbo 308 lasted 4 laps! I hear on the radio that Tony will pit with 'vibrations.' He comes in on lap 20 - a quick check - Ken and Ron fill 'em up fast and the right front tire is changed. There are still 'vibrations' so he pits on the next lap and the left front is changed. On examination the tire does not show a flat spot so it must have thrown a weight.

Silvia Wilkinson was doing our timing and scoring and she was a miracle worker - we could see that the car was gaining places as attrition took its toll. Paul kept a complete lap chart in the pit so that at a glance we knew the record of each pit stop, their length, on what lap, the status of the tires and brakes, the gas and oil added, when the next stop will occur and, of course, which driver was out.

Our pit stops were going extremely well and regular since all the crew had been through it before. Jim and Francois re-padded the front brakes 8.5 hours into the race. All was well and by 7pm #65 was on the scoreboard in 5th overall. 4th overall came up a couple of hours later - then 3rd where the car stayed for a long time. We passed the half way point of the race at 3:30 am. The complete reliability of the car up to now filed all of us with hope that a spectacular finish was on the cards - it was so unbearably exciting.

On lap 379 Tony was due to pit about 4:40 am. He was in 2nd place on the scoreboard! Quite suddenly at 3:30 am the caution light came on at the S/F and I called Tony immediately on the radio to pit. We could use the caution light and the resultant slowdown for our benefit since it was time to gas in a few laps. There was no response from Tony. Silvia told us he was past due. We all strained to catch sight of the car.

The unthinkable had happened! Gianpiero Moretti in a Porsche 935 had a tire puncture on the banking, went down low, and then came up again as Tony tried desperately to avoid him by running up near the wall. The Porsche tagged the left door of the Ferrari; poor Tony was spun and was going backwards at a frightening rate of speed. The left rear brushed the wall knocking off the wheel. Tony arrived back at the pits unhurt, thank God, but visibly shaken after such a terrifying incident.

Our effort was over. The 512BB/LM that had been so meticulously prepared so well crewed and so superbly driven by Tony and Rick, will be repaired to race again another day.

(Think about this - how do you feel in those circumstances? All that work, weeks of preparation, high expectations; all wiped out because of someone-else's misfortune.)

The team wishes to thank the following sponsors: Spanair, Eastport Erection Co., FAF Motorcars, Sea World, Longford Leasing, Western Motor Works and Bill and Pat Kiernan.

The entry would not have been possible without the assistance of Alberto Pedretti and Wide World of Cars for arranging acquisition of the car.

Others who deserve very special recognition for unselfish devotion include Paul Pappalardo, Ken Sindall, Ron Clark, Mark deFriece, Lee Dykstra, Walt Medlin, Silvia Wilkinson, Pam Sicard, Vicki Adamowicz, Leslie Knoop, Ross Earle, Howard Jones, Buzz Kulicek, Bruce Lavacheck, Bob Rapp, Ken Richardson, Sam Smith, Jon Masterson, Bob Donner lll, Ron Spangler Jr., Dick and Robert Schmitter and Elaine Williamson. Jim Robinson and Francois Sicard gave unstintingly of their time and talent to prepare a fast and reliable Ferrari. And to Patti and Ron Spangler - you must be the ultimate in car owners - though we didn't finish at Daytona this year, the entry of your 512BB/LM brought many Ferrari enthusiasts together for an unforgettable week, with a remarkable resurgence of pride in our love of automobiles Ferrari. Bless you all!!"

34445 raced again one year later at the 1982 Daytona 24hrs. The BB was 18th fastest in practice (1:55) but because they had not set a time within 110% of the fastest in their class they had to run a pre-qualifying race on the Friday. In this they finished third and therefore qualified to start 51st. (A bit of a stupid regulation?)

Their pace though showed up during the race as they moved up to 11th at the end of the first hour, and by the eight hour mark were up to 5th! Three hours later they were 4th! Sadly that is as high as they were going to get, as the gear-box gave out and the team retired at 337 laps.

The following extract is reproduced courtesy of BOB RAPP and PRANCING HORSE magazine, and will help the reader to appreciate just how much work and expense is involved in a project of this type.

"Ron Spangler is quite an organizer, along with Patti, and the preparation for the race started many months prior to it. Ron sent out a preparation brochure which listed practically everything that one could have thought of. The table of contents on this list included sponsors and patrons, preparation items, race items, crew and expenses, pass lists, hotel, track and restaurant information, rooms, travel to and from Daytona, race jacket lists and sizes, financial analysis, final checklist items, and participants' names and addresses. Incidentally the scene of some 30 Ferrari enthusiasts all wearing the Prancing Horse Farm jackets was one of the most exciting scenes I have ever seen in racing, and probably the some 50,000 people who witnessed us pushing the car onto the grid were similarly impressed.

If you are interested just in the cost of such an effort the budget showed about $60,000 not including the car or parts. In addition, it didn't include meals or hotel or travel expenses for the majority of the people who were there, as they paid their own ways. With some 30 people having come to the race in support of Car Number 65, and considering the car and parts cost in excess of $150,000, I figured the total effort was at least $250,000 total (at 1982 prices remember!) without counting anything for the free time of the volunteers. And do you know what you get should you end up in first place as prize money? $15,000 That's what! And had we finished in fourth place we would have received all of $3,250...."

Despite the disappointment of Daytona the team were out again for the Sebring 12hrs. They qualified a very strong 12th, five places ahead of the Henn BB. Yet again they were to be disappointed, retiring on the 60th lap.

Undeterred by previous failures, and even by the age of the Ferrari, the Prancing Horse Farm team again turned up at Daytona (1983) with their always immaculately prepared car. They qualified well in 19th place, but went even better in the race. At the 6hr. mark the BB was in the lead!! Yes, ahead of the Porsches, and even the GTP cars. O.K. so one or two of the faster cars had had problems, but it was still number 1, the only BB/LM ever to lead a major race! The BB continued to run strongly, holding on to second for a long time until just after half distance (377 laps) when the crank broke, and ended a remarkable run.

Looking at the performance of 34445 makes one wonder what could have been achieved if the factory had REALLY developed and explored the full potential and possibilities of the BB/LM.

2006: Owned by John Goodman (USA) and exhibited at Cavallino Classic XV

31/1/81	Daytona 24 Hrs	65	PHF	Adamowicz/Knoop	DNF
29/1/82	Daytona Prelim	65	PHF	Knoop	1
30/1/82	Daytona 24 Hrs	65	PHF	Knoop/Pumpelly/Baird	DNF
30/3/82	Sebring 12 Hrs	65	PHF	Baird/Pumpelly/Mead	DNF
5/2/83	Daytona 24 Hrs	65	PHF	Baird/Pumpelly/Mead	DNF

At Le Mans 35523 ran an attractive white colour scheme. The twin blue stripes were in recognition of the American driver Steve Earle, and the red and blue stripes recognised the two English drivers. (NB Colln)

35523 was brought new from the factory in 1981 by Simon Phillips. This is his story, based on an interview conducted by the author.

"I bought the BB/LM because in 1980 I was involved in an abortive foray to Le Mans with an Aston Martin. This was to be a DB V8 Aston road car converted to make a competition car, but in late May the entry was withdrawn and with three to four weeks to go I was without any sort of involvement at Le Mans. Paul Watson, who was organising the entries for me at the time, put me in touch with Steve O'Rourke who was looking for someone to drive his BB/LM (s/n 27577) and it was really a last minute arrangement. My initial reaction was one of delight because I thought I'd blown Le mans for 1980, and instead there I was going out with a Ferrari, so that was pretty good in itself. The race was an incredible mixture, the nose being damaged in the first hour and requiring a great deal of tank tape to secure it. Subsequently it lost its tail, and we borrowed one from the Italian BB which was already out. However this didn't fit Steve's car without quite a lot of cutting and shutting plus a lot more tank tape. By now the car looked rather like a tank tape special with a British racing Green nose and a red tail.

I can't remember now whether it was my first or second stint, I think my second, there was an incredible BANG at full chat on the Mulsanne straight and the entire passenger floor blew out! I thought the back axle had gone or something but then I realized that we still had drive so it couldn't be that. This damage was repairable without too much difficulty, but through all this the car kept going very well. Most of my long distance sports car experience at that time had been in either a DFV engined Lola, which was something of a pig to drive, or the RSR Porsche in which you learnt very early on to get your braking finished before you tried turning-in, other wise it just spun like a top. So to find a car that you could brake and turn-in simultaneously was super. That may be state-of-the-art now, but in the early 1980s, at least to me with the particular cars that I was experienced with, it was unheard of. The Ferrari did it with great safety and predictability.

But now we come to why I subsequently bought a BB myself. It was quite late on in the race, probably my last or last but one stint. I'd come up behind a BMW M1 at the beginning of the Mulsanne Straight, and although he stayed on the left-hand side when he should have moved over, I presumed, given the length of the straight that he must have seen me. The cars were of similar performance down the straight so my rate of progress past him was slow and gradual. By the 'kink' I had the nose of the Ferrari level with his passenger door and I thought he must have known I was there. Unfortunately he didn't, and he came right across to take the apex. The only way of avoiding him was to get all four wheels on the grass on the inside of the 'kink' at about 200mph. The BB/LM never even wavered! It went straight across on the grass, came out on the inside of the track without any drama whatsoever. The M1 driver must have practically come to a stop, because despite having been on the grass I came out of the 'kink' about 200yds ahead of him. I don't think there are many long distance sports-racing cars that could safely be put on the grass at that sort of speed, and that's why I decided there and then that I had to have one!"

At Silverstone 1981 Simon Phillips privately owned car appeared with very little sponsorship, and looked unusual with a mainly white colour scheme. In the next garage can be seen the nose of 27577 (NB Colln)

The order was placed through Maranello Concessionaires in August 1980. Simon visited Ferrari in December to make the final arrangements and 35523 made its competition debut in May 1981 in the Silverstone 6hrs event. Simon takes up the story,

"The Six Hour race went very well on the whole until the last half hour. Michael Salmon did the first stint in extraordinarily heavy rain. I did the middle one when it was beginning to dry and we were able to speed up a bit. Steve Earle did the last stint and we were lying in something like 8th or 9th place overall with half an hour to go. Suddenly Steve didn't come round. Some of us went to the various corners of the circuit and we found Steve stopped just after Copse. He had got the back of the car up, and was having to support it on his back whilst he tried to find out what was the matter. we subsequently found out that it was simply and solely a wire that had come off the alternator. It also taught us a simple lesson; you had to carry a prop in the car in case it was necessary to raise the back of the car in the middle of a race and the driver had to do it on his own. So by Le Mans that year we had a specially fitted prop that could be used in that kind of situation. It would have been a good result but for that small thing!"

After Silverstone the BB went back to Vic Norman's Rosso outfit to be prepared for Le Mans. Simon's team for the big event was run by Richard Williams with a team of six mechanics. Sharing the driving were Le Mans veteran Mike Salmon and Monterey Historic event organizer Steve Earle.

In practice gearbox problems caused by a faulty selector left the car starting in 40th position, although the BB was equal on top speed to the NART Boxer which was quickest of the five BBs entered. Eleven hours into the race the #48 car was placed 19th when the gearbox seized. Simon and the team were very disappointed as it was felt that the failure was due to a design fault rather than any oversight on the part of the team. As Simon's telex to the factory after Le Mans explained, 'The retirement of our BB512LM was caused by two drop gears breaking up due to inadequate cooling of the gearbox. This in turn was due to failure of one or both of the Bendix electrical pumps, thus stopping the flow of oil through the cooler. Since the pumps were wired in tandem the failure of one is enough to cause the cooling system to fail. The pumps were unable to withstand the very high temperature (180+). We noticed that some, if not all of the other BBs have modified the gearbox cooling arrangement either by substituting mechanical pumps or adding additional radiators. This together with our own experience suggests a design weakness and we recommend that you consider notifying all owners known to use the BB512 in endurance racing that one or other of these modifications be carried out....please don't think from the above that we are bitter over our experience....our overall impression is that the car is magnificent...'

One area of considerable comment and speculation at Le Mans was the identity of one of Simon's sponsors, Sheila Wong Chong; who was she? (We should say, 'who is she?') Simon explained that although he had sold some space on the car to sponsors for the 24 hour epic he had been unable to sell the most expensive and conspicuous part, that on the nose. So rather than leave it blank he donated the space to his wife who is a fully qualified chartered surveyor. (Wong Chong is her maiden and business name)

After Le Mans the BB returned to England where Simon entered it in a typically eccentric British event, the Silverstone Six Hour Relay. The variety to be found in this event can be amply demonstrated by looking at Simon's own team which contained a 1938 BMW 328, a 1951 Frazer-Nash Le Mans replica, a lightweight Ferrari 250SWB, a 1972 Porsche RSR, a 1970 Chevron B16 and the BB/LM. Simon remembers the event well: "Our handicap reflected the potential times of the older and slower cars, but also the BB/LM was precluded from doing more than 50 laps under the rules of the handicap. For all that however with about twenty minutes left we were leading on handicap, and it was quite evident that we were about to take the lead on scratch as well, because Mike Salmon in the BB/LM was catching the leading Porsche at a great rate of knots. It was at this point that he unfortunately had his accident." And some accident it was! Coming into Woodcote Corner (which on the club circuit was a sharp right-hander) Salmon clipped a slower car and flipped the BB into a complete 360 degree barrel roll. Happily the car came to rest right side up against the barrier and a dazed Mike Salmon was helped away from the car. The car though didn't fare so well with every panel dented, including the roof!!

After this mishap the BB was stripped of all mechanical parts, and the rest of the car was returned to Ferrari to be re-chassied and re-bodied. Simon asked the Assistenza Tecnica in Modena if it would be possible to save weight during the rebuild to make the car more competitive in 1982. After a number of Telexes it became apparent that the factory felt there was little that could be done, only suggesting that Simon's mechanics may be able to reduce the weight of each component during final assembly. Nevertheless Simon ordered the re-build to go ahead, and ordered some spare engine parts for the coming season.

The first and, as it turned out, only event for Simon's BB in 1982 was the Silverstone 1000kms the annual Le Mans warm-up thrash. Sponsorship was obtained from Algarve Beach Villas and the car appeared in an unusual sand coloured paint finish, which I thought looked quite appropriate in view of the sponsor. But as Simon says it wasn't quite like that:

35523 pictured here in primer during practice for Silverstone 6hrs 1982. Although a sponsor was found for the race there wasn't enough money to make it worthwhile repainting the car. (NB Colln)

"When it was rebodied after the Relay accident I asked for it to be finished in primer because I was hoping to get an overall sponsor for the 1982 season, and then we'd paint it up in the colours of the sponsor. We left it until the last possible moment for the race at Silverstone, then in the end the sponsor we got certainly wasn't prepared to pay enough money for us to spray the car as well. The 'colour' was in fact primer! After the race I had it resprayed in its 1981 Le Mans colours except without all the sign-writing. What then about the race? Simon continues "Everything went pretty smoothly on the whole. We had some problems with the clutch which had to be treated with a lot of care. It turned out to be the clutch release valve which was the problem, so the gearchange was a bit baulky, but we eventually finished second in class. Since it was the first time the car finished during my ownership I felt pretty good about that. We were only beaten by a very fast Porsche 935 in the IMSA class, which wasn't really fair in comparison."

And so on a bright note ended the competition career of 35525. Simon then became involved in the Aston Martin Nimrod project and competed with that car and his own team at Le Mans in 1982. The BB stayed with Simon until it was sold at the Christies Ferrari auction in May 1987.

35523 resurfaced in 2005 competing in the Shell Ferrari Historic Historic Challenge Series in Europe.

10/ 5/81	Silverstone 6 Hrs	41	Phillips	Phillips/Salmon/Earle	DNF
13/ 6/81	Le Mans 24 Hrs	48	Phillips	Phillips/Salmon/Earle	DNF
18/10/81	Silverstone Relay	5F	Phillips	Phillips/Salmon	DNF
18/ 5/82	Silverstone 6 Hrs	80	Phillips	Phillips/Salmon/Earle	17

35525 – Engine 021

Bob Donner's second BB/LM pictured from high in the stands at Le Mans in 1981 (NB Colln)

35525 shown here winning the 1986 Virginia City Hillclimb. (Donner)

35525 was finished in February 1981, and purchased by Bob Donner of Colorado Springs U.S.A. Bob took delivery at the Ferrari factory and transported it to Belgium to be prepared for Le Mans. The drivers were three Belgians, the experienced Pierre Dieudonne, Jean Xhenceval and Jean-Paul Libert, and the BB was entered by Rennod Racing which you've probably realised is the name Donner contra posed Dieudonne (3m56.72) and Xhenceval (3m58.78) both qualified in under 4mins, but Libert was a bit off the pace with a 4m11.35. The race went really well for the team, but not so well for poor Pierre Dieudonne, who was taken ill and only drove for about 4 out of the 24 hours. This left the main burden on Xhenceval and the slower, but reliable Libert. Yet despite this setback the Ferrari was in 18th place after one hour and never ran lower. There were no problems; just regular stops for petrol, tyres and oil, and an eventual 9th place overall and 3rd. in class.

Bob had the engine rebuilt by the factory and then ran in a few club events, setting the fastest time in the Ferrari Owners Club Virginia City Hill-Climb.

35525 began a new competition career in 2004 when it was regularly entered in European rounds of the Shell Ferrari Historic Challenge Series.

13/6/81   Le Mans 24 Hrs   46   Rennod Xhenceval/Libert/Dieudonne   9

35527's first competition appearance was at Le Mans 1981 where it ran as high as 4th place before retiring. (NB Colln)

35527 was delivered to Chinetti in time to run its first race at Le Mans 1981. The NART cars always seemed to run well, and again the team was the fastest of the Ferrari entries, with Alain Cudini recording a very strong 3m52.60. During the race the team performed brilliantly, running in 4th place after only four hours!! During the next ten hours they dropped a couple of spots as the quicker cars picked up pace, but they were still heading for a good finish when just after 9 in the morning Phillipe Gurdjian hit a patch of oil and damaged the BB enough to cause its retirement.

35527 returned to Le Mans for its second competition outing in 1982, where the unfortunate Gurdjian was swapped for the soon to be notorious John Paul Snr., but otherwise the driver team remained the same. Cudini was again the quickest qualifier with a 3m54.07 lap, good enough for 4th in class.

Again the team ran extremely well, and again they got as high as fourth, and again problems intervened. Just two hours from the end the gearbox began to seize. At 2:40pm Cudini parked the BB at Post 129 less than 700 yds. from the finish line, and at one minute to four started her up, shoved her into gear and trundled round to the finish line to be classified 9th overall.

- 35527 was then retired from active competition, and didn't crop up again until 1989 when it was sold at Coy's of Kensington Nurburgring auction for $1,304,480. It was purchased by Nicklen Bank Group, Sweden
- 1993 : Sold to Tom CELANI through Ferrari of Los Gatos.
- 1997 : Sold to Steve BARNEY.
- 1998 : Sold to Chris COX.
- 1998 : Overall winner in American Ferrari Historic Challenge.
- 1998 : Sold to NEUMAN.
- 1999 : Sold to Todd MORICI
- Sold to GTC/ Jean GUIKAS- France.
- 2005 : Competed in the rounds of the Shell Ferrari Historic Challenge series
- 2006 : For sale by Jean Guikas (GTC Marseille France)

| 13/6/81 | Le Mans 24 Hrs | 49 | NART | Morton/Cudini/Gurdjian | DNF |
| 19/6/82 | Le Mans 24 Hrs | 72 | NART | Morton/Cudini/Paul | 9 |

35529

These photos from 1981 Le Mans show the unique swoopy Bellancauto bodywork. Bellancauto's unusual bodywork seemed to work well as they qualified 2nd of the 5 BB/LMs, only bested by the new lighter weight NART car. (NB Colln)

The second Bellancauto Boxer was built by Ferrari and delivered in February 1981. The team set to work immediately and created some radically modified aerodynamic bodywork. The nose dipped down low to the ground, and the tail was lowered and smoothed to create better air-flow. The design was the work of engineer Armando Palanca, who had well-known ex-factory mechanic Giulio Borsari along to help. Photos taken during testing suggest that it was originally intended to run without a rear wing, but by the time Monza came round the original wing was back in place. In recognition of their hard-work the team renamed their car a BBB (BB Bellancauto) 512.

The team must have been quite heartened by the Monza result, as 6th overall and 1st in class was no doubt encouraging. The next event was Le Mans where a real comparison could be made, and the team would be able to compare their work with that of the factory. At least they were no heavier than the standard BBs. Practice times for an event like Le Mans can be a little bit misleading as one never knows how hard a team is really trying, whether they are going just fast enough to qualify or whether they are really going for a quick lap, but the BBB was second quickest of the Ferraris although slowest on the Mulsanne.

Practice though was about as successful as the BBB would get. During the race the team stumbled from problem to problem, losing time with the electrics and the fuel-injection being the main problem areas. At just after 2am the BBB stopped out on the circuit having never run higher than 20th

A couple of weeks later the Bellancauto boys turned up at Enna for the Six Hours where the BBB returned to it's Monza form and again finished 6th

In 1982 there was only the one appearance at Mugello, where the BBB again finished, this time in tenth place.

The next time 35529 appeared was not until Imola 1984 where it was obvious that the body had been developed yet again. The nose was visibly shorter, and the tail had also been chopped. A new, larger rear wing had also been added. The suspension was also modified to use the new Michelin rubber to best effect. The new shorter, squatter BBB was now more than 30kgs lighter.

Bellancauto's Ferrarelle pictured at Imola 1984 (Collezione Maranello Rossa)

Testing was carried out at Vallelunga where the modifications proved effective in lowering lap times, and the top speed was tested, in the time honoured method, on a stretch of unopened motorway - achieving a claimed 206mph.

For Imola, and Le Mans for that matter, the BBB ran as No27, the number made famous on the Ferrari Grand Prix cars by the late, great Gilles Villeneuve. (A friend of mine said that I couldn't get Gilles name in a book about the BBs. Wrong!) But the BBB needed more than the famous number and retired.

At Le Mans the team entered the IMSA GTX class, on their own, so a class win was definitely a possibility, and needless to say they also qualified fastest in their class, but also slowest! By 1984 Group C was very strong and so Marazzi's 4m00.2 was only good enough for 43rd. starting position. Mind you, they very nearly didn't make that. The engine blew up during the Saturday morning warm-up period and the team only just managed to fit the spare in time to take the start.

The first few laps were considerably enlivened by Roger Dorchy who hurled his WM down the Mulsanne and into the lead; he then went even further and on the fourth lap hurled it into the Armco. Still the little French team had their moment of glory in front of the millions of French TV viewers.

Anyway I digress, what about the BBB boys? Well they ran reliably for nearly six hours, getting up to 32nd place before retiring with gearbox maladies. And with the end of the BBB came the end of the great BB adventure at Le Mans.

35529 in detail, at its final Le Mans appearance in 1984. (Bluemel)

35529 in detail, at its final Le Mans appearance in 1984. (Bluemel)

The BBB has now retired to Fabrizio Violati's Maranello Rosso Exhibition in San Marino. Go visit, and see a little bit of Ferrari history.

26/4/81	Monza 1000 kms	15	B'auto	Flammini/Dini/Violati	6
13/6/81	Le Mans 24 Hrs	45	B'auto	Violati/Flammini/Truffo	DNF
28/6/81	Enna 6 Hrs	5	B'auto	Violati/Truffo	5
19/9/82	Mugello 1000 Kms	5	B'auto	Truffo/Violati	10
6/5/84	Imola	27	B'auto	Micangeli/Micangeli/'Gero'	DNF
16/6/84	Le Mans 24 Hrs	27	B'auto	Micangeli/Marazzi/Lacaud	DNF

35529 at Le Mans 1981. (Bluemel)

38179 arrives at Le Mans. Notice the narrow slave wheels and tyres used during transportation (Robidoux)

In its only race appearance the PHF car heads for an impressive 6th place finish. (NB Colln)

38179 was finished in November 1981 and delivered to Jacques Swaters in Belgium. It was purchased in 1982 by Ron Spangler of Prancing Horse Farm Racing and ran only one event - the 1982 Le Mans 24 hrs

It would appear that there was nothing particularly special about 38179 and it was in fact the heaviest of the four BB/LMs at Le Mans that year, but the talented Pierre Dieudonne knocked out a 3m56.52 practice lap in it.

Come the race the P.H.F. team did a knock-out job. Apart from a 23min. stop on the mid-night hour to change the petrol pump the pit-stops went like clock-work, and so did the BB. The beautiful red and gold machine charged on through the night, and into the long daylight hours of a Le Mans Sunday. By the end it was a brilliant sixth and the first non-Porsche home, the race being dominated by the Rothmans sponsored, works entered 956s which finished 1-2-3.

Le Mans 1982 was its only competition appearance and in 1990 it was offered for sale at $1.45 million.

| 19/6/82 | Le Mans 24 Hrs | 70 | PHF | Dieudonne/Libert/Baird | 6 |

38181

38181 (Keith Bluemel)

Not much known about this particular car. Built at the end of 1981 and sold through Alberto Pedretti's dealership. In 1986 it was offered for sale at $150,000, and in 1987 appeared at the Ferrari Club of America's Annual Meet where it won 1st in class, entered by Ed Wettach of Jackson, MS.

In 2006 it competed in the American Shell Ferrari Historic Challenge series.

38739

38739 was never raced – It is pictured here at Imola in 1989. (Bluemel)

Finished in December 1981 and sold to the Roman Ferrari dealer Roberto Crepaldi. It was never raced and is still owned by Crepaldi. It has a red body with the same distinctive striping of the 1979 Daytona BBs, except this has the Italian green/white/red stripes instead of the red/white/blue of the 1979 cars. It appeared at Imola in June 1989 for the special Ferrari Sports and Prototypes meet.

38739 began a late competition history in 2004, since when it has made a regular appearances in the Shell Ferrari Historic Challenge series.

41263

Was delivered to Charles Pozzi in March 1982, and its only race was at Le Mans the same year. It was sponsored by Pioneer, and was turned out in a splendid blue and white colour scheme. Despite troubles with fluctuating oil pressure all three drivers managed to get below 4mins.

Perhaps the practice problems should have alerted the team to change the engine; it expired less than five hours into the race.

(For Ballot-Lena this was his 17th Le Mans and his fifth in a BB/LM. Back in 1972 and 1973 he'd also been in Ferraris, Pozzi's Daytonas, having first raced at Le Mans back in 1966 in a Mini-Marcos. His best result was 3rd. overall in 1977 driving a Po***he)

At Le Mans 1982 Pozzi's new 41263 looked fabulous with sponsorship from Pioneer (NB Colln)

44023   Engine 032

And finally the factory built 44023. It was delivered to Jacques Swaters, never raced, but driven in a few club events by Jean Beurlys. It was then sold to American Gary Kohs, and has been through a number of owners since.

44023 was built by the factory in 1982 and was photographed here at Mas du Clos in 1983 (Bluemel)

BB/LM on the Track

by George Nuse

It must surely be assumed that the 512BB/LM is one of the more purposeful appearing GT racing cars ever built and it is one of the most contemporary of Ferrari's GT racers. At the time of its manufacture, like so many of the greatest Ferrari GT racers, it had as its greatest potential for winning its ability to reliably race for long distances, and it achieved relatively good fuel economy when compared to the turbo powered Porsches.

With race cars there is always a weak link and in the BB/LM it was excessive weight which caused the weak links to appear. The rather step-child approach which Ferrari took in the development of these races (as in the case of the fifteen Daytona race cars preceding them) is somewhat surprising because it has become the expectation of onlookers that Ferrari race cars are capable of winning. The lack of support from Ferrari for these 'custom' racers only allowed occasional glimpses of their potential to appear. At the Le Mans and Daytona races the cars were certainly capable of very high speeds (200+mph) and better fuel economy than the hordes of Porsches, but by now constant technical advances and testing were required to be competitive, and the BB/LM never came home a winner.

The subject of this article is the 512BB/LM (s/n 34445) which ran as high as 3rd in 1981, 4th in 1982, and 1st after six hours in 1983 at the Daytona 24hr race. These achievements were not turned into finishes due to various problems encountered with the design of the cars. It must be remembered that Ferrari cars tend to be very strong but unfortunately that also meant heavy! In the first encounters with the high-banked turns at Daytona the NART team found the Michelin tyres were not up to the extreme forces generated by these cars. Our test car was modified by Lee Dykstra (Group 44 Jaguar designer and Indy car engineer) to allow for the use of the proven tyre/wheel setup of the 935 Porsche turbo. Also the suspension geometry was modified to optimise the contact patch of the tyres on both the road courses and the 30° banking found at the Daytona tri-oval. Again the lack of technical support and development caused these magnificent cars to fall short of their potential winning abilities, of which only short glimpses were seen at Le Mans and other racing venues where the long legs of the Ferrari tradition should have brought the cars to victory.

And now to test this car (which is maintained by Mike Gourley at his facility, Continental Coachworks in Conyers, Georgia) we go to the beautiful, exciting race track, Road Atlanta for the annual Walter Mitty Challenge and Vintage Car Races where the cars will not be limited by the public highways. Upon entering the driver's seat the large size of the car becomes apparent. The controls are all readily available and the typical Ferrari external shift-gate is used. All of the controls are readily at hand and the pertinent gauges are arranged both logically and visibly. The controls for the auxiliaries are mounted next to the seat where there are switches for ignition, fuel pumps, oil cooling pump, lights etc. Upon executing the proper sequence of switches the car starts up and is ready to drive off. Immediately the large dimensions of the car and the high level of noise

demand your attention. At lower speeds the very wide Goodyear slicks tend to follow every irregularity in the pavement, and of course the heavy low speed steering adds to the chore of staying on line. Once the temperatures start to come up to the operating range specified the addition of throttle shows the car has substantial torque and power and is very tractable. With the lower speed gear set the transmission provides 55, 73, 102, 135 and 171mph at 7000rpm which is adequate for the long back straight at Road Atlanta. The car is easy to drift through long fast corners such as Turns One and Six, and only the Esses and the sharp, slow Turn Seven makes the cars bulk known by excessive steering effort and input. Braking requires some planning because the brakes, while certainly adequate for the job, simply require some distance to slow this large mass down. Once up to speed and upon getting comfortable with (a) the car's handling, and (b) owner Bruce Vineyard's nervous stare, the car turns in the fastest timed run overall and wins its class in the Sports timed runs with a time of 1m34s. Of course these days Paul Newman takes the Nissan Turbo 300ZX round about 7secs faster, but the sound of the BB/LM at full song is worth more than mere seconds.

Heading down the front straight at Road Atlanta we enter Turn One at close to full throttle in 4th gear at about 6000rpm, and at the apex of Turn Two hard braking and a shift to 3rd prepare the car for acceleration through Turn Three and the sweeping left-hand Turn Four. As the car is turned into the beginning of the Esses we shift up to 4th gear and the neutral handling of the car comes into play as the rapid right and left turns are taken at approximately 115mph. At the approach to Turn Five hard braking and a shift to 3rd are accomplished in the brief time the car is held in a straight line. Exiting Turn Five under hard acceleration the car rifts out to the edge of the track and quickly 4th gear is needed cresting the hill and we are up to the redline at the end of the short straight approaching Turn Six. Although Turn Six is banked to the right and can be taken at a rapid pace, very hard braking and a shift to 3rd gear are needed and a nice sideways attitude is taken up in the short chute to the braking point of Turn Seven, which is the slowest and most important turn, leading onto the long back straight. Taking Turn Seven never feels as though it is done correctly, but the BB/LM comes out in 2nd and here the power of the engine is most apparent. Redline is use in 2nd then 3rd gear and at the top of 3rd the car clears the rise on the straight and the steering becomes very light due to the combination of hard acceleration and the curvature of the hill. (It is here that several Can-Am cars did back-flips) Continuing down the straight 4th gear and then 5th gear are used and mental preparation begins for the charge, at what is already very high speed, down into The Dip at the top of 5th gear. The car is very stable on the back straight and only the fast pace, heavy weight, and driver anxiety causes dramatic rise in pulse rate coming up to The Bridge under heavy braking with a shift into 3rd gear. Down the hill into Turn Twelve a shift into 4th gear at full throttle and the lap is complete with the car accelerating and Turn One approaching very rapidly. The car is a delight to drive; with excellent response, neutral handling and mediocre brakes.

Considering the BB/LM as a road car, driver comfort isn't too bad except for the heat generated inside the enclosed cockpit, but passenger access leaves a little to be desired. Rear vision is lacking due to the extreme angle of the rear window and the neat rear wing. Going through our local McDonalds is a problem due to the fixed windows, a car too loud for the driver to be heard at the drive-through speaker, and a width greater than the opening at the drive through, but then when this car was conceived it was hoped that the car would be used mainly on the track.

If you ever get the chance to visit with one of these special Ferraris please take your time. They are very functional, very Ferrari-like, and best of all they make that magic sound for which all 12 cylinder Ferraris are famous.

(Reprinted with the Permission of Prancing Horse magazine)

Brochures, Books, Memorabilia & Models

Factory Literature

The foremost items in any Ferrari owner's collection are usually those produced by the Ferrari factory and directly associated with their particular tipo. The most common item is usually a hand-book, but then most owners like to add the original sales brochure for their car, and then some even go so far as to have the workshop manual as well.

Following is a list of Ferrari produce literature relating directly to the various Boxers.

For those unfamiliar with Ferrari literature a brief explanation might help. The first number is known as the Ferrari Print Number. Ferrari started producing sales brochures and printed literature in 1946 but didn't begin numbering them until 1965 when they began with 1/65. The print number can usually be found in very small type on the rear cover of the brochures, and the last page of the hand-books. On the brochures there will sometimes be another number, for example 15M/9/81 on the BB512i brochure. This indicates that 15,000 (15M) copies were printed in September 1981.

83/73		BB*	Sales Brochure
no#/73		365GT4/BB	Gearbox Assembly (11/73)
84/74		365GT4/BB	Owners Manual
89/73		365GT4/BB	Spare Parts Catalogue (11/73)
89/74		365GT4/BB	Spare Parts Catalogue
no#/74		365GT4/BB	Parts Book Revisions (Luglio 1974)
106/75		365GT4/BB	Workshop Manual
109/75		365GT4/BB	Warranty Card
118/75		365GT4/BB	Spare Parts Catalogue (inc Body Parts)
130/76		BB512	Owners Manual
130/80		BB512	Owners Manual (reprint of 130/76)
131/76		BB512	Spare Parts Catalogue (inc Body Parts)
133/76[1]		BB512	Sales Brochure
158/78[1]		BB512	Sales Brochure
159/78		BB512	Spare Parts Catalogue (inc Body Parts)
200/80		BB512	Sales Brochure
221/81		BB512i	Sales Brochure
221/81	15M/09/81	BB512i	Sales Brochure
221/81	10M/09/82	BB512i	Sales Brochure
221/81	8M/11/83	BB512i	Sales Brochure
224/81		BB512i	Owners Manual
230/82		BB512i	Parts Manual
234/82		BB512i	Poster
288/83		BB512i	Owners Manual (Swiss)
301/84		BB512i	Times Reference Book

* Although the first BB is commonly referred to as the 365GT4/BB the Ferrari sales brochure and the Pininfarina press release refer to it only as 'BB berlinetta boxer'.
[1] A comparison of these two brochures – produced only 2 years apart - show some interesting information;

133/76 shows; 0-400metres = 13.7s, 0-1000metres = 24.0s, maximum speed (5th @ 6800rpm) = 188mph
158/78 shows; 0-400metres = 14.2s, 0-1000metres = 25.1s, maximum speed (5th @ 6400rpm) = 176mph

The Ferrari brochure for the BB512 featured a simple cover. Size is 270mm x 270mm and is 12 sheets inside, including 2 in tracing paper, and 2 fold-out sheets. (NB colln)

BB512i handbook is 150mm x 210mm and 115pages. (NB Colln)

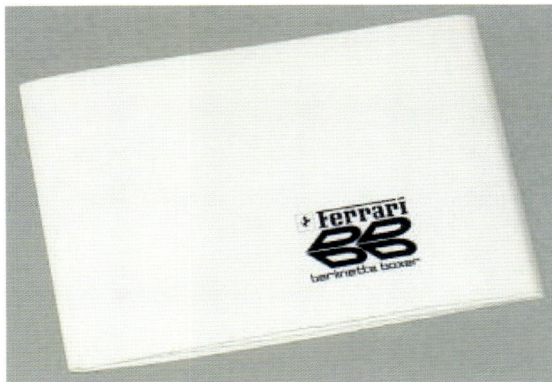

This rare Press Pack was produced by Pininfarina in 1971 and featured a set of sepia printed cards as well as a draughtman's side elevation.

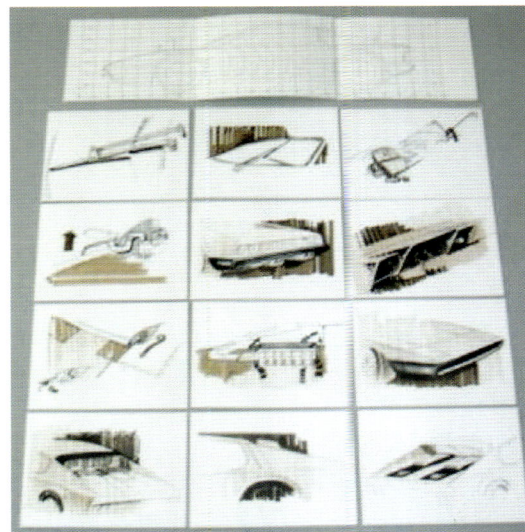

Books

Surprisingly, there have been few books about the Boxers (which is why I've written this one!), but those that have been published are listed below;

Ferrari Berlinetta Boxer 365 & 512 Series *by Mel Nichols* - Osprey Autohistory -1979
Nichols 'in' at Maranello allowed him to include some interesting back-ground information about the research and development behind the BB, but as the book was published in 1979 it inevitably can tell only half the story. Likewise the competition aspect is incomplete.

Ferrari Berlinetta Boxer *by Mel Nichols & Serge Bellu* – EPA – 1983
This is the French language update of the book listed above. Many of the photos are the same but it does have a chapter about the BB512i and an updated section about the racing BB/LMs. Again, this was published too early to be complete.

The Engine; Ferrari 365GT/4 BB *by Ray Ichiro Fukuno* –
Nigensha Publishing Co Ltd – 2005 - ISBN 544-40002-3
This is a fabulous book of 128 pages filled with lavish photos of the 365GT4/BB engine. The Japanese owner of 17903 had the engine totally stripped down, even taking the Weber carburettors apart, photographed and rebuilt. The photos are stunning quality with many photos of the components, down to the last washer, laid out in relative position to their rebuilt state. The text, in Japanese and English, describes in detail the mechanical components and the rebuilding process. A great book.

Boxer the Ferrari Flat 12 Racing and GT Cars *by Jonathan Thompson* – NP Osprey - 1981
It is really more about the flat twelve engined Grand Prix and 312PB sports racing cars than the BB, although it does have some info on the BB/LMs, but was written before the BB512i appeared, and therefore before the story was complete.
ISBN 0-930880-05-6

Flat Twelve *by Alan Henry* - MRP - 1981
Is about the flat twelve engined Grand Prix and sports racing cars, and has no BB content at all. (Still a good book, mind you)

Ferrarissima 3 – *Automobilia* – 1985 (ISSN 0393-3318)
Has a 14pp feature on the BB512i and includes a reprint of the BB512i handbook (224/81)

Naturally there have been many, many articles in magazines about the various BBs although these by nature usually only cover a road test or description of one car. A couple worth looking out for are:

Forza 9 (Feb 1998) features a 7pg article covering (very briefly) topics such as 'Good and Bad', 'What to look for', 'Buyers Checklist', with some nice colour photos.

Cavallino 22 carried a 14page article "A History and Appreciation" about the various BBs, and a further 3page article about the BB and the American grey market.

Other memorabilia

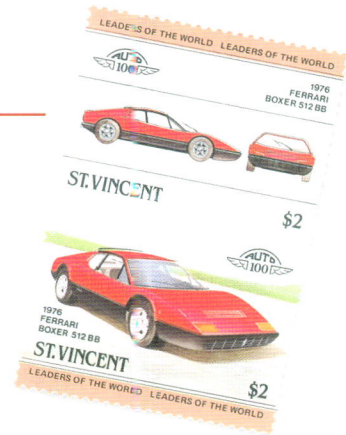

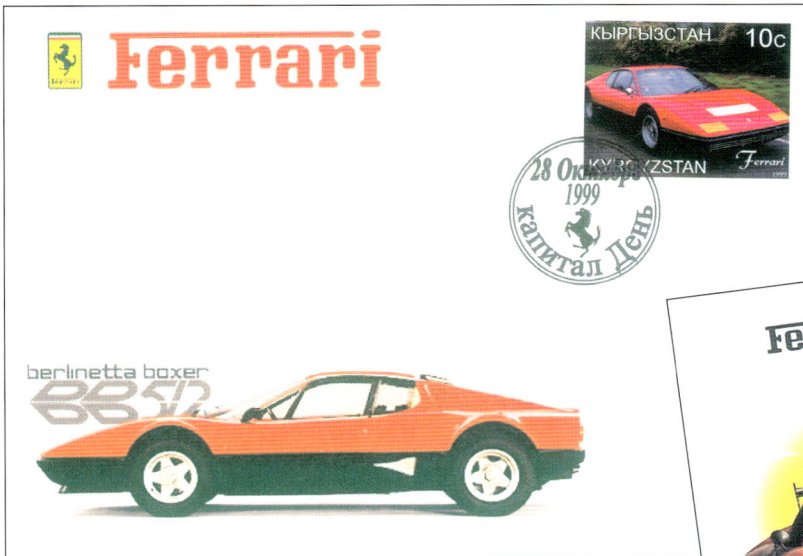

The Boxer has appeared on postage stamps and first day covers

London car dealer HR Owen featured the Boxer on one of their publicity postcards

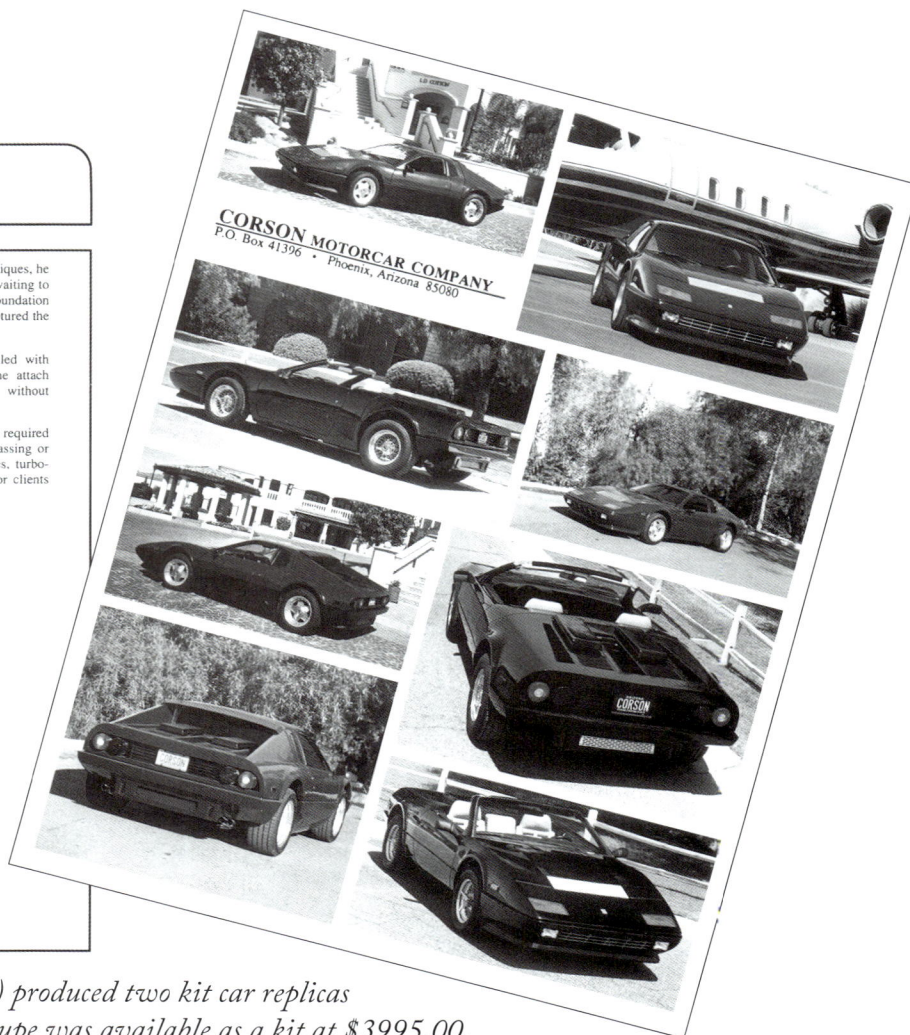

Corson
STYLED ★ FIERO

When designer Randy Corson first saw the Pontiac Fiero and its construction techniques, he was sure this was the car he had been waiting for. For several years Randy had been waiting to design a kit that was stylish, affordable and simple to assemble. The Fiero is the perfect foundation for a styling kit. The Corson styling kit creates the beautiful European look that has captured the imagination of automobile lovers for years.

If you are familiar with the Fiero, you know that the body panels are installed with innovative hardware and attach points. The Corson styling kit utilizes those same attach points for the Installation of the kit. This method allows the kit to be installed without disturbing the integrity of the stock Fiero chassis and running gear.

The deluxe kit consists of 11 fiberglass panels, eight custom aluminum grills, required lights, trim and hardware. It is easily installed without special tools, and no fiberglassing or welding is required. Options available include Hayashi racing wheels, Goodyear tires, turbochargers, mirrors and other after-market items. Turn-key models will be produced for clients who feel they don't have the time or qualifications to assemble a kit.

PONTIAC FIERO CHASSIS SPECIFICATIONS (1984 through 1988)
- Wheelbase: 93.4 inches
- Overall Length: 171.0 inches (with Corson kit)
- Width: 74.0 inches (with Corson kit)
- Height: 46.9 inches
- Track F/R: 57.8/58.7 inches
- Weight: 2600 - 2750 lbs.
- Fuel Capacity: 10.2 - 11.9 gallons
- Luggage Capacity: 5.85 - cu. ft.
- Engine
  - 2.5 Liter 4 Cyl. 98HP 135 lb. ft. Torque
  - 2.8 Liter V-6 135HP 165 lb. ft. Torque
- Transmission
  - 4-Speed Manual   1984-1986
  - 5-Speed Manual   1985-1988
  - 3-Speed Automatic 1984-1988

* For Color Brochure Send $5.00 in U.S. Funds To:
CORSON MOTORCAR COMPANY
P.O. BOX 41396
Phoenix, Arizona 85080
602-375-2544

© Copyright 1987

The Corson Motorcar Company (who they?) produced two kit car replicas that were based on the Pontiac Fiero. The coupe was available as a kit at $3995.00, and the spyder was available built only at $33,000!! (and this was in 1987) (NB Colln)

Models

365GT4/BB

7-11 Japan Limited Supercars		?	Toy
AMR 3		43	Mblt
Aoshima Super Mini Car 5		60	Pkit
Arii 63B		20	Pkit
Bandai Mini Mini Car	NART	43	Plast
Bandai Mini Mini Car 2199		40	Plast
Betta		32	Slot
Bolink		12	P/RC
Brianza 5a		14	Resin
Buby-Solido 44		43	M/DC
Century Models 2		43	Mblt
Chiera	Koenig	43	Rkit
Classico (Shell Colln)		36	M/DC
Crown 2 - C544		24	Pkit
Crown 4		35	Pkit
Eidai Grip Technica		24	Pkit
Eidai Grip Technica 19		28	M/DC
Entex 9101F		43	Pkit
Hasbro Autobot			P/toy
Hilario 001	Koenig	43	Rkit
I.S.		60	Plast
Ideal			Pl/m
Kawai 1002		38	Pkit
Kyosho 08173		18	Mblt
Matchbox 40385		32	PKit
MS Moulage 009		43	Rkit
Nanyung	Gp5 #58	12	Plast

Nanyung NY2400	yellow Gp5	16	Plast
Nanyung NY2458R	red Gp5 #58	16	Plast
Nanyung NY2458S	silver Gp5 #58	16	Plast
Nichimo MW2404		24	Pkit
Nitto 642	Gp5 #58	28	Pkit
Nomura Toy			Plast
R Schreiber		24	Pkit
Revell 7301		24	Pkit
Revell-Takara 1416		24	Pkit
Revell-Takara 1419		24	Pkit
Rigo		43	blt
Sakura		66	M/DC
Sakura Super Car 3		43	M/DC
Sakura-Mania		43	Mkit?
Solido 44		43	M/DC
Solido 1515		43	M/DC
Solido Duo 7038 (F)		43	M/DC
Solido Duo 7039 (F)		43	M/DC
Solido Duo 7040 (GB)		43	M/DC
Solido Duo 7041 (D)		43	M/DC
Solido Duo 7042 (USA)		43	M/DC
Solido Duo 7043 (I)		43	M/DC
Tron P23		43	Mkit
Airfix 8140 (US)		24	Pkit
Unknown (J)		65	Plast
Unknown (J)		75	M/DC
Unknown (J)		90	M/DC
Verem 411		43	M/DC
Verem 411(promo)		43	M/DC
Zee Toys D70		60	M/DC

BB512

ABC CBR005	512BB	14	Rblt
AMR-X 444		43	Mkit
AMR-X 445	NART Spyder	43	Mkit
AMR-X 446	Targa	43	Mkit
AMT 8687		24	Pkit
Alps		22	Tin
Annecy Miniatures	Zender	43	Rkit
Annecy Miniatures	1983 Geneva	43	Blt
Annecy Miniatures	IMSA	43	Rkit
Annecy Miniatures	Koenig	43	Rkit
Annecy Miniatures 5		43	Blt
Annecy Miniatures 6	NART Spyder	43	Blt
Annecy Miniatures 7	Targa	43	Blt
Annecy/AMR		43	Mkit
Aoshima Midship-3 G8-37		20	Pkit
Aoshima SC02		20	Pkit
Aoshima Silhouette Racing 7		24	Pkit
Arii 63D		20	Pkit
Arii 904		24	Pkit
Arii AR102-8		32	Pkit
Arii Remocon Series 68D		28	Pkit
Asahi AS54		55	M/DC
Asahi Tsusho-Atokomi		20	P/RC
Asahi Tsusho-Sigma 500		50	M/DC
Best BE9305		43	M/DC
BOF/Esdo	JL Chateau	43	Rkit
Esdo	JL Chateau	43	Rkit
BBR 1	Koenig	43	Rblt
BBR 33		43	Rblt
BBR 098A	512BB Targa	43	Rblt
BBR BBR140A/B	512BB Targa	43	Rblt
BBR BBP190	512BB Targa	43	Rblt
BBR BBP256	512BB Targa	43	Rkit
BBR Valko 2	Anliker	43	Rblt
Bandai BEC2		43	M/DC
Bandai Wind-Up Series		32	Pkit
Best 9265		43	M/DC
Burago 0133		24	M/DC
Burago 4133		43	M/DC
Carat	Koenig	43	Resin
? (Chinese)	(Official Licensed Product)	72	M/DC
Ciemme 43 CMK4309	512BB Turbo Chateau	43	Rkit
Co-Hog	racer	40	Wood
Co-Hog	street	40	Wood
Cox		12	P/RC
Diapet G68, 1410		40	M/DC
Editions Fabbri		43	M/DC
Entex 9100F		32	Pkit
Entex 9101B		43	Pkit
Entex 9583		24	Pkit
Ertl/AMT 8687		24	Pkit
Esci		24	Pkit
Franklin Mint		64	Pewter
Fujimi 103		16	Pkit
Fast FAS001	512BB	43	Rblt
Fast FAS002	512BB Uderzo	43	Rblt
Fast FAS004	512BB Eastwood	43	Rblt
Grand Prix Racing		60	Slot
Guisval 301	Shell Oil	43	M/DC
Guisval 342	SKF	43	M/DC
Guisval 343	Gulf	43	M/DC
HE14		14	Resin
Herbes	Lorenz Spyder	43	Resin
Hilario 002-1	Lorenz Spyder	43	Rkit

Hilario 002-2	Lorenz Spyder #2	43	Rkit
Hilario 004	Emblem Turbo	43	Rkit
Hilario 005-1	USA	43	Rkit
Hilario 002-5	Targa	43	Rkit
Hilario 010	European	43	Rkit
Ikko Mokei 1006		24	Pkit
Imai 2		55	Pkit
Imai 623		24	Pkit
Imai 629, 1329		24	Pkit
Ixo FER005		43	M/DC
Jimson		48	Ptoy
Kawai 1007		38	Plast
Kermi/Marcus (Hungary)		24	Plast
Kusan Wrapper racer		50	M/DC
Kyosho		18	M/DC
Kyosho		64	M/DC
Kyosho		43	M/DC
Kyosho Mini Z MZG37Y		?	Toy
LS 2		40	Pkit
MA Scale Models	NART Spyder	43	Blt
MA Scale Models	Targa Turbo	43	Blt
MOG 4A	Uderzo long-nose	43	Rkit
MOG 4B	Uderzo short-nose	43	Rkit
MOG 4C	Swiss	43	Rkit
MPC 1-0553		24	Pkit
MPC 1-0556		24	Pkit
MS Moulages 006	Koenig	43	Rkit
Marui 12		24	Pkit
Marui 14		24	Pkit
Masuday 02		87	Mkit
Matchbox - Avon/BBX			M/DC
Mattel Drive Command 2444		24	P/RC
Metal 43 - 1444		43	Mblt
Metal 43 - 1445	NART Spyder	43	Mblt
Metal 43 - 1446	Straman Spyder	43	Mblt
Nakamura 5301-135		24	Pkit
Niko		40	Pkit
Nitto 609	Gp5	24	Pkit
Nitto 615		28	Pkit
Nitto 620		24	Pkit
Nitto 622	Wolf	24	Pkit
ODK		32	Pkit
Otaki 95		24	Pkit
PCM Creation		24	transkit
Piccolino GT21		76	Mkit
Playart Model Power		64	M/DC
Playart Charmerz		64	M/DC
Raccoon RAC014	BB512 Koenig	43	Rkit
Revell 7510		16	Pkit
Roadace Replicas		100	Plstr
Sakura SP1		43	M/DC
Speedy Sports 7930/3B		50	M/DC
Spurn		160	M/DC
Studio 27 FR2404		24	Rkit
Taiyo	Sears Roebuck	24	P/RC
Takora		66	Plast
Testor-Burago 154		24	M/DC
Tilt MT77-WS-07		24	Pkit
Tilt MT82-CB3		24	Pkit
Tomica (Tomy) F57		62	M/DC
US Models 15		87	Blt
Unknown (HK)		38	M/DC
Unknown (I)		43	Crystal
Unknown (Taiwan)		24	Plast
Waco		24	P/RC
Yonezawa		43	Slot??
Yunica 85-2		050	M/DC

BB512i

Amacar 2	1984 Koenig	43	Resin
Brianza		14	Resin
Conti		10	Metal
HE14 002		14	Resin
Nitto 14045		24	Pkit

HE14s BB512 was nearly a foot long (30cms); with opening doors and engine cover. It was a hand built limited edition that featured superb paint finish and very fine photo-etched detail. (NB Colln)

BB/LMs

ABC ABC1403	1982 LM #70	14	Rkit	38179
ABC ABC1403B	1982 Daytona #65	14	Rkit	34445
ABC ABC1403C	1983 LM #47 (sic)	14	Rkit	
ABC CBR013B	1982 Daytona #65	14	Rblt	34445
ABC CBR013C	1983 LM #47 (sic)	14	Rblt	
Airfix 6407-5	NART	24	Pkit	18139
AMR RUFT1202	1981 LM #46	12	Rkit	35525
AMR-X	1980 LM #79	43	Mkit	28601
AMR-X	1981 LM #49	43	Mkit	35527
AMR-X	1982 LM #73	43	Mkit	30559
AMR-X 452	1981 LM #45	43	Mkit	35529
AMR-X 452	1982 LM #70	43	Mkit	38179
Annecy Miniatures	1980 LM #74	43	Resin	30559
Annecy Miniatures	1980 LM #76	43	Resin	32129
Annecy Miniatures	1980 LM #77	43	Resin	31589
Annecy Miniatures	1981 Daytona #65	43	Resin	34445
Annecy Miniatures	1981 LM #47	43	Resin	31589
Annecy Miniatures	1981 LM #48	43	Resin	35523
Annecy Miniatures	1981 Mugello #29	43	Resin	34157
Annecy Miniatures	1981 Silverstone #41	43	Resin	35523
Annecy Miniatures	1982 Daytona #6	43	Resin	30559
Annecy Miniatures	1982 Daytona #65	43	Resin	34445
Annecy Miniatures	1982 LM #71	43	Resin	41263
Annecy Miniatures	1982 LM #72	43	Resin	35527
Annecy Miniatures	1982 LM #73	43	Resin	30559
Annecy Miniatures	1982 Mt Fuji #12	43	Resin	30559
Annecy Miniatures	1983 Daytona #65	43	Resin	34445
Antonietti/Bossac		8	Metal	
BAM	1979 LM #63	43	Mkit	26685
BAM-X	1975 NART Sebring #111	43	Mkit	18139
BAM-X	1977 NART LM #75	43	Mkit	18139
BAM-X	1978 NART LM	43	Mkit	24131
BAM-X	1979 Daytona #68	43	Mkit	26683
BAM-X	1979 LM #64	43	Mkit	26683
BAM-X	1981 LM #47	43	Mkit	31589
BAM-X	1982 Daytona #6	43	Mkit	30559
BAM-X	1982 LM #71	43	Mkit	41263
Bandai Silhouette Formula		24	Pkit	18139
Best BE9279	1980 Monza #31	43	M/DC	28601
Best BE9297	1980 Daytona #69	43	M/DC	26683
Best BE9299	1980 LM #79	43	M/DC	28601
Best BE9300	1979 Daytona #67	43	M/DC	26685
Best BE9306	1979 LM #62	43	M/DC	26681
Best BE9317	1980 LM #75	43	M/DC	26685
Best BE9318	1979 Daytona #66	43	M/DC	26681
Bill Tong Models BTM001	1977 LM #75	24	Rblt	18139
Bill Tong Models BTM002	1975 Sebring #111	24	Rblt	18139
Bill Tong Models BTM003	1975 Daytona #1	24	Rblt	18139
Bill Tong Models BTM004	1978 LM #86	24	Rblt	18139
BOF/Esdo	1981 Daytona #79	43	Rkit	17577

Model	Description	Scale	Type	No.
Brumm Borsa Verona	Yellow no #s	43	M/DC	
Brumm R210	red/no #s	43	M/DC	
Brumm R211	1980 LM #78	43	M/DC	27577
Brumm R212	1981 LM #48	43	M/DC	35523
Brumm R212B	1980 LM #78 (w/race damage)	43	M/DC	27577
Brumm R212C	1979 LM #61	43	M/DC	27577
Brumm R213	1981 LM #47	43	M/DC	31589
Brumm R213B	1982 Daytona #6	43	M/DC	30559
Brumm R214	1980 LM #77	43	M/DC	31589
Brumm S021	black/no #s	43	M/DC	
Burago 4106	1979 Daytona #66	43	M/DC	26681
Burago 4133	1979 LM #64	43	M/DC	26683
Burago 5133	1979 Daytona #66	43	M/DC	26681
Carrera 25727	1979 LM #64	24	Slot	26683
Carrera 25728	1979 LM #61	32	Slot	27577
Carrera 27126	1980 LM #77	32	Slot	31589
Carrera 27101	1980 LM #78	32	Slot	27577
CG Hobby K24	1978 LM #88	43	transkit	24127
CG Hobby K24	1978 LM #89	43	transkit	24129
Cioni	1979 LM #62	14	Resin	26681
Cioni	1979 LM #63	14	Resin	26683
Classic Toys (Joel Fumy)		43	Blt	
Co-Hog	1979 Daytona #68 (toy)	40	Wood	26683
DRS Manou 16		43	Rkit	
Editions Fabbri	1980 LM #76	43	M/DC	32129
Eidai Grip Technica 30	NART	28	M/DC	18139
Entex 9504	NART	25	Pkit	18139
FDS 611	1980 LM #76	43	Mkit	32129
FDS 613	1981 LM #45	43	Mkit	35529
FDS 614	1981 LM #46	43	Mkit	35525
FDS 617	1982 Daytona #6	43	Mkit	30559
FDS 619	1982 LM #71	43	Mkit	41263
FDS 623	1980 LM #79	43	Mkit	28601
FDS 625	1980 LM #78	43	Mkit	27577
Guichard	1979 LM #62	43	transkit	26681
Guichard	1979 LM #63	43	transkit	26683
Gunze Sangyo 110	NART	24	Pkit	18139
Gunze Sangyo 140	1975 NART LM	24	Pkit	18139
Gyl 003	1978 LM #85	43	Mkit	22715
Gyl 005	1979 LM #61	43	Mkit	27577
Gyl 007	1981 LM #46	43	Mkit	35525
HiFi 51	1984 LM #27	43	Mkit	35529
Ixo LMC078	1981 LM #47	43	Rblt	31589
Ixo FER006	1982 LM #71	43	Rblt	41263
Ixo LMC077	1980 LM #76	43	Rblt	32129
Ixo FER016	1982 LM #72	43	Rblt	35527
Mad 001	Henn	43	Rkit	30559
Mad 001M	Henn	43	Rblt	30559
Mad 002	1982 Daytona #47	43	Rkit	31589
Mad 002M	1982 Daytona #47	43	Rblt	31589
Mad 003	1982 Daytona #65	43	Rkit	34445
Mad 003M	1982 Daytona #65	43	Rblt	34445
Mad 005	365BB	43	Rkit	17577
Mad 005M	365BB	43	Rblt	17577
Mad 006	1982 Daytona #79 (sic)	43	Rkit	
Mad 006M	1982 Daytona #79 (sic)	43	Rblt	
Mad 008	1980 Monza #31	43	Rkit	28601
Mad 008M	1980 Monza #31	43	Rblt	28601
Marui	NART	24	Pkit	18139
Marx 6135	NART	24	Plast	18139
Matchbox 3	1982 LM #71	40	M/DC	41263
Matchbox 4	1981 LM #46	40	M/DC	35525
Matchbox Special (China)	#147	38	M/DC	
Matchbox Turbo AM-2400		40	M/DC	
Meri MK018	1978 LM #86	43	Rkit	18139
Meri 18	1977 NART LM #75	43	Mkit	18139
Meri 19	1978 LM #86	43	Mkit	18139
Meri 45	1984 LM #27	43	Mkit	35529
Meri MKFR001	1977 LM #75	43	Rkit	18139
Meri MKFR002	1978 LM #86	43	Rkit	18139
Meri MKFR003	1982 Daytona #6	43	Rkit	30559
Meri MKFR004	1979 LM #62/63	43	Rkit	26681/85
Meri MKFR005	1980 LM #75	43	Rkit	26685
Meri MKFR006	1980 LM #76/77	43	Rkit	32129/31589
Meri MKFR007	1981 LM #46	43	Rkit	35525
Meri MKFR008	1981 LM #48	43	Rkit	35523
Meri MKFR009	1982 LM #72	43	Rkit	35527
Meri MKFR010	1982 LM #71	43	Rkit	41263
Meri MKFR011	1980 LM #78	43	Rkit	27577
Meri MKFR012	1981 LM #47	43	Rkit	31589
Meri MKFR013	1982 LM #70	43	Rkit	38179
Meri MKFR014	1984 Lime Rock #21	43	Rkit	29511
Meri MKFR015	1985 Sebring #21	43	Rkit	29511
Meri MKFR016	1980 Silverstone #11	43	Rkit	27577
Meri MKFR027	1984 LM #27	43	Rkit	35529
Meri MKS008	1981 LM #?	43	Rkit	
Meri/Bam MP009	1979 LM #62/63	43	Mkit	26681/85
MG		18	Rkit	
MG M038	1981 LM #79	43	Rkit	28601
MG M039	1981 Monza #15	43	Rkit	35529
MG S032	1975 Sebring #111	43	Rkit	18139
MG S033	1975 Daytona #1	43	Rkit	18139
MG S042	1975 Lime Rock #111	43	Rkit	18139
MG S043	1978 Daytona #5	43	Rkit	18139
MG S045	1978 LM #86	43	Rkit	18139
MG Firenze 5	1975 NART IMSA	43	Mkit	18139
MG Firenze 6	1976 NART Road Atlanta	43	Mkit	18139
Museum Collection	1977 LM #75	24	RKit	18139
Nichimo	NART	24	Pkit	18139
Nitto 630	NART	28	Pkit	18139
Provence Moulage K1618	1979 LM #64	43	Rkit	26683
Provence Moulage PM2566	1984 LM #27	43	Rkit	35529
Provence Moulage PM2618	1979 LM #64	43	Rkit	26683
Provence Moulage PM2722	1981 LM #48	43	Rkit	35523
Provence Moulage PM2780	1979 LM #61	43	Rkit	27577
Provence Moulage PMCD012	1982 LM #73	43	Rkit	30559
Provence Moulage ST0272	1979 LM #63	43	Rkit	26685
RD Marmande	1975 NART Sebring #111	43	Wood	18139
Record	1984 LM #27	43	Rkit	35529
Remember	1981 Silverstone #42	43	Rblt	27577
Serie 78 7802TR	1978 LM #88	43	transkit	24127
Serie 78 7802TR	1978 LM #89	43	transkit	24129
SHMR 51205	1980 LM #74	43	Rkit	30559
SHMR 51207	1982 Monza #98	43	Rkit	34157
SHMR 51208	1983 Bellancauto Test	43	Rkit	35529
SHMR 51209	1982 LM #70	43	Rkit	38179
SHMR 51210	1984 LM #27	43	Rkit	35529
SHMR 51211	1979 LM #61	43	Rkit	27577
SHMR 51212	1979 Daytona #66/67	43	Rkit	26681/85
SHMR 51213	1984 LM #27	43	Rkit	35529
Solido 5044 1978 LM #87		43	Mkit	24131
Solido 5044 1978 LM #89		43	Mkit	24129
Studio 27 C285	1979 Daytona #67	24	Rkit	26685
Studio 27 C286	1979 Daytona #68	24	Rkit	26683
Studio 27 C287	1982 Daytona #6	24	Rkit	30559
Studio 27 C288	1979 LM #61	24	Rkit	27577

Studio 27 C289	1979 LM #62/63	24	Rkit	
				26681/85
Studio 27 C290	1979 LM #64	24	Rkit	26683
Studio 27 C292	1980 LM #75/76/77	24	Rkit	
Studio 27 C293	1980 LM #78	24	Rkit	27577
Studio 27 C294	1980 LM #79	24	Rkit	28601
Studio 27 C296	1981 LM #47	24	Rkit	31589
Studio 27 C298	1981 LM #49	24	Rkit	35527
Studio 27 C301	1982 LM #72	24	Rkit	35527
Studio 27 C302	1982 LM #73	24	Rkit	30559
Taiyo 7855		20	Tin	18139
TAV001	1980 Daytona #69	43	?blt	26683
TAV002	1981 Silverstone #42	43	?blt	27577
TAV006	1981 Silverstone #41	43	?blt	35523
Tilt MT78-W-17	NART	24	Pkit	18139
Tilt MT82-CB5	NART (no decals)	24	Pkit	
Tokoloshe TOK002	1984 Test #27	43	Rblt	35529
Tokoloshe TOK011	1977 NART LM #75	43	Rblt	18139
Tokoloshe TOK015	1984 LM #27	43	Rblt	35529
Tokoloshe	1978 Daytona #5	43	Rblt	18139
Tomy	NART	22	Tin	18139
Tron AT01	1979 LM #62/63	43	Mkit	
				26681/85
Tron AT04	1980 LM #75	43	Mkit	26685
Tron AT05	1980 LM #78	43	Mkit	27577
Tron AT05SP	1980 LM #78	43	Mkit	27577
Tron AT07	1979 Daytona #68	43	Mkit	26683
Tron AT08	1981 LM #48	43	Mkit	35523
Tron AT09	1979 Daytona #67	43	Mkit	26685
Tron AT10	1978 LM #88	43	Mkit	24127
Tron AT11	1978 LM #85	43	Mkit	22175
Tron AT12	1980 LM #76	43	Mkit	32129
Tron AT12	1980 LM #77	43	Mkit	31589
Tron AT13	1978 LM #88	43	Mkit	24127
Tron AT14	1978 LM #87	43	Mkit	24131
Tron LE03	1982 Silverstone #80	43	Mkit	35523
Tron LE06	1981 Silverstone #42	43	Mkit	27577
Tron LE08	1985 Daytona #21	43	Mkit	29511
Tron LE09	1985 Daytona #51	43	Mkit	30559
Tron P24	1975 LM #99	43	Mkit	18095
Tron TRO174P	1978 LM #88	43	Rkit	24127
Tron TRO174PM	1978 LM #88	43	Rblt	24127
Tron TRO175P	1978 LM #87	43	Rkit	24131
Tron TRO175PM	1978 LM #87	43	Rblt	24131
Tron TRO176P	1978 LM #89	43	Rkit	24129
Tron TRO176PM	1978 LM #89	43	Rblt	24129
Tron TRO184P	1978 LM #85	43	Rkit	22715
Tron TRO184PM	1978 LM #89	43	Rblt	22715
Tron/Beehl	1978 LM #89	43	Mkit	27577
Yaxon 806	1979 LM #62	43	M/DC	26681
Yaxon 807	Jolly Club	43	M/DC	
Yaxon 811	Yaxon	43	M/DC	

Carrera's 1:32nd scale slot car faithfully captures the look of the 1978 BB/LMs and is available in 4 versions (NB Colln)

The Provence Moulage BB/LM has a stunning level of detail for a 1:43rd scale model (NB Colln)

Toy	=	Toy		blt	=	Built
Mblt	=	Metal Built		crystal	=	Glass
Pkit	=	Plastic kit		Metal	=	Metal hand-built
Plast	=	Plastic		P/toy	=	Plastic toy
Slot	=	Slot car		Pewter	=	Pewter
P/RC	=	Plastic Radi Control		plaster	=	Plaster
Resin	=	Resin built		Tin	=	Tin plate
M/DC	=	Metal DieCast		tkit	=	Transkit
Rkit	=	Resin Kit		wood	=	Wood
Mkit	=	Metal Kit				

Italian Andrea Cioni created these beautiful models of the Pozzi Le Mans cars. Handbuilt in 1:14th scale they were more than 12" (30cms) long with excellent detail (Cioni)

BB Register

VIN #	ENG #	MODEL	YEAR	COLOUR	INTERIOR	DRIVE	REG No.	LOCATION	COUNTRY	COMMENTS
365GT4/BB	365GT4/BB	365GT4/BB	365GT4/BB	365GT4/BB	365GT4/BB	365GT4/BB	365GT4/BB	365GT4/BB	365GT4/BB	365GT4/BB
17185		BB	1973	Rosso/Nero	Beige	LHD	UOT 2M (UK)	Tokyo	Japan	
17223		BB	1973	Rosso/Nero	Beige	LHD		Rome	Italy	
17257	00005	BB	1973	Rosso/Nero	Nero	LHD		Georgia	US	
17269	00007	BB	1973	Rosso/Nero	Nero	LHD	276691 RE	Milan	Italy	
17301	00009	BB	1973	Rosso/Nero	Nero	LHD		Oslo	Denmark	ex Gene Hackman
17321	00011	BB	1973	Giallo/Nero	Tan	LHD		Tokyo	Japan	
17359		BB	1973	Rosso/Nero	Tan/Nero	LHD		Honolulu	US	
17373		BB	1973	Verde Pino Met	Tan	LHD		STOLEN '80		
17401	00019	BB	1973	Grigio Ferro	Bordeaux	RHD	YSA 211	Melbourne	Australia	1973 Melbourne Show Car
17403		BB	1973	Argento/Nero	Nero	LHD			Japan	
17411		BB	1973			LHD			Italy	
17417		BB	1973			LHD			Italy	
17427		BB	1973			LHD		Wisconsin	US	Imported US by Dick Fritz
17439		BB	1973	Rosso/Nero	Tan	LHD	JJG 829		Belgium	
17445		BB	1973	Giallo/Nero	Nero	LHD		Maryland	US	
17447		BB	1973			LHD			Italy	
17461		BB	1973	Argento/Nero	Nero	LHD			France	1974 Monaco GP Course car
17471		BB	1973	Rosso Corsa	Tan	LHD		California	US	
17479		BB	1973			LHD			Italy	
17493		BB	1973			LHD			Italy	
17501		BB	1973			LHD			Belgium	
17511		BB	1973	Rosso/Nero	Nero	LHD		California	US	
17519		BB	1973			LHD			Italy	
17527		BB	1973	Rosso/Nero	Nero	LHD			US	
17535		BB	1973	Rosso/Nero	Nero	RHD	SNO 130K		UK	
17543		BB	1974	Blu Sera Met	Tan	LHD		Vermont	US	
17553		BB	1974	Giallo/Nero	Nero	LHD	575 TKG	Massachusetts	US	
17561	DEST	BB	1974	N/A	N/A	LHD	N/A	DESTROYED	N/A	
17569		BB	1974			LHD			US	
17577		BB/LM	1974	Rosso/NART	Nero	LHD			US	See BB/LM Chassis history
17585		BB	1974	Rosso/Nero	Nero	LHD	36 20	Yokohama	Japan	
17593		BB	1974			LHD			Italy	
17617		BB	1974	Rosso/Nero	Tan/Nero	LHD			Switzerland	1974 Geneva Show Car
17625		BB	1974	Rosso/Nero	Nero	RHD	TNR 595M		UK	
17633		BB	1974	Rosso/Nero	Nero	LHD		Georgia	US	
17641		BB	1974	Blu Sera Met	Nero	LHD	NZ 06 GF	Vermont	US	
17649		BB	1974	Rosso/Nero	Tan/Rosso	RHD	RLJ 565M		UK	
17655		BB	1974			LHD			Italy	
17659		BB	1974			LHD		Rome	Italy	
17665		BB	1974	Rosso/Nero	Nero/Rosso	LHD	05 TT 95		Netherlands	
17671		BB	1974	Rosso/Nero	Nero	LHD			France	
17677		BB	1974			LHD			Italy	Koenig conv
17683		BB	1974	Rosso/Nero	Nero	LHD			Sweden	
17689		BB	1974	Argento/Nero	Nero	LHD	8855 QS 64		France	
17693		BB	1974	Rosso/Nero	Nero	LHD	DE 28 12		Netherlands	

365GT4/BB	365GT4/BB	365GT4/BB	365GT4/BB	365GT4/BB	365GT4/BB	365GT4/BB	365GT4/BB	365GT4/BB	365GT4/BB
VIN #	ENG #	MODEL	YEAR	COLOUR	INTERIOR	DRIVE	REG No.	LOCATION	COUNTRY	COMMENTS
17697		BB	1974			LHD			Switzerland	
17701		BB	1974	Rosso/Nero	Nero	RHD	VPC 235M		UK	
17705		BB	1974			LHD			Italy	
17709		BB	1974	Rosso/Nero	Tan	LHD			Italy	
17713	00055	BB	1974	Argento/Nero	Nero	LHD	N/A	DESTROYED	N/A	
17717		BB	1974			LHD			Brazil	
17721		BB	1974	Nero Tropicale	Nero	LHD			Italy	
17725		BB	1974			LHD			Switzerland	
17729		BB	1974	Argento/Nero	Nero	RHD		Jersey	UK	
17733		BB	1974			LHD		Wisconsin	US	
17737		BB	1974			LHD			Brazil	
17741		BB	1974	Rosso Rubino	Tan	RHD	VLK 484M		UK	
17743		BB	1974			LHD			Belgium	
17745		BB	1974	Giallo/Nero	Nero	LHD			Germany	
17747		BB	1974			RHD	VPC 238M		UK	modified for comp
17749		BB	1974			LHD		Rome	Italy	
17751		BB	1974	Rosso/Nero	Tan	LHD			Amman	
17755	00025	BB	1974	Rosso/Nero	Crema	LHD		Maryland	US	
17759		BB	1974	Giallo/Nero	Nero	RHD			UK	
17761		BB	1974	Blu Sera Met	Bordeaux	LHD		Florida	US	
17765		BB	1974			LHD			Italy	
17767		BB	1974	Rosso/Nero	Nero	LHD			Germany	
17771		BB	1974			LHD			Italy	
17773		BB	1974	Nero Tropicale	Blu Scuro	LHD			Italy	
17777		BB	1974			LHD			France	
17779		BB	1974	Blu Sera Met	Tan	RHD			Australia	
17783		BB	1974			LHD			Italy	
17785		BB	1974			LHD			Italy	
17789		BB	1974	Rosso/Nero	Tan	LHD		Rome	Italy	
17791		BB	1974			RHD			UK	
17793		BB	1974			RHD	VEN 15		UK	
17797		BB	1974			LHD			Italy	
17799		BB	1974	Rosso/Nero	Nero	RHD			UK	
17801		BB	1974			LHD			US	
17805		BB	1974			LHD			Germany	
17807		BB	1974	Rosso Corsa	Zegna Cloth	LHD			Belgium	
17809		BB	1974			LHD			Switzerland	
17813		BB	1974	Rosso Chiaro	Tan	RHD	P 53		UK	
17817		BB	1974	Rosso Corsa	Nero	RHD		Wellington	New Zealand	
17821	00071	BB	1974			LHD			Italy	
17825		BB	1974	Rosso Corsa	Nero	LHD			Germany	
17827		BB	1974	Rosso Corsa	Nero	RHD	365 BBF		South Africa	
17829		BB	1974	Blu Sera Met	Tan	LHD				
17831		BB	1974			LHD			Italy	
17837		BB	1974			LHD			US	
17839		BB	1974			RHD			Australia	
17841		BB	1974	Rosso/Nero	Tan	RHD	KVE 39		UK	
17845		BB	1974	Argento/Nero	Nero	RHD			Australia	
17847		BB	1974			RHD			UK	
17851		BB	1974	Giallo/Nero	Nero	LHD		Georgia	US	
17853		BB	1974			LHD			Italy	
17857		BB	1974	Rosso/Nero	Crema	LHD		Pennsylvania	US	
17859		BB	1974	Rosso/Nero	Tan	LHD	8511VK72		France	
17861		BB	1974	Marrone	Tan/Nero	RHD	RPL 647R	Rouen	France	
17865		BB	1974	Rosso/Nero	Nero/Grigio	LHD		Zurich	Switzerland	

365GT4/BB	365GT4/BB	365GT4/BB	365GT4/BB	365GT4/BB	365GT4/BB	365GT4/BB	365GT4/BB	365GT4/BB	365GT4/BB
VIN #	ENG #	MODEL	YEAR	COLOUR	INTERIOR	DRIVE	REG No.	LOCATION	COUNTRY	COMMENTS
17867		BB	1974	Rosso/Nero	Nero/Rosso	RHD			Australia	
17869		BB	1974	Rosso/Nero	Nero	RHD	SOL 715M		UK	
17873		BB	1974			RHD			UK	
17875		BB	1974			RHD			UK	
17877		BB	1974	Rosso/Nero	Nero	RHD			New Zealand	
17881		BB	1974			LHD			Germany	
17883		BB	1974	Rosso/Nero	Nero/Tan Cloth	LHD			Italy	
17885		BB	1974			LHD			Switzerland	
17887		BB	1974			RHD			Belgium	
17889		BB	1974	Rosso/Nero	Tan	RHD			UK	
17891		BB	1974	Rosso/Nero	Tan	RHD			Belgium	
17893		BB	1974	Rosso/Nero	Tan	RHD	400 BOX		UK	
17897		BB	1974			LHD			Japan	
17899		BB	1974	Rosso/Nero	Tan	RHD		Ireland	UK	
17901		BB	1974			LHD			Italy	
17903		BB	1974			RHD	VEC 690M		UK	
17905		BB	1974	Giallo/Nero	Nero	LHD		California	US	
17909		BB	1974	Rosso/Nero	Nero	RHD	WPG 17M		UK	
17911		BB	1974			RHD	KBC 242N		UK	
17913		BB	1974	Verde Pino Met	Tan	LHD			Japan	
17915		BB	1974	Rosso Corsa	Tan	RHD	BOX 44B	Sydney	Australia	
17917		BB	1974	Rosso/Nero	Nero	LHD		Texas	US	
17921		BB	1974	Rosso/Nero	Nero	LHD			Italy	
17923		BB	1974			LHD			Italy	
17925		BB	1974			LHD			France	
17927		BB	1974	Rosso Dino	Tan	LHD		Zurich	Switzerland	
17929		BB	1974			LHD		California	US	
17933		BB	1974	Rosso Corsa	Nero	RHD	MCT 2		US	
17935		BB	1974			LHD			Italy	
17937		BB	1974	Argento/Nero	Nero	LHD			Italy	
17941		BB	1974			RHD			Australia	
17943		BB	1974	Rosso/Nero	Tan	RHD	XMC 28M		UK	
17945		BB	1974	Rosso/Nero	Nero	LHD	JUT 335		Belgium	
17947		BB	1974	Nero Tropicale	Nero	LHD		Connecticut	US	
17951		BB	1974			LHD			France	
17953		BB	1974			LHD			Italy	
17955		BB	1974	Nero Tropicale	Tan	RHD			UK	
17959		BB	1974			RHD			UK	
17961		BB	1974			LHD			Italy	
17963		BB	1974			LHD			Italy	
17967		BB	1974			RHD	BB 365		UK	
17969		BB	1974	Rosso/Nero	Tan	LHD			US	
17971		BB	1974			LHD			Italy	
17975		BB	1974	Nero Tropicale	Tan	LHD			Italy	
17977		BB	1974	Rosso/Nero	Tan	RHD	JOJ 979N		UK	
17979		BB	1974			LHD			Italy	
17983		BB	1974	Bianco Avus	Blu Scuro	LHD			Italy	
17985		BB	1974			LHD			Italy	
17987		BB	1974			LHD			Italy	
17991		BB	1974	Rosso/Nero	Nero/Rosso	LHD	352 W 13	Marseille	France	
17993		BB	1974			LHD			France	
17995		BB	1974	Rosso/Nero	Tan	LHD		Colorado	US	
17999		BB	1974			LHD			Switzerland	
18001		BB	1974	Nero Tropicale	Nero	LHD		California	US	

VIN #	ENG #	MODEL	YEAR	COLOUR	INTERIOR	DRIVE	REG No.	LOCATION	COUNTRY	COMMENTS
18003		BB	1974	Rosso/Nero	Nero	LHD			France	
18007		BB	1974			LHD			Italy	
18009		BB	1974	Rosso/Nero	Tan	LHD			Italy	
18011		BB	1974			LHD			France	
18015		BB	1974			LHD			France	
18017		BB	1974			LHD			Japan	
18019		BB	1974	Rosso/Nero	Nero	LHD			France	
18023		BB	1974			LHD			Italy	
18025		BB	1974			LHD		Firenze	Italy	
18027		BB	1974			LHD			Canada	
18031		BB	1974	Giallo/Nero	Nero	LHD	DPX 4197	New York	US	
18033		BB	1974			LHD			Spain	
18035		BB	1974			LHD			Switzerland	
18039	00033	BB	1974	Nero Tropicale	Nero	LHD		Texas	US	
18041		BB	1974			LHD			Switzerland	
18043		BB	1974			LHD			Germany	
18047		BB	1974			LHD			Italy	
18049		BB	1974			LHD			Italy	
18051		BB	1974	Rosso/Nero	Crema	RHD			UK	
18055		BB	1974	Rosso/Nero	Nero	LHD		Cassis	France	
18057		BB	1974	Rosso/Nero	Nero	LHD			Switzerland	
18059		BB	1974			LHD			France	
18063		BB	1974			LHD			Japan	
18065		BB	1974			LHD			Switzerland	
18067		BB	1974	Giallo/Nero	Nero	LHD		Illinois	US	
18071		BB	1974	Rosso/Nero	Nero/Tan	RHD	SB 350		UK	
18073		BB	1974			RHD	557 BOX		UK	
18075		BB	1974			RHD	6 BPE		UK	
18079		BB	1974			LHD			Switzerland	
18081		BB	1974	Blu Dino Met	Tan	LHD		California	US	
18083		BB	1974			LHD			Germany	
18087		BB	1974	Rosso/Nero	Nero	RHD	KLC 879N		UK	
18089		BB	1974	Rosso/Nero	Tan	LHD			Austria	ex Niki Lauda
18091		BB	1974	Rosso/Nero	Nero	LHD		California	US	
18095	DEST	BB/LM	1974	Rosso/Nero	Nero	LHD	N/A	DESTROYED	N/A	
18097		BB	1974			LHD			Germany	
18099		BB	1974			LHD			Switzerland	
18103		BB	1974	Giallo/Nero	Nero	RHD	700 FLY		UK	
18105		BB	1974			LHD			Germany	
18107		BB	1974			RHD			UK	
18111		BB	1974	Bianco Avus	Nero	RHD	BVU 696N		UK	
18113		BB	1974			LHD			Germany	
18115		BB	1974			RHD			UK	
18119		BB	1974	Blu Sera Met	Nero	LHD			France	
18121		BB	1974			LHD			Switzerland	
18123		BB	1974			RHD	JEF 83		UK	
18125		BB	1974			RHD	16 BOX		UK	
18127		BB	1974	Giallo/Nero	Nero	LHD	4RE BB	Virginia	US	
18129		BB	1974	Rosso Corsa	Nero/Rosso	RHD	JPM 845N		UK	
18131		BB	1974			RHD	GPE 634N		UK	
18133		BB	1974	Argento/Nero	Bordeaux	LHD		California	US	
18135		BB	1974	Rosso/Nero	Nero	LHD		California	US	conv to LHD
18137		BB	1974			RHD			UK	
18139		BB/LM	1974	Rosso/NART	Nero	LHD			US	
18141		BB	1974			RHD		Jersey	UK	

365GT4/BB	365GT4/BB	365GT4/BB	365GT4/BB	365GT4/BB	365GT4/BB	365GT4/BB	365GT4/BB	365GT4/BB	365GT4/BB
VIN #	ENG #	MODEL	YEAR	COLOUR	INTERIOR	DRIVE	REG No.	LOCATION	COUNTRY	COMMENTS
18143		BB	1974	Giallo/Nero	Nero	LHD			Italy	
18145		BB	1974	Rosso Corsa	Beige/Nero	RHD	HLD 15N		UK	Autokraft Targa conv
18147		BB	1974			RHD	4 MBM		UK	
18149		BB	1974			LHD	MPH 70P		UK	
18151		BB	1974			LHD				
18153		BB	1974	Rosso/Nero	Nero	RHD	KPJ 960P		UK	
18155		BB	1974			RHD			UK	
18157		BB	1974			RHD			UK	
18159		BB	1974	Rosso/Nero	Nero	RHD			Australia	
18161		BB	1974	Argento/Nero	Nero	LHD				
18163		BB	1974			RHD			UK	
18165		BB	1974			RHD	ORH 271P		UK	
18167		BB	1974			LHD				
18169		BB	1974	Rosso/Nero	Nero	LHD			Canada	
18171		BB	1974			LHD			Denmark	
18173		BB	1974			LHD	TSY 364M		UK	
18177		BB	1974	Rosso/Nero	Tan/Nero	LHD		Florida	US	
18179		BB	1974			LHD			Italy	
18181		BB	1974			LHD			Amman	
18185		BB	1974			LHD			Switzerland	
18187		BB	1974	Argento/Nero	Nero	LHD			US	
18189		BB	1975	Rosso Rubino	Tan	LHD		Ohio	US	
18193		BB	1974			RHD	JMH 565N		UK	ex Sir George Burton
18195		BB	1974	Giallo/Nero	Nero	LHD		Paris	France	
18197	00221	BB	1974	Rosso/Nero	Nero/Rosso	LHD		California	US	
18201		BB	1974	Grigio Ferro	Nero	LHD			UK	
18203		BB	1974			LHD			Italy	
18205		BB	1974			LHD		Firenze	Italy	
18209		BB	1974			LHD			Switzerland	
18211		BB	1974	Rosso/Nero	Tan	LHD		Pennsylvania	US	
18213		BB	1974			LHD			Switzerland	
18217		BB	1974			LHD				
18219		BB	1974	Rosso/Nero	Nero	LHD	TZD 808		Belgium	1975 Brussels Show Car
18221		BB	1974	Rosso/Nero	Nero	LHD			France	
18225		BB	1974			LHD				
18227		BB	1974			LHD			Germany	
18229		BB	1974			LHD			Italy	
18233		BB	1974	Rosso/Nero	Nero	RHD	PEG 200		UK	
18235		BB	1974			RHD	307 AWD		UK	
18237		BB	1974			RHD	JJH 574N		UK	
18241		BB	1974			RHD	LYD 303P		UK	
18243		BB	1974	Rosso Rubino	Nero	LHD			France	ex Prince Sangusko
18259		BB	1974	Azzurro Chiaro	Nero	RHD			UK	
18261		BB	1974	Nocciola Met	Beige/Nero	LHD		Pennsylvania	US	
18265		BB	1974	Blu Dino Met		LHD		New York	US	
18267		BB	1974	Chiaro Blu Met	Crema/Nero	RHD	HPG 919N		UK	
18297		BB	1974			LHD		California	US	
18299		BB	1974	Rosso/Nero	Tan	LHD			Switzerland	
18301		BB	1974			LHD				
18303		BB	1974			RHD			Australia	
18307		BB	1974	Rosso/Nero	Tan	LHD	BPA 6348	New Hampshire	US	
18311		BB	1974			LHD	AGU 430N		UK	
18315		BB	1975			LHD				
18319		BB	1975			LHD			Italy	
18321		BB	1975			LHD			Italy	

VIN #	ENG #	MODEL	YEAR	COLOUR	INTERIOR	DRIVE	REG No.	LOCATION	COUNTRY	COMMENTS
18327		BB	1975			LHD			France	
18329		BB	1975			LHD			Sweden	
18333		BB	1975			RHD			UK	
18337		BB	1975	Rosso/Nero	Nero	LHD			Italy	
18341		BB	1975			LHD			Italy	
18349		BB	1975			LHD			Italy	
18355		BB	1975			RHD			South Africa	
18357		BB	1975			LHD			Italy	
18363		BB	1975			LHD			Italy	
18367		BB	1975	Rosso Dino	Tan	LHD		California	US	
18373		BB	1975	Rosso/Nero	Tan	LHD			Italy	Koenig conv
18375		BB	1975			RHD			Australia	
18377		BB	1975	Blu TdF	Nero	LHD			Switzerland	
18381		BB	1975	Blu Sera Met	Nero	LHD		Marseille	France	1975 Barcelona Show Car
18385		BB	1975			LHD		Bologna	Italy	
18389		BB	1975			LHD			Germany	
18391		BB	1975	Rosso/Nero	Tan	LHD			Italy	
18393	00310	BB	1975	Rosso/Nero	Nero	LHD		New Jersey	US	
18397		BB	1975	Rosso/Nero	Tan	LHD		California	US	
18401		BB	1975	Rosso Corsa	Nero	LHD			Germany	Koenig conv
18405		BB	1975			LHD			Italy	
18407		BB	1975			LHD			Italy	
18411		BB	1975			LHD			Italy	
18413		BB	1975			LHD			Switzerland	
18417		BB	1975	Rosso Chiaro	Nero	LHD		New Jersey	US	
18419		BB	1975			LHD			Italy	
18423		BB	1975			LHD			Germany	
18427		BB	1975	Rosso/Nero		LHD			Italy	
18429		BB	1975	Rosso/Nero	Nero	LHD		California	Italy	
18431		BB	1975	Rosso/Nero	Nero	LHD			Holland	
18435		BB	1975	Grigio Ferro		LHD		Rome	Italy	
18437		BB	1975			LHD			Germany	
18441		BB	1975			LHD			France	
18443		BB	1975			LHD				
18445		BB	1975			LHD			Germany	
18453		BB	1975			LHD				
18457		BB	1975	Grigio Ferro	Nero	LHD			Switzerland	
18459	DEST	BB	1975	N/A	N/A	LHD	N/A	DESTROYED	N/A	
18463		BB	1975			LHD			Italy	
18467		BB	1975			LHD			Germany	
18471		BB	1975			LHD			Belgium	
18475		BB	1975	Giallo/Nero	Nero	LHD			Germany	
18479		BB	1975	Rosso/Nero	Nero	LHD		Arizona	US	
18481		BB	1975	Argento/Nero	Nero	RHD			Australia	
18487		BB	1975	Rosso/Nero	Tan	LHD			Switzerland	
18491		BB	1975	Rosso/Nero	Tan	LHD			US	
18495		BB	1975	Rosso/Nero	Nero	LHD			Belgium	
18499		BB	1975			LHD			Switzerland	
18503		BB	1975			LHD			Italy	
18507		BB	1975			LHD			Italy	
18511		BB	1975			LHD			Italy	
18515		BB	1975			LHD			Germany	
18521		BB	1975			RHD			Australia	
18523		BB	1975			LHD			Italy	

	365GT4/BB	365GT4/BB	365GT4/BB	365GT4/BB	365GT4/BB	365GT4/BB	365GT4/BB	365GT4/BB	365GT4/BB
VIN #	ENG #	MODEL	YEAR	COLOUR	INTERIOR	DRIVE	REG No.	LOCATION	COUNTRY	COMMENTS
18529		BB	1975			LHD			Italy	
18533		BB	1975	Argento/Nero	Blu Scuro	LHD		New Jersey	US	
18535		BB	1975			LHD			Belgium	
18543		BB	1975			LHD		California	Italy	
18545		BB	1975			LHD		Rome	Italy	
18547		BB	1975			LHD			Italy	
18549		BB	1975	Ross/Nero	Nero	LHD			Italy	
18553		BB	1975	Rosso/Nero	Nero	LHD		Oregon	US	Spyder conv
18555		BB	1975			RHD			Australia	
18557		BB	1975			RHD			Australia	
18567		BB	1975	Rosso/Nero	Nero	LHD		Rome	Italy	
18569		BB	1975			LHD			Italy	
18571		BB	1975			LHD			Italy	
18577		BB	1975			LHD			Germany	
18581		BB	1975			LHD			Italy	
18587	00340	BB	1975	Rosso/Nero	Nero	LHD		Illinois	US	
18591		BB	1975			LHD			Italy	
18597		BB	1975			LHD			Italy	
18599		BB	1975			LHD			Italy	
18605		BB	1975			LHD			Germany	
18611		BB	1975	Rosso/Nero	Nero	LHD			Germany	1975 Frankfurt Show Car
18613		BB	1975	Bianco/Nero	Nero	LHD		Brescia	Italy	
18623		BB	1975	Rosso/Nero	Tan	LHD			Italy	
18625		BB	1975			LHD			UK	
18629		BB	1975			LHD			Germany	
18631		BB	1975	Giallo/Nero	Nero	LHD		Tennesee	US	
18635		BB	1975			LHD			France	
18639		BB	1975			LHD			Germany	
18641		BB	1975	Argento/Nero	Nero	LHD			Belgium	
18645		BB	1975			LHD			Germany	1975 Frankfurt Show Car
18647		BB	1975	Rosso/Nero	Nero	LHD		Colorado	Italy	
18649		BB	1975	Argento/Nero	Nero	LHD			France	
18655		BB	1975	Rosso/Nero	Tan	LHD			US	
18657		BB	1975	Rosso/Nero	Tan	LHD		Colorado	US	
18659		BB	1975			LHD			Italy	
18663		BB	1975	Rosso/Nero	Nero	LHD			Italy	
18665		BB	1975	Blu TdF	Tan/Nero	LHD			Germany	
18671		BB	1975			LHD			Italy	
18685		BB	1975	Rosso/Nero	Crema/Nero	RHD	BOX 365		UK	1975 London Show Car
18687		BB	1975			LHD			Germany	
18691		BB	1975	Nero Tropicale	Nero	LHD			Sweden	
18695		BB	1975	Rosso/Nero	Tan	RHD			UK	
18701		BB	1975			LHD			Italy	
18707		BB	1975			LHD			Italy	
18709		BB	1975	Argento/Nero	Nero	LHD			Belgium	
18713		BB	1975			LHD			Belgium	
18719		BB	1975	Rosso/Nero	Tan	RHD	MMW 25R		UK	
18727		BB	1975	Rosso/Nero	Nero	RHD			UK	
18743		BB	1975	Rosso Corsa	Tan	LHD		Pennsylvania	US	
18745	00378	BB	1975	Giallo/Nero	Nero	LHD		Illinois	US	
18749		BB	1975			LHD			Italy	
18757		BB	1975			LHD			Italy	

VIN #	ENG #	MODEL	YEAR	COLOUR	INTERIOR	DRIVE	REG No.	LOCATION	COUNTRY	COMMENTS
18763		BB	1975			LHD			Italy	
18787		BB	1975			LHD			Italy	
18955		BB	1976	Rosso/Nero	Nero	LHD	MTK F 365		Germany	
18959		BB	1976			LHD			Germany	
18995		BB	1976			LHD			Switzerland	
19005		BB	1976	Rosso/Nero	Nero	LHD			Italy	
19071		BB	1976	Azzurro Chiaro	Nero	LHD		New York	US	
19085		BB	1976	Grigio Ferro	Nero	LHD			Italy	
19153		BB	1976	Rosso/Nero	Nero	RHD			Australia	
19177		BB	1976	Argento/Nero	Blu Scuro	RHD			Australia	
19199		BB	1976	Rosso/Nero	Nero	LHD		Zurich	Switzerland	
19239		BB	1976	Rosso Corsa	Nero	RHD			Australia	
19247		BB	1976	Argento/Nero	Nero	RHD			Australia	
19257		BB	1976	Giallo Fly	Nero	LHD			Italy	
19323		BB	1976	Rosso Corsa	Nero	LHD			Belgium	
19343	00395	BB	1976	Nero Tropicale	Tan	RHD	365 BOX	Hertfordshire	UK	
19445		BB	1976	Rosso Corsa	Crema/Rosso	LHD		Milan	Italy	

VIN #	ENG #	MODEL	YEAR	COLOUR	INTERIOR	DRIVE	REG No.	LOCATION	COUNTRY	COMMENTS
19271	00004	BB	1976	Rosso/Nero	Nero	LHD				
19677		BB	1976	Rosso Chiaro	Nero	LHD				
19711		BB	1976	Rosso/Nero	Nero	LHD				
19807		BB	1976	Argento/Nero	Nero/Crema	LHD		Florida	US	
19839		BB	1976			LHD				
19865		BB	1976	Rosso/Nero		LHD			US	
19879		BB	1976			LHD				
19885	00011	BB	1976	Rosso/Nero	Nero	RHD	JHW 3		UK	
19915		BB	1976	Rosso/Nero	Tan	LHD		California	US	
19927		BB	1976	Argento Met	Nero	LHD		Berlin	Germany	
19985		BB	1976	Rosso/Nero	Tan	LHD			US	
19995		BB	1976	Rosso/Nero	Tan	LHD		California	US	
20017		BB	1976	Rosso/Nero	Nero	LHD			France	
20019		BB	1976			LHD				
20021		BB	1976	Rosso/Nero	Tan	LHD	31 SJ 21		France	
20039		BB	1976	Rosso/Nero	Nero	LHD				
20085		BB	1976	Rosso/Nero	Crema	RHD	ABW 749R		UK	
20143		BB	1976	Rosso/Nero	Nero	LHD				1977 Amsterdam Show Car
20145		BB	1976			LHD				
20147		BB	1976	Rosso/Nero	Nero	LHD			Germany	
20149		BB	1976	Rosso/Nero	Nero	LHD			Germany	
20151		BB	1976			LHD				
20153		BB	1976	Nero Met	Bordeaux	LHD		Atlanta	US	
20193		BB	1976	Nero Met	Bordeaux	LHD		New York	US	
20257		BB	1976	Rosso/Nero	Nero	LHD		Texas	US	
20285		BB	1976	Rosso/Nero	Bordeaux	LHD				
20287		BB	1976			LHD				
20289		BB	1976	Giallo/Nero	Nero	LHD			US	
20309		BB	1976	Rosso Chiaro	Crema	LHD	JJ RZ 29		Netherlands	
20339		BB	1976	Rosso/Nero	Tan	LHD	YNE 274S		UK	
20367		BB	1976	Rosso/Nero	Tan	LHD			France	
20487		BB	1976	Argento/Nero	Tan	LHD				
20489		BB	1976			LHD				
20491		BB	1976	Rosso/Nero	Nero	LHD				
20509		BB	1976	Rosso Corsa	Nero	LHD		Florida	US	
20529		BB	1976	Rosso/Nero	Nero	LHD			France	

VIN #	ENG #	MODEL	YEAR	COLOUR	INTERIOR	DRIVE	REG No.	LOCATION	COUNTRY	COMMENTS
BB512	BB512	BB512	BB512	BB512	BB512	BB512	BB512	BB512	BB512	BB512 BB512 BB512 BB512 BB512 BB512
20553		BB	1976	Rosso/Nero	Nero	LHD		California	US	
20647		BB	1976	Rosso/Nero	Nero	LHD				
20657		BB	1976	Rosso/Nero	Nero	RHD	YAF 60T		UK	
20679		BB	1976	Rosso/Nero	Crema	LHD				
20693		BB	1976	Rosso/Nero	Crema	LHD	BOX 512		UK	
20747		BB	1976	Blu TdF	Tan	LHD			Netherlands	
20769		BB	1976	Rosso/Nero	Nero	LHD				
20807		BB	1977			LHD			Italy	
20809		BB	1977			RHD			UK	
20811		BB	1977	Rosso/Nero	Nero	RHD	NEY 180		UK	
20825		BB	1977	Rosso/Nero	Nero	RHD			New Zealand	
20873		BB	1977	Rosso/Nero	Nero	LHD			Canada	1979 FCA Concours Winner
20903		BB	1977	Rosso/Nero	Tan	LHD				
20933		BB	1977	Rosso/Nero	Tan	LHD				
20981		BB	1977	Rosso/Nero	Nero/Rosso	LHD				
21033		BB	1977	Blu TdF	Tan	LHD		Colorado	US	
21067		BB	1977	Rosso/Nero	Tan	LHD				
21087		BB	1977	Rosso/Nero	Nero	LHD				
21101		BB	1977	Giallo Fly	Nero	LHD	XPF 563S		UK	
21123		BB	1977	Giallo/Nero	Nero	LHD				
21125		BB	1977			LHD				
21133		BB	1977	Rosso/Nero	Nero	RHD	UES 603S		UK	
21137		BB	1977	N/A	N/A	RHD		DESTROYED	N/A	
21149		BB	1977	Argento Met	Bordeaux	RHD	3037 PJ		UK	
21167		BB	1977	Rosso Corsa	Nero	LHD				
21171		BB	1977	Rosso Corsa	Nero	LHD				
21257		BB	1977	Grigio Ferro	Nero	LHD				
21281		BB	1977			LHD				
21295		BB	1977	Rosso Corsa		LHD				
21317		BB	1977	Rosso Corsa	Nero	LHD				Koenig conv
21331		BB	1977	Rosso Corsa	Nero	RHD			UK	
21351		BB	1977	Rosso Corsa	Tan	LHD				Koenig conv
21363		BB	1977	Rosso Corsa	Nero	LHD				
21401		BB	1977	Rosso Corsa	Nero	LHD				
21425		BB	1977	Rosso Corsa	Nero	LHD				
21437		BB	1977	Rosso Corsa	Nero	LHD				
21445		BB	1977	Argento Met	Bordeaux	LHD				
21475		BB	1977	Rosso Corsa	Nero	LHD				
21485		BB	1977	Rosso Corsa	Nero	RHD	371 R		UK	
21495		BB	1977	Rosso Corsa	Nero	LHD				
21513		BB	1977			LHD			Italy	Modified body
21523		BB	1977	Rosso Corsa	Nero	LHD		California	US	
21549		BB	1977	Rosso Corsa	Nero	LHD				
21559		BB	1977			RHD			Netherlands	
21587		BB	1977			LHD		California	US	
21613		BB	1977	Rosso Corsa	Nero	LHD			Germany	
21617		BB	1977	Rosso Corsa	Nero	LHD			France	
21623		BB	1977	Rosso/Nero	Nero/Rosso	RHD			UK	
21625		BB	1977			RHD	ATM 799S		UK	Spyder conv
21647		BB	1977	Bianco Avus	Nero	LHD				Targa conv
21659		BB	1977	Rosso/Nero	Nero	LHD		Edmonton	Canada	
21667		BB	1977	Argento/Nero	Nero/Rosso	LHD	BE 288796		Switzerland	
21675		BB	1977	Nero Met	Nero	LHD				
21709		BB	1977	Rosso Corsa	Bordeaux	LHD				

	BB512	BB512	BB512	BB512	BB512	BB512	BB512	BB512	BB512	BB512	BB512	BB512	BB512	BB512	BB512
VIN #	ENG #	MODEL	YEAR	COLOUR	INTERIOR	DRIVE	REG No.	LOCATION	COUNTRY	COMMENTS					
21715		BB	1977	Azzurro/Nero	Bordeaux	LHD	FR 11960		Switzerland						
21725		BB	1977	Rosso Corsa	Nero	RHD	VOC 651S		UK						
21727		BB	1977	Rosso/Nero	Tan	LHD		California	US						
21749		BB	1977	Rosso Rubino	Tan	LHD									
21791		BB	1977	Rosso Corsa	Nero	LHD		Paris	France						
21793		BB	1977			LHD									
21795		BB	1977			RHD	NFC 395		UK						
21859		BB	1977	Blu Sera Met	Nero	LHD									
21873		BB	1977	Giallo/Nero		LHD			Holland	ex Switzerland, 2006: BB/LM conv, Engine #0014 (ex 30559); G/box #16					
21901		BB	1977	Rosso/Nero	Nero/Rosso	LHD		Florida	US						
21903	00156	BB	1977	Blu Chiaro	Crema	LHD			France						
21921		BB	1977	Rosso Corsa	Nero	LHD									
21939		BB	1977	Rosso Corsa	Crema/Nero	LHD		North Carolina	US						
21941		BB	1977	Rosso/Nero	Nero	LHD									
21951		BB	1977	Rosso/Nero	Tan	RHD	ANX 926S		UK						
21953		BB	1977	Blu Sera Met	Tan	LHD		California	US						
21975		BB	1977	Argento Met	Nero	RHD			UK						
21989		BB	1977	Nero Met	Tan	LHD		Los Angeles	US						
22007		BB	1977	Rosso Corsa	Tan	LHD									
22023		BB	1977	Rosso Corsa	Tan	LHD									
22049		BB	1977	Rosso Corsa	Tan	LHD									
22059		BB	1977	Rosso/Nero	Nero	LHD		California	US	Koenig conv					
22069		BB	1977	Rosso Corsa	Nero	LHD									
22083		BB	1977	Rosso/Nero	Nero	LHD		Monaco	France	Gp.4 Modified					
22085		BB	1977	Rosso Corsa	Crema	RHD	PDR 7		UK						
22087		BB	1977	Rosso Corsa	Nero	RHD			UK						
22153		BB	1977	Rosso Corsa	Nero	RHD	HAB 463S	Surrey	UK						
22169		BB	1977	Rosso Corsa	Tan/Rosso	RHD	AH 66		UK						
22177		BB	1977	Rosso Corsa	Nero	LHD									
22241		BB	1977	Nero Met	Tan	LHD		Illinois	US						
22243		BB	1977	Rosso/Nero	Nero	LHD			New Mexico						
22247		BB	1977	Rosso/Nero	Nero	LHD									
22251		BB	1977	Rosso/Nero	Crema/Nero	RHD	30 BOH		UK						
22253		BB	1977	Rosso Corsa	Bordeaux	LHD				Koenig conv					
22255	98145.452		1977			98145.452	98145.452		98145.452	98145.452					
22289		BB	1977	Rosso Corsa	Nero	LHD									
22299		BB	1977	Rosso Corsa	Nero	LHD				Koenig conv					
22315		BB	1977	Giallo Fly	Nero	LHD		California	US						
22337		BB	1977	Rosso Corsa	Crema	RHD	FWL 936S		UK						
22339		BB	1977	Rosso Corsa	Nero	LHD									
22363		BB	1977	Rosso Corsa	Tan	LHD									
22385		BB	1977	Nero Met	Tan	LHD		New Mexico	US						
22401		BB	1977			LHD									
22419		BB	1977	Rosso Corsa	Nero	LHD		Florida	US						
22431		BB	1977	Rosso/Nero	Nero	RHD	MIA 512		UK						
22447		BB	1977	Rosso Corsa	Nero	LHD									
22469		BB	1977	Giallo Fly	Nero	LHD		Maryland	US						
22481		BB	1978	Rosso/Nero	Nero	RHD	UPR 850S		UK						
22503		BB	1978			RHD			Singapore						
22505		BB	1978	N/A	N/A	RHD		DESTROYED	N/A						
22507		BB	1978	Rosso Corsa	Nero	RHD			UK						
22511		BB	1978	Rosso/Nero	Nero	RHD	UYR 3S		UK						

BB512	**BB512**	**BB512**	**BB512**	**BB512**	**BB512**	**BB512**	**BB512**	**BB512**	**BB512**	**BB512**	**BB512**	**BB512**
VIN #	ENG #	MODEL	YEAR	COLOUR	INTERIOR	DRIVE	REG No.	LOCATION	COUNTRY	COMMENTS		
22527		BB	1978	Rosso/Nero	Nero	RHD		Melbourne	Australia			
22541		BB	1978	Rosso/Nero	Tan	RHD	UHX 834S		UK			
22543		BB	1978	Blu Sera Met	Tan	RHD	155 MPH		UK			
22549		BB	1978	Rosso Rubino	Bordeaux	RHD	8 HAO		UK			
22551		BB	1978	Rosso/Nero	Nero	RHD	YJF 530S		UK			
22553		BB	1978	Rosso Chiaro	Rosso	LHD	K BB 512		Belgium			
22555		BB	1978	Rosso/Nero	Nero	LHD			Canada	Ex Roger Penshe; later conv to BB/LM replica		
22557		BB	1978	Nero Met	Nero	RHD		Surrey	UK			
22713		BB	1978	Rosso Rubino	Bordeaux	LHD		California	US			
22715		BB/LM	1978	Giallo/Nero	Nero	LHD	N/A	Munich	Germany			
22749		BB	1978	Rosso Corsa	Nero	LHD						
22789		BB	1978			LHD						
22803		BB	1978	Nero Met	Tan/Nero	LHD		California	US			
22863		BB	1978	Rosso Corsa	Nero	LHD						
22865		BB	1978	Rosso Corsa	Nero/Rosso	LHD		New York	US			
22889		BB	1978	Rosso/Nero	Nero	LHD	4409 AS	California	US			
22897		BB	1978	Rosso/Nero		LHD						
22901		BB	1978	Blu Sera Met	Tan	LHD		California	US			
22913		BB	1978	Ross/Nero	Nero	LHD						
22941		BB	1978	Rosso Corsa	Nero	RHD	WJU 880S		UK			
22997		BB	1978	Bianco Avus	Nero	LHD		North Carolina	US			
23005		BB	1978	Bianco Avus	Nero	LHD		San Francisco	US	ex Stan Nowak		
23015		BB	1978	Rosso Corsa	Nero	LHD		Conneticut	US	Original colour Nero Met		
23025		BB	1978	Rosso Corsa	Nero	LHD		New Jersey	US			
23091		BB	1978	Rosso Corsa	Tan	LHD			US			
23125		BB	1978	Rosso Corsa	Nero	LHD						
23273		BB	1978			LHD			Canada			
23275		BB	1978	Nero Met	Nero	LHD			US			
23283	DEST	BB	1978	N/A	N/A	LHD		DESTROYED	N/A			
23383		BB	1978	Rosso Corsa	Tan	LHD						
23415		BB	1978	Rosso Corsa	Nero	LHD		Conneticut	US	Amerispec conv		
23497		BB	1978	Azzurro Met	Tan/Nero	LHD			US			
23527		BB	1978			RHD	115 BOX		UK			
23583		BB	1978	Nero Met	Nero	LHD			Australia			
23665		BB	1978	Rosso Corsa	Nero	LHD		New Jersey	US			
23681		BB	1978	Rosso Corsa	Nero	LHD						
23689		BB	1978	Rosso Corsa	Crema	LHD						
23711		BB	1978	Rosso Chiaro	Nero	LHD		Missouri	US			
23713		BB	1978			LHD						
23715		BB	1978	Rosso Corsa	Nero	LHD						
23717		BB	1978	Rosso Corsa	Nero	LHD			US			
23745		BB	1978			RHD	AND 15		UK			
23767		BB	1978			RHD	11 VKR		UK			
23769		BB	1978	Rosso Corsa	Tan	LHD			France			
23779		BB	1978	Rosso Corsa	Nero	LHD			Netherlands			
23799		BB	1978	Rosso Corsa		LHD						
23841		BB	1978	Rosso Corsa	Nero	RHD	MEL 8		UK			
23853		BB	1978	Rosso Corsa	Crema	LHD		Florida	US			
23861		BB	1978	Argento/Nero	Blu Scuro	LHD		California	US			
23897		BB	1978	Blu Sera Met	Crema	RHD	VPH 680S		UK			
23899		BB	1978			LHD						
23901		BB	1978	Rosso Corsa	Tan/Rosso	LHD			US			
23903		BB	1978			LHD			Germany			

VIN #	ENG #	MODEL	YEAR	COLOUR	INTERIOR	DRIVE	REG No.	LOCATION	COUNTRY	COMMENTS
23905		BB	1978	Rosso Corsa	Tan	LHD		Munich	Germany	
23935		BB	1978	Rosso Corsa	Tan	LHD		California	US	Koenig conv
23959		BB	1978	Rosso/Nero	Nero	LHD		California	US	
23991		BB	1978			LHD			US	
24009		BB	1978	Rosso/Nero	Crema	RHD	YUT 35T		UK	
24031		BB	1978	Rosso Corsa	Tan	LHD		California	US	Original colour Blu Sera
24043		BB	1978			RHD	XLW 524S		UK	
24099		BB	1978	Rosso Corsa	Crema	LHD	VSU 511		UK	
24121		BB	1978	Nero Met	Nero	LHD				
24123		BB	1978			LHD			Italy	
24125		BB	1978			LHD				
24127		BB/LM	1978	Bianco Avus	Nero	LHD	#88	Marseille	France	
24129		BB/LM	1978	Rosso/Nero	Nero	LHD	N/A		Japan	
24131		BB/LM	1978	Rosso/Nero	Nero	LHD	N/A	Florida	US	
24167		BB	1978	Nero Met	Nero	LHD				
24201		BB	1978	Rosso Corsa	SaBBia	RHD	78 BBX	Ireland	UK	
24239		BB	1978			RHD	BJD 894T		UK	
24287		BB	1978			LHD				
24315		BB	1978	Rosso/Nero	Nero	RHD	BTW 852T		UK	
24317		BB	1978			LHD				Zender conv
24323		BB	1978	Rosso Corsa	Nero	LHD		Atlanta	US	
24351	00270	BB	1978	Nero Met	Tan	LHD	MI 92818G	Milan	Italy	
24405		BB	1978			LHD				
24445	00274	BB	1978	Rosso/Nero	Nero	LHD		Nevada	US	
24465		BB	1978	Rosso/Nero	Nero	LHD			Italy	
24477		BB	1978	Rosso/Nero	Nero	RHD	XPB 490S		UK	
24519		BB	1978	Rosso Corsa	Tan	LHD				
24577		BB	1978	Rosso/Nero	Tan	RHD	WYV 422T	Bucks	UK	Original colour Argento
24611		BB	1978			LHD		California	US	
24641		BB	1978	Nero Met	Tan	RHD			Australia	
24655		BB	1978	Rosso/Nero	Tan	LHD		California	US	
24693		BB	1978			LHD		Rhode Island	US	
24711		BB	1978	Rosso Corsa	Nero	LHD				
24731		BB	1978	Argento Met	Bordeaux	LHD				
24771		BB	1978	Rosso Corsa	Nero	LHD	65 RD FV		Netherlands	
24773		BB	1978	Rosso Corsa	Tan	LHD			Italy	
24775		BB	1978	Rosso Corsa	Crema	RHD	BYP 521T		UK	
24789		BB	1978	Grigio Ferro		LHD				
24839		BB	1978	Rosso/Nero		LHD			Switzerland	
24915		BB	1978	Rosso Corsa	Tan	LHD				
24923		BB	1978	Argento Met	Nero	LHD		Pennsylvania	US	
24927		BB	1978	Rosso/Nero	Crema	RHD	148 BBX		UK	
24975		BB	1978	Rosso Corsa		LHD				
24979		BB	1978	Nero Met	Tan	LHD		Boston	US	Targa conv
25113		BB	1978	Giallo Fly	Crema	LHD				
25131		BB	1978			LHD				
25155		BB	1978	Nero Met	Nero	LHD			US	
25185		BB	1978	Rosso/Nero	Nero	LHD			US	
25191		BB	1978	Rosso/Nero	Nero	LHD		Detroit	US	
25209		BB	1978	Rosso/Nero	SaBBia	RHD	6969 PT		UK	
25225		BB	1978			LHD				
25259		BB	1978	Rosso Corsa	Crema	LHD				
25291		BB	1978	Rosso Corsa	Nero	RHD	ERY 971T (UK)	Melbourne	Australia	
25387		BB	1978	Blu Sera Met	Tan	LHD				
25435		BB	1978	Rosso Corsa	Nero	LHD		Los Angeles	US	

VIN #	ENG #	MODEL	YEAR	COLOUR	INTERIOR	DRIVE	REG No.	LOCATION	COUNTRY	COMMENTS
25489		BB	1978	Nero Met	Nero	LHD				
25571		BB	1978	Grigio Ferro		LHD				
25697		BB	1978	Rosso/Nero	Nero	LHD			US	
25835		BB	1978	Rosso Corsa	Nero	RHD	DTW 903T		UK	
25881		BB	1978	Bianco Avus	Tan	LHD		San Francisco	US	
25913		BB	1978	Rosso Corsa	Nero	LHD	512 TV 42		France	Original colour Nero
25915		BB	1978			LHD				
25917		BB	1978	Rosso Corsa	Nero/Rosso	LHD			Austria	
25919		BB	1978			LHD				
25921		BB	1978	Blu Sera Met	Tan	LHD		New Jersey	US	
25923		BB	1978	Rosso Corsa	Nero	LHD		New York	US	
25925		BB	1978			LHD				
25927		BB	1978			LHD				
25999		BB	1978	Rosso Corsa	Tan	LHD				
26201		BB	1978	Rosso Corsa	Tan	RHD	BOX 534		UK	
26229		BB	1978			LHD			US	
26243		BB	1978	Rosso/Nero	Nero	LHD		New Jersey	US	
26301		BB	1978			LHD				
26315		BB	1978	Rosso/Nero	Tan	RHD	512 NTM		UK	
26357		BB	1978	Argento Met	Bordeaux	LHD		California	US	
26389		BB	1978	Rosso Corsa	Nero	LHD		California	US	
26455		BB	1978	Nero Met	Crema/Nero	LHD		Conneticut	US	Original Colour Rosso/ Nero
26637		BB	1978	Rosso Corsa	Crema	LHD				
26643		BB	1978	Rosso Corsa		LHD				
26657		BB	1978	Rosso Corsa	Crema	RHD	BB 512 (UK)		UK	
26681		BB/LM	1978	Rosso Corsa	Nero	LHD	N/A		US	
26683	00001	BB/LM	1978	Rosso Corsa	Nero	LHD	N/A		US	
26685		BB/LM	1978	Rosso Corsa	Nero	LHD	N/A		UK	
26947		BB	1978	Argento/Nero	Nero	LHD		Detroit	US	Ex Chuck Jordan
26949		BB	1978	Blu Sera Met	Crema	LHD	BB 512		Belgium	
26989		BB	1978	Rosso/Nero	Tan	LHD	FI 970394	Firenze	Italy	
26999		BB	1978	Rosso Rubino	Nero	LHD				
27001		BB	1978	Rosso/Nero	Tan/Nero	LHD		Washington	US	
27019		BB	1978	Rosso/Nero	Nero	RHD	OUF 84W		UK	
27021		BB	1978	Rosso/Nero	Tan	LHD		Maryland	US	
27063		BB	1978	Nero Met	Nero	RHD	AYT 2T		UK	
27097		BB	1978	Rosso/Nero	Nero	RHD			US	Koenig conversion
27109		BB	1978	Rosso/Nero	Tan	LHD				
27133		BB	1978	Nero Met	Bordeaux	LHD	VD 128667	Vaud	Switzerland	
27141		BB	1978	Rosso/Nero	Nero/Rosso	RHD	DPL 203T		UK	
27235		BB	1978	Rosso Corsa	Crema	LHD				
27237		BB	1978	Blu Sera Met	Tan/Nero	LHD			France	
27239		BB	1978	Rosso Corsa	Nero	LHD				
27279		BB	1978	Giallo Fly	Nero	LHD				
27289		BB	1978	Argento Met	Bordeaux	RHD	NOT 112		UK	
27321		BB	1978	Rosso/Nero	Crema/Nero	LHD				C
27323		BB	1978	Rosso/Nero	Tan	LHD			Netherlands	
27325		BB	1978	Rosso/Nero	Crema	LHD	NR JZ 82		Netherlands	Original Colour Nero
27343		BB	1978	Nero Met	Tan	LHD				
27375		BB	1978	Rosso/Nero	Nero	LHD	JRU 273V		UK	
27379		BB	1978	Rosso/Nero	Nero	LHD		Minnesota	US	
27377		BB	1978	Rosso/Nero	Crema	RHD	512 GUW		UK	
27381		BB	1978			RHD	BPD 175T		UK	
27399		BB	1978	Rosso/Nero	Crema	LHD		Los Angeles	US	

	BB512	BB512	BB512	BB512	BB512	BB512	BB512	BB512	BB512	BB512	BB512	BB512	BB512	BB512	BB512
VIN #	ENG #	MODEL	YEAR	COLOUR	INTERIOR	DRIVE	REG No.	LOCATION	COUNTRY	COMMENTS
27447		BB	1978	Rosso/Nero	Nero	LHD		Los Angeles	US	
27449		BB	1978	Giallo Fly	Blu Scuro	LHD			Netherlands	
27501		BB	1978	Rosso/Nero	Nero	RHD	WHY 92	Derbyshire	UK	
27505		BB	1978	Nero Met	Nero	LHD	VELOCI	Illinois	US	
27551		BB	1978	Argento Met	Nero	LHD				
27553		BB	1978	Giallo Fly	Nero	LHD		Wisconsin	US	
27577		BB/LM	1978	Verde Met	Tan	LHD	N/A	Berkshire	UK	
27579		BB/LM	1978	Rosso Corsa	Nero	LHD	N/A		Switzerland	
27611		BB	1978	Rosso/Nero	Nero	LHD		Conneticut	US	
27693		BB	1978			LHD				
27699		BB	1978	Rosso Rubino	Tan	LHD				
27773		BB	1978	Nero Met	Nero	LHD			France	
27775		BB	1978			LHD				
27777		BB	1978	Rosso Corsa	Tan	LHD				
27861		BB	1978	Rosso/Nero	Nero	RHD	512 FLU		UK	
27863		BB	1978	Blu Sera Met	Crema	LHD				
27865		BB	1978			LHD				
27869		BB	1978	Argento Met	Nero	LHD				
27935		BB	1978	Argento/Nero	Nero	LHD		California	US	
27939	DEST	BB	1978	N/A	N/A	LHD	HEV 575T	DESTROYED	US	
27941		BB	1978	Bianco Avus	Blu Scuro	LHD	512 C	Melbourne	Australia	
28011		BB	1978			LHD				
28033		BB	1978	Giallo/Nero	Nero	LHD			US	
28051		BB	1978	Blu Sera Met	Tan/Blu	RHD	FJF 512V		UK	
28053		BB	1978			RHD	DPM 222V		UK	
28145		BB	1978	Rosso/Nero	Crema/Nero	LHD		Essen	Germany	
28147		BB	1978	Rosso Corsa	Nero	LHD			US	
28149		BB	1978	Rosso/Nero	Tan	LHD		California	US	
28151		BB	1978	Rosso/Nero	Tan	LHD		Oregon	US	
28183		BB	1978	Rosso/Nero	Nero	LHD		California	US	
28229		BB	1978			LHD				
28233		BB	1978	Grigio/Nero	Nero	LHD		California	US	
28235		BB	1978	Blu Chiaro	Tan	RHD	512 RMM		UK	Modified for comp
28237		BB	1978	Rosso/Nero	Bordeaux	LHD				
28283		BB	1978			LHD			US	
28301		BB	1978	Rosso/Nero		LHD				
28377		BB	1978			RHD	LAH 777V		UK	
28379		BB	1978	Nero Met	Nero	LHD				
28441		BB	1978	Rosso/Nero	Nero	LHD				
28443		BB	1978			LHD				
28445		BB	1978			RHD	EHD 573V		UK	
28537		BB	1978	Rosso/Nero	Nero	LHD		Alabama	US	
28541		BB	1978	Nero Met	Tan	LHD				
28543		BB	1978	Rosso/Nero	Nero	LHD		Indianapolis	US	
28573		BB	1978	Rosso/Nero	Tan	LHD			Switzerland	
28601		BB/LM	1978	Rosso Corsa	Nero	LHD	#110		France	
28631		BB	1979	Rosso/Nero	Tan	LHD			HK	
28633	00459	BB	1979	Rosso Corsa	Nero	LHD		California	US	Original Colour Rosso/ Nero
28637		BB	1979	Rosso/Nero	Nero	RHD	KNN 150V		UK	
28639		BB	1979	Rosso Corsa	Tan	LHD		Texas	US	
28703		BB	1979	Rosso/Nero	Nero	LHD				
28705		BB	1979	Rosso/Nero	Nero/Rosso	LHD	TNX BR	California	US	
28707		BB	1979	Rosso/Nero	Tan/Rosso	LHD	7666 KW		UK	
28767		BB	1979	Blu Sera Met	Tan	LHD				

VIN #	ENG #	MODEL	YEAR	COLOUR	INTERIOR	DRIVE	REG No.	LOCATION	COUNTRY	COMMENTS
28789		BB	1979	Rosso/Nero		LHD				
28873		BB	1979	Rosso/Nero	Tan/Nero	LHD				
28879		BB	1979	Rosso Corsa	Nero	RHD			Australia	Original Colour Oro Met
28981		BB	1979	Rosso/Nero	Nero	RHD		DESTROYED	N/A	
28983		BB	1979	Rosso/Nero	Nero	RHD	EPE 692V		UK	
28985		BB	1979			LHD				
28987		BB	1979	Rosso Dino	Nero	LHD				
29053		BB	1979	Rosso Corsa	Crema	LHD		New York	US	
29055		BB	1979	Rosso Corsa	Crema	RHD	BOT 287V	Surrey	UK	Ex Adrian Newey
29057		BB	1979	Rosso/Nero	Tan	LHD		New Jersey	US	
29175		BB	1979			RHD	600 XBB		UK	
29177		BB	1979	Rosso Corsa	Nero	LHD				Koenig conv
29181		BB	1979	Nero Met	Tan	LHD		Florida	US	
29183		BB	1979	Nero Met	Tan	LHD				Koenig conv
29191		BB	1979	Nero Met	Tan	LHD				
29271		BB	1979	Rosso Corsa	Crema	LHD				
29271		BB	1979	Rosso/Nero	Crema	RHD	NWY 326V		UK	
29273		BB	1979	Nero Met	Nero	LHD				
29365		BB	1979	Nero Met	Nero	LHD				
29367		BB	1979			LHD				
29373		BB	1979	Rosso/Nero	Tan	RHD			UK	
29423		BB	1979	Rosso/Nero	Nero	LHD				
29507		BB/LM	1979	Rosso Corsa	Nero	LHD	N/A	Germany		
29509		BB/LM	1979	Rosso/Blu Str	Nero	LHD	N/A	Wisconsin	US	
29511		BB/LM	1979	Rosso Corsa	Nero	LHD	N/A		US	
29543		BB	1979	Argento Met	Tan	LHD				
29545		BB	1979	Rosso/Nero	Tan	LHD		Indiana	US	
29601		BB	1979			LHD			US	
29643		BB	1979	Argento Met	Nero	LHD				Koenig conv
29663		BB	1979			LHD		Detroit	US	
29695		BB	1979	Rosso/Nero		LHD	PR 9	Jersey	UK	
29717		BB	1979			RHD	BOX 65V		UK	
29719		BB	1979	Grigio Ferro	Tan	LHD		California	US	Koenig conv
29753		BB	1979	Rosso/Nero	Nero	LHD		Conneticut	US	
29823		BB	1979	Argento Met	Bordeaux	LHD				
29897		BB	1979	Argento Met		LHD				
30013		BB	1979	Rosso/Nero	Nero	LHD		Atlanta	US	
30057		BB	1979			RHD			HK	
30079		BB	1979			LHD		California	US	
30131		BB	1979			LHD			US	
30155		BB	1979	Rosso/Nero	Nero	LHD				
30197		BB	1979	Marrone	Tan	LHD		California	US	
30235		BB	1979	Rosso Corsa	Tan	LHD		Washington	US	
30251		BB	1979	Grigio Ferro	Nero	LHD		California	US	
30269		BB	1979	Rosso/Nero	Crema	RHD	VSX 86V		UK	
30311		BB	1979	Rosso Chiaro	Nero	RHD	EYN 12V	Surrey	UK	Ex Chris Rea, LM Spec Engine
30313		BB	1979	Blu Sera Met	Crema	RHD	DH 8504		UK	
30335		BB	1979	Rosso Corsa	Nero	LHD		Texas	US	
30337		BB	1979			LHD				
30387		BB	1979	Nero Met	Tan	LHD		California	US	
30393		BB	1979	Rosso/Nero	Crema	LHD			US	
30401		BB	1979	Rosso/Nero	Nero	LHD		Boston	US	
30463		BB	1979			LHD				

BB512	BB512	BB512	BB512	BB512	BB512	BB512	BB512	BB512	BB512	BB512	BB512	BB512	BB512	BB512	BB512

VIN #	ENG #	MODEL	YEAR	COLOUR	INTERIOR	DRIVE	REG No.	LOCATION	COUNTRY	COMMENTS
30467		BB	1979	Rosso/Nero	Nero/Rosso	LHD				
30509		BB	1979	Rosso/Nero	Nero	LHD		California	US	
30517		BB	1979	Rosso Corsa	Crema	LHD				
30559	00010	BB/LM	1979	Rosso Corsa	Nero	LHD	N/A		France	
30611		BB	1979	Rosso Corsa	Nero	LHD				
30633		BB	1979	Rosso Corsa	Nero	LHD				
30661		BB	1979	Rosso/Nero	Nero	LHD			Canada	Original Colour Argento Met
30667		BB	1979	Nero Met	Crema	LHD		Florida	US	
30709		BB	1979	Rosso Corsa	Crema	RHD			UK	
30713	00568	BB	1979	Rosso Corsa	Crema/Nero	LHD		Oregon	US	
30715		BB	1980	Rosso Corsa		RHD	LOG 46		UK	
30717		BB	1980	Rosso Corsa	Nero	LHD				
30757		BB	1980	Rosso Corsa	Crema	RHD	PMW 69		UK	
30761		BB	1980			LHD		California	US	
30765		BB	1980	Rosso Corsa	Nero	LHD				
30815		BB	1980	Blu TdF	Nero	LHD				
30817		BB	1980			RHD	VOW 11	Jersey	UK	
30821		BB	1980	Giallo Fly	Nero	LHD				
30839		BB	1980	Nero Met	Nero	LHD	512 VP 59		France	
30865		BB	1980	Rosso/Nero	Tan	LHD			Switzerland	
30931		BB	1980	Nero Met	Tan	LHD		California	US	
30933		BB	1980	Rosso Corsa	Nero/Rosso	RHD	CVK 959V		UK	
30967		BB	1980	Nero Met	Crema	LHD			US	
30971		BB	1980	Rosso Corsa		LHD		Pennsylvania	US	
30973		BB	1980	Rosso Corsa	Nero	LHD				
30981		BB	1980	Nero Met	Tan	LHD				
31061		BB	1980	Grigio Ferro	Bordeaux	LHD		Oregon	US	
31063		BB	1980	Rosso Corsa		LHD				
31067		BB	1980	Nero Met	Nero	LHD		California	US	
31075		BB	1980			LHD				
31113		BB	1980			LHD			US	
31151		BB	1980	Nero Met	Crema/Nero	RHD	11 UKR		UK	
31153		BB	1980			RHD			UK	
31155		BB	1980			RHD	SRP 1G		UK	
31157		BB	1980			LHD				
31159		BB	1980	Rosso Corsa	Nero	LHD	S LP 999	Basel	Switzerland	Koenig conversion, BBLM Replica
31181		BB	1980			LHD				
31207		BB	1980	Rosso Chiaro	Nero	LHD				
31221		BB	1980	Rosso Corsa	Crema	LHD				
31227		BB	1980	Rosso Corsa		LHD				
31293		BB	1980	Rosso Corsa	Nero	LHD		Oregon	US	
31295		BB	1980			LHD		New Jersey	US	
31299		BB	1980	Rosso Corsa		LHD				
31363		BB	1980	Rosso Corsa	Nero	LHD				
31363		BB	1980	Rosso/Nero	Nero	LHD		California	US	
31453		BB	1980			LHD			Netherlands	
31455		BB	1980			LHD				
31457		BB	1980			LHD				
31459		BB	1980	Rosso/Nero	Nero	LHD			US	
31539		BB	1980			LHD				
31547		BB	1980	Rosso/Nero	Tan	LHD		California	US	
31549		BB	1980	Rosso/Nero	Nero	LHD			US	
31589	00023/105	BB/LM	1980	Rosso Corsa	Nero	LHD	N/A	Toronto	Canada	

BB512	BB512	BB512	BB512	BB512	BB512	BB512	BB512	BB512	BB512	BB512	BB512	BB512	BB512	BB512	BB512
VIN #	ENG #	MODEL	YEAR	COLOUR		INTERIOR	DRIVE	REG No.		LOCATION		COUNTRY		COMMENTS	
31641		BB	1980	Nero Met		Tan	LHD								
31643		BB	1980	Bianco Avus		Nero	LHD	DLA 101		Dresden		Germany		Spyder conversion	
31699		BB	1980	Rosso Corsa		Crema	LHD								
31785		BB	1980	Nero Met		Nero	LHD							Koenig conv	
31787		BB	1980	Rosso/Nero		Nero	LHD								
31867		BB	1980	Rosso/Nero		Bordeaux	RHD	512 BAB				UK			
31973		BB	1980	Rosso/Nero		Tan/Nero	LHD								
31975		BB	1980	Rosso/Nero		Nero	LHD					US		Spyder conversion	
32097		BB	1980				RHD	89 BAD				UK			
32101		BB	1980	Rosso/Nero		Nero	LHD								
32103		BB	1980				LHD			California		US			
32129	00013	BB/LM	1980	Pozzi Blu		Nero	LHD	#111		London		UK			
32131		BB/LM	1980	Rosso Corsa		Nero	LHD	N/A				US			
32187		BB	1980				LHD					US			
32189		BB	1980	Nero Met		Crema/Tan	LHD	VD 279205				Switzerland			
32191		BB	1980	Bianco Avus		Bordeaux	LHD			California		US		Original Colour Rosso Corsa	
32237		BB	1980	Nero Met		Bordeaux	LHD			California		US			
32277		BB	1980				RHD	ORY 30W				UK			
32279		BB	1980				LHD	HYU 618W				UK			
32281		BB	1980	Rosso/Nero		Nero	LHD			California		US		Original Colour Azzurro Chiaro	
32435		BB	1980				LHD								
32437		BB	1980	Rosso/Nero		Tan	LHD			Massachusetts		US		Original Colour Argento	
32545		BB	1980	Nero Met		Tan	LHD			Idaho		US			
32623		BB	1980	Nero Met		Crema/Nero	LHD								
32671		BB	1980				LHD			Florida		US		Rebodied as a BBLM Replica '81	
32679		BB	1980	Rosso/Nero		Tan	LHD								
32683		BB	1980	Rosso/Nero		Nero	LHD								
32763		BB	1980	Rosso Corsa		Nero	LHD	512BB		Idaho		US			
32831		BB	1980				LHD								
32833		BB	1980	Rosso/Nero		Nero	LHD			New Jersey		US			
32837		BB	1980	Argento Met		Nero/Rosso	LHD			California		US			
32839		BB	1980	Rosso/Nero		Nero	LHD								
32917		BB	1980	Rosso/Nero		Nero	LHD								
32975		BB	1980	Argento Met		Nero	LHD								
32977		BB	1980	Nero Met		Tan	LHD			Los Angeles		US			
32981		BB	1980	Rosso Corsa		Tan	LHD								
33053		BB	1980	Rosso/Nero		Nero	LHD								
33131		BB	1980	Rosso/Nero		Nero	LHD	512 OAD				UK		Rebodied as a BBLM Replica	
33287		BB	1980	Nero Met		Nero	LHD								
33321		BB	1980	Argento Met		Nero	LHD								
33351		BB	1980	Argento Met		Nero	LHD			New Jersey		US			
33353		BB	1980	Rosso/Nero		Tan	LHD								
33355		BB	1980	Rosso/Nero		Nero	LHD								
33443		BB	1980	Argento Met		Nero	LHD								
33445		BB	1980	Rosso Corsa			LHD								
33513		BB	1980	Rosso/Nero		Nero	LHD	BL 555				Switzerland			
33515		BB	1980	Bianco Avus		Nero	LHD								
33517		BB	1980	Rosso/Nero		Nero	LHD			Bern		Switzerland			
33621		BB	1980	Rosso/Nero		Nero	RHD	LVR 570W				UK			
33623		BB	1980	Rosso/Nero		Tan	LHD			Texas		US			

BB512	BB512	BB512	BB512	BB512	BB512	BB512	BB512	BB512	BB512	BB512	BB512	BB512	BB512	BB512	BB512
VIN #	ENG #	MODEL	YEAR	COLOUR	INTERIOR	DRIVE	REG No.		LOCATION	COUNTRY		COMMENTS			
33625	00731	BB	1980	Rosso/Nero	Nero	LHD			California	US					
33647		BB/LM	1980	Rosso Corsa	Nero	LHD	N/A			Netherlands					
33713		BB	1980			LHD									
33715		BB	1980	Rosso/Nero	Nero	LHD			New York	US					
33719		BB	1980	Rosso/Nero	Nero	LHD									
33799		BB	1980	Rosso/Nero	Tan	LHD			Florida	US					
33803		BB	1980			LHD									
33893		BB	1980	Rosso/Nero	Nero	LHD	RHV 088			Belgium					
33965		BB	1980	Rosso Corsa	Tan	RHD	XVU 73X			UK					
33967		BB	1980	Rosso Corsa	Nero	LHD	DF 512			Germany					
33969		BB	1980			LHD									
33971		BB	1980	Grigio Ferro	Bordeaux	LHD			California	US		Original Colour Argento Met			
34059		BB	1981			LHD									
34063		BB	1981	Rosso Corsa	Tan	LHD									
34065		BB	1981	Nero Met	Bordeaux/Nero	LHD			Collorado	US					
34151		BB	1981			LHD			New Jersey	US					
34153		BB	1981	Nero Met		LHD						Targa conversion			
34157	00017/19	BB/LM	1981	Rosso Corsa	Nero	LHD	N/A			Germany					
34201		BB	1981	Rosso Corsa	Tan/Nero	LHD			Rhode Island	US					
34245		BB	1981	Giallo Fly	Tan	LHD									
34351		BB	1981	Ross/Nero	Nero	LHD									
34355		BB	1981	Rosso/Nero	Nero	LHD									
34357		BB	1981	Rosso Corsa	Nero	LHD			Florida	US					
34445		BB/LM	1981	Rosso/Nocciola	Nero	LHD	N/A			US					
34469		BB	1981	Nero Met	Tan	LHD									
34471		BB	1981	Nero Met	Tan/Nero	LHD			New York	US					
34473		BB	1981	Nero Met	Nero/Rosso	LHD			Florida	US					
34517		BB	1981	Rosso/Nero	Nero	LHD				France					
34615		BB	1981	Nero Met	Nero/Rosso	LHD									
34619		BB	1981	Rosso/Nero	Nero	LHD			Los Angeles	US					
34621		BB	1981	Rosso/Nero	Nero	LHD			San Francisco	US					
34672		BB	1981	Rosso/Nero	Nero	LHD			San Francisco	US					
34705		BB	1981	Rosso/Nero	Nero	LHD			Oklahoma	US					
34707		BB	1981			LHD									
34709		BB	1981	Nero Met	Tan	LHD			Alabama	US					
34711		BB	1981	Blu Sera Met	Tan	LHD									
34775		BB	1981	Argento Met	Nero	LHD									
34815		BB	1981	Nero Met	Nero	LHD				Netherlands		ex John Hugenholtz			
34817		BB	1981			LHD									
34937		BB	1981	Rosso/Nero	Tan	LHD			California	US					
35007		BB	1981	Nero Met	Nero	LHD			Wisconsin	US					
35101		BB	1981	Giallo Fly	Nero	LHD						Koenig conv			
35103		BB	1981	Rosso/Nero	Nero	LHD			Alabama	US					
35145		BB	1981	Rosso/Nero	Tan	LHD			Los Angeles	US					
35171		BB	1981	Rosso/Nero	Tan	LHD									
35177		BB	1981	Bianco Avus	Nero	LHD				Holland					
35201		BB	1981	Rosso/Nero	Tan	LHD									
35269		BB	1981	Rosso/Nero	Nero	LHD									
35271		BB	1981	Rosso/Nero	Nero	LHD									
35415		BB	1981	Rosso/Nero	Tan/Nero	LHD									
35523	00020	BB/LM	1981	Bianco Avus	Nero	LHD	N/A			Switzerland					
35525	00021	BB/LM	1981	Rosso Corsa	Nero	LHD	N/A			France					
35527	00023/24	BB/LM	1981	Rosso Corsa	Nero	LHD	N/A		Marseille	France					
35529		BB/LM	1981	Rosso Corsa	Nero	LHD	N/A			Italy					

VIN #	ENG #	MODEL	YEAR	COLOUR	INTERIOR	DRIVE	REG No.	LOCATION	COUNTRY	COMMENTS
35539		BB	1981	Rosso/Nero	Tan	LHD		New York	US	
35541		BB	1981	Rosso Corsa	Nero	LHD				
35647		BB	1981	Rosso Corsa	Nero	LHD				
35649		BB	1981	Rosso Corsa	Tan	LHD		Florida	US	
35651		BB	1981			LHD				
35653		BB	1981	Rosso Corsa	Nero	LHD				
35655		BB	1981	Nero Met	Nero	LHD			US	
35761		BB	1981	Rosso Corsa	Tan	LHD			US	
35763		BB	1981	Nero Met	Crema	LHD	MI 61230Y	Milan	Italy	
35765		BB	1981	Rosso/Nero	Nero	LHD				
35795		BB	1981			LHD				
35873		BB	1981	Rosso/Nero	Tan	LHD		Los Angeles	US	
35875		BB	1981	Bianco Avus	Nero	LHD	MR CV 3		Germany	
35877		BB	1981			LHD				
35879		BB	1981	Rosso/Nero	Nero	LHD		New York	US	
35881		BB	1981	Rosso/Nero	Nero	LHD		California	US	
35999		BB	1981	Nero Met	Tan	LHD				
36001		BB	1981			LHD			US	
36003		BB	1981			LHD				
36005		BB	1981	Rosso Corsa	Nero	LHD	274 BEV 77		France	Rebodied in '91 as a BBLM Replica
36169		BB	1981	Rosso Corsa	Crema	LHD				
36255		BB	1981			LHD				
36259		BB	1981	Rosso Corsa	Tan	LHD				
36261		BB	1981			LHD		California	US	
36263		BB	1981	Rosso/Nero	Nero	LHD				
36445		BB	1981	Grigio Ferro	Nero	LHD				
35447		BB	1981	Rosso/Nero	Nero	LHD				
36449		BB	1981	Rosso/Nero	Nero	LHD		Oregon	US	
36451		BB	1981	Blu Chiaro	Crema	LHD			France	
36663		BB	1981			LHD			US	
36665		BB	1981	Rosso/Nero	Tan	LHD		California	US	
36685		BB	1981			LHD				
36775		BB	1981	Rosso/Nero	Nero	LHD				
36777		BB	1981			LHD		Boston	US	
36779		BB	1981	Rosso Corsa	Tan	LHD		Texas	US	
36781		BB	1981	Rosso Corsa	Tan	LHD			Netherlands	modifed for comp
36863		BB	1981	Nero Met	Tan	LHD		California	US	Original Colour Rosso Rubino
36865		BB	1981	Rosso Corsa	Tan	LHD				
36867		BB	1981	Argento Met	Tan	LHD				
36869		BB	1981	Giallo Fly	Nero	LHD	MDT 325W	Yorkshire	UK	
36916		BB	1981			LHD		California	US	
36959		BB	1981	Rosso/Nero	Nero	LHD		California	US	
36961		BB	1981	Rosso/Nero	Crema/Rosso	LHD		Florida	US	
36963		BB	1981	Blu Chiaro	Tan	LHD		California	US	
37059		BB	1981	Argento Met	Nero	LHD	TRK 429W		UK	
37061		BB	1981	Rosso Corsa	Tan	LHD				
37089		BB	1981	Rosso Corsa	Tan	LHD			US	
37123		BB	1981	Rosso/Nero	Nero	LHD		California	US	
37125		BB	1981	Rosso/Nero	Nero	LHD				
37239		BB	1981	Rosso/Nero	Nero	LHD				
37347		BB	1981	Rosso/Nero	Nero	LHD				
37351		BB	1981			LHD				
37585		BB	1981	Rosso/Nero	Tan	LHD		San Francisco	US	

	BB512	BB512	BB512	BB512	BB512	BB512	BB512	BB512	BB512	BB512	BB512	BB512	BB512	BB512	BB512
VIN #	ENG #	MODEL	YEAR	COLOUR	INTERIOR	DRIVE	REG No.		LOCATION	COUNTRY		COMMENTS			
37587		BB	1981	Rosso Corsa	Nero	LHD	SUB 933			Belgium					
37591		BB	1981	Rosso/Nero	Tan	LHD				Switzerland					
37715		BB	1981	Argento/Nero	Rosso/Nero	LHD			Michigan	US					
37717		BB	1981	Rosso Corsa	Tan	LHD									
37719		BB	1981	Rosso/Nero	Tan	LHD			Missouri	US					
37721		BB	1981	Blu Sera Met	Nero	LHD				Germany					
37759		BB	1981	Rosso/Nero	Crema	LHD			Florida	US					
37795		BB	1981	Rosso Corsa	Nero	LHD			California	US		Original Colour Bianco Avus			
37859		BB	1981			LHD									
37861		BB	1981	Rosso/Nero	Nero	LHD			Alabama	US					
37863		BB	1981	Rosso Corsa	Nero	LHD	57 DLL		Maryland	US					
37881		BB	1981			LHD			Pennsylvania	US					
37889		BB	1981	Rosso Corsa	Tan	LHD									
38005		BB	1982	Rosso/Nero	Nero	LHD				US					
38007		BB	1982	Rosso/Nero	Tan	LHD				France					
38009		BB	1982	Rosso Corsa	Nero	LHD			Texas	US					
38011		BB	1982			LHD									
38059		BB	1982	Rosso/Nero	Tan	LHD									
38115		BB	1982	Rosso/Nero	Tan	LHD			Los Angeles	US					
38117		BB	1982			LHD				Italy					
38119		BB	1982	Rosso Corsa	Tan	LHD			Florida	US					
	BB512i	BB512i	BB512i	BB512i	BB512i	BB512i	BB512i	BB512i	BB512i	BB512i	BB512i	BB512i	BB512i	BB512i	BB512i
38121		BBi	1982	Rosso Corsa	Nero	LHD				Italy					
38179		BB/LM	1982	Rosso Corsa	Nero	LHD	N/A			US					
38181	00031	BB/LM	1982	Rosso Corsa	Nero	LHD	N/A		California	US					
38199		BBi	1982	Nero Met	Tan	LHD			California	US					
38201		BBi	1982	Rosso/Nero	Nero	LHD									
38203		BBi	1982	Rosso/Nero	Tan/Nero	LHD			New Jersey	US					
38205		BBi	1982	Rosso/Nero	Tan	LHD									
38291		BBi	1982	Rosso/Nero	Tan	LHD			Colorado	US					
38295		BBi	1982	Grigio Ferro	Nero	LHD			California	US					
38383		BBi	1982	Nero Met	Tan	LHD			New Jersey	US					
38385		BBi	1982	Nero Met	Crema/Nero	LHD									
38387		BBi	1982	Rosso Chiaro	Nero/Rosso	LHD			Texas	US					
38487		BBi	1982			LHD									
38619		BBi	1982	Rosso Corsa	Tan	LHD	LXA 25 (UK)		Florida	US					
38623		BBi	1982	Rosso Corsa	Nero	LHD									
38713		BBi	1982	Rosso Corsa	Tan	LHD			New Jersey	US					
38715		BBi	1982	Blu Sera Met	Nero	LHD									
38717		BBi	1982	Rosso Corsa	Tan/Nero	LHD				US					
38719		BBi	1982	Rosso/Nero	Nero	LHD			New Jersey	US					
38723		BBi	1982	Rosso/Nero	Nero	LHD									
38729		BBi	1982	Rosso/Nero	Nero	LHD			California	US					
38739		BB/LM	1982	Rosso Corsa	Nero	LHD	#112			Italy					
38823		BBi	1982	Blu Sera Met	Tan	LHD									
38831		BBi	1982	Rosso/Nero	Nero	LHD	9492 WWJ 06			France					
38833		BBi	1982	Rosso/Nero	Tan	LHD			Denver	US					
38839		BBi	1982	Nero Met	Nero	LHD			New York	US		Original Colour Rosso/Nero			
38961		BBi	1982	Rosso Corsa	Tan	LHD									
38963		BBi	1982			LHD			Minnesota	US					
39065		BBi	1982	Bianco Avus	Tan	LHD				Germany					
39071		BBi	1982			LHD			California	US					
39073		BBi	1982	Rosso Corsa	Tan/Nero	LHD	39073		Munich	Germany					

BB512i	BB512i	BB512i	BB512i	BB512i	BB512i	BB512i	BB512i	BB512i	BB512i	BB512i	BB512i	BB512i	BB512i	BB512i
VIN #	ENG #	MODEL	YEAR	COLOUR	INTERIOR	DRIVE	REG No.		LOCATION		COUNTRY		COMMENTS	
39181		BBi	1982			LHD								
39183		BBi	1982	Rosso/Nero	Tan	LHD			New Hampshire		US			
39303		BBi	1982	Rosso/Nero	Tan	LHD			Washington		US			
39305		BBi	1982			LHD								
39307		BBi	1982			LHD								
39309		BBi	1982			LHD					Italy			
39311		BBi	1982	Rosso/Nero	Nero/Rosso	LHD			California		US			
39411		BBi	1982	Nero Met	Tan	LHD								
39415		BBi	1982	Rosso/Nero	Nero	LHD								
39417		BBi	1982	Rosso/Nero	Nero	LHD			California		US		Spyder conversion	
39421		BBi	1982			LHD			Alabama		US			
39523		BBi	1982	Bianco Avus	Nero	LHD					US			
39527		BBi	1982	Nero Met	Nero	LHD			California		US			
39629		BBi	1982	Argento Met	Nero	LHD			San Diego		US			
39633		BBi	1982			LHD								
39723		BBi	1982	Argento Met	Nero	LHD								
39727		BBi	1982	Rosso Corsa	Nero	LHD					US			
39729		BBi	1982	Rosso Corsa	Nero	LHD								
39837		BBi	1982			LHD								
39839		BBi	1982	Rosso/Nero	Tan	LHD			New York		US			
39843		BBi	1982	Nero Met	Nero	LHD			Atlanta		US			
39845		BBi	1982	Rosso/Nero	Nero	LHD								
39929		BBi	1982	Argento Met	Tan/Grigio	LHD			Texas		US			
39931		BBi	1982	Grigio Ferro	Crema	LHD								
40033		BBi	1982	Rosso/Nero	Bordeaux	LHD							Rebodied as a BBLM Replica	
40037		BBi	1982	Rosso Corsa	Tan/Grigio	LHD			San Diego		US			
40041		BBi	1982	Rosso Corsa	Nero	LHD					France			
40141		BBi	1982	Nero Met	Nero	LHD								
40145		BBi	1982	Grigio Ferro	Bordeaux	LHD			Ohio		US			
40147		BBi	1982	Grigio Ferro	Nero	LHD	TI 21801 U		Ticino		Switzerland			
40149		BBi	1982	Grigio/Nero	Bordeaux/ Grigio	LHD			Illinois		US			
40241		BBi	1982	Rosso Corsa	Tan	LHD	VD 393599				Switzerland			
40329		BBi	1982	Rosso/Nero	Tan	LHD			Oregon		US			
40331		BBi	1982	Rosso Corsa	Tan	RHD	CAR 512				UK			
40333		BBi	1982	Rosso/Nero	Tan	LHD			Texas		US			
40335		BBi	1982	Rosso Corsa	Nero/Crema	LHD			Denver		US			
40401		BBi	1982	Nero Met	Nero	LHD								
40415		BBi	1982	Blu Sera Met	Tan	LHD	HHC 317Y				UK			
40417		BBi	1982	Rosso Corsa	Tan	LHD								
40453		BBi	1982	Nero Met	Tan	LHD			California		US			
40467		BBi	1982	Rosso/Nero	Tan	LHD								
40475		BBi	1982	Rosso/Nero	Tan	LHD							modifed for comp	
40505		BBi	1982	Rosso Corsa	Nero	LHD			Florida		US		Original Colour Nero Met	
40509		BBi	1982	Rosso/Nero	Tan	LHD								
40565		BBi	1982	Nero Met	Tan	LHD	703 4137		Illinois		US			
40569		BBi	1982	Rosso/Nero	Tan	LHD					US			
40661		BBi	1982	Rosso/Nero	Nero	LHD			Los Angeles		US			
40663		BBi	1982			LHD								
40665		BBi	1982	Rosso/Nero	Bordeaux	LHD								
40707		BBi	1982	Rosso Corsa		LHD							Koenig conversion	
40731		BBi	1982	Rosso/Nero	Nero	LHD								
40773		BBi	1982	Rosso Corsa	Crema	RHD					UK		Twin Turbo conversion	

	BB512i	BB512i	BB512i	BB512i	BB512i	BB512i	BB512i	BB512i	BB512i	BB512i	BB512i	BB512i	BB512i
VIN #	ENG #	MODEL	YEAR	COLOUR	INTERIOR	DRIVE	REG No.	LOCATION	COUNTRY	COMMENTS			
40775		BBi	1982			LHD							
40777		BBi	1982	Nero Met	Nero	LHD		New Jersey	US				
40847		BBi	1982			LHD							
40849		BBi	1982			LHD							
40915		BBi	1982	Rosso/Nero	Nero	LHD							
40917		BBi	1982	Rosso/Nero	Nero	LHD							
40999		BBi	1982	Rosso/Nero	Nero	LHD							
41001		BBi	1982	Rosso/Nero	Nero	LHD		New York	US				
41003		BBi	1982	Rosso Corsa	Nero/Grigio	LHD							
41039		BBi	1982			RHD	MUV 306X		UK				
41041		BBi	1982	Rosso Corsa	Nero	LHD			Netherlands	Being converted into BBLM '06-'07			
41043		BBi	1982			LHD							
41045		BBi	1982	Rosso Rubino	Tan	LHD		California	US				
41049		BBi	1982			LHD							
41061		BBi	1982	Argento Met	Nero/Grigio	LHD							
41125	00139	BBi	1982	Argento/Nero	Nero/Grigio	LHD		Milan	Italy				
41131	00141	BBi	1982	Rosso Corsa	Nero/Rosso	RHD	HVF 956X	Oxfordshire	UK				
41161		BBi	1982	Rosso Corsa	Tan	LHD							
41189		BBi	1982	Rosso Corsa	Tan	LHD		Texas	US				
41191		BBi	1982	Rosso Corsa	Crema	LHD			France				
41193		BBi	1982	Rosso Corsa	Nero	LHD							
41195		BBi	1982	Rosso Corsa	Nero	LHD							
41257		BBi	1982	Rosso Corsa	Crema	LHD	N 040329		Germany				
41263		BB/LM	1982	Pozzi Blu	Nero	LHD	#114	Paris	France				
41347		BBi	1982	Rosso Corsa	Nero	LHD							
41351		BBi	1982	Rosso Corsa	Nero	LHD			Canada	Original Colour Nero Met			
41353		BBi	1982	Nero Met	Tan	LHD		California	US				
41355		BBi	1982	Rosso Corsa		LHD							
41405		BBi	1982	Rosso Rubino	Tan	LHD		California	US				
41409		BBi	1982	Nero Met	Nero	LHD							
41415		BBi	1982	Rosso/Nero	Nero	LHD							
41503		BBi	1982	Rosso/Nero	Nero	LHD		San Diego	US				
41507		BBi	1982	Rosso/Nero	Nero	LHD							
41601	00189	BBi	1982	Argento Met	Nero/Grigio	LHD	JRV 479V	Surrey	UK				
41609		BBi	1982			LHD							
41677		BBi	1982	Rosso/Nero	Crema	LHD			Italy				
41729		BBi	1982	Rosso/Nero	Nero	RHD	BOX 989	Sussex	UK				
41735		BBi	1982	Rosso/Nero	Tan	LHD							
41825		BBi	1982	Nero Met	Tan	LHD							
41869		BBi	1982	Blu Sera Met	Crema	LHD	D FF 512		Germany				
41873		BBi	1982	Rosso Corsa	Tan	LHD							
41875		BBi	1982	Nero Met	Nero	LHD							
41927		BBi	1982	Grigio Ferro	Nero	LHD			Italy				
41931		BBi	1982	Nero Met	Crema	LHD		California	US				
41933		BBi	1982	Rosso Corsa	Crema	LHD							
42003		BBi	1982	Grigio Ferro	Nero	LHD							
42029		BBi	1982	Rosso/Nero	Nero	LHD							
42033		BBi	1982	Argento Met	Nero	LHD							
42085		BBi	1982			RHD	OVK 90X		UK				
42099		BBi	1982			LHD							
42123		BBi	1982			LHD							
42211		BBi	1982	Bianco Avus	Nero	LHD							
42213	00203	BBi	1982	Rosso Corsa	Tan	LHD	82 BOXER	Atlanta	US				

VIN #	ENG #	MODEL	YEAR	COLOUR	INTERIOR	DRIVE	REG No.	LOCATION	COUNTRY	COMMENTS
42295		BBi	1982			LHD				
42301		BBi	1982	Rosso Corsa	Nero/Grigio	LHD				
42369		BBi	1982	Rosso Corsa	Tan	LHD				
42373		BBi	1982	Rosso Corsa	Tan	LHD				
42419		BBi	1982	Rosso Corsa	Nero	LHD				
42423		BBi	1982	Rosso Corsa	Nero	LHD				
42507		BBi	1982	Rosso Corsa	Crema	LHD		New York	US	
42509	00216	BBi	1982	Rosso/Nero	Tan	LHD	WND 273	Ontario	Canada	
42565		BBi	1982	Rosso Corsa	Nero/Rosso	LHD	50	New Jersey	US	
42581		BBi	1982	Rosso/Nero	Nero	LHD				
42583		BBi	1982			LHD				
42585		BBi	1982			LHD				
42587		BBi	1982	Rosso Corsa	Tan	LHD	BL 113131		Switzerland	
42619		BBi	1982			LHD				
42713	00233	BBi	1982	Azzurro Met	Blu Scuro	RHD	BBX 48	Surrey	UK	
42715		BBi	1982			LHD				
42717		BBi	1982			LHD				
42719		BBi	1982	Bianco Avus	Blu Scuro	LHD				
42767		BBi	1982	Rosso/Nero	Crema	LHD		Conneticut	US	
42769		BBi	1982	Rosso Corsa	Crema	LHD				
42841		BBi	1982	Nero Met	Tan	LHD				
42843		BBi	1982	Nero Met	Crema	LHD		Atlanta	US	
42845		BBi	1982	Rosso/Nero	Tan	LHD		Florida	US	
42847		BBi	1982	Rosso/Nero	Tan	LHD		Atlanta	US	
42849		BBi	1982	Bianco Avus	Nero	LHD				
42857		BBi	1982	Rosso Corsa	Tan	LHD				
42869		BBi	1982			RHD	XE 33		UK	
42871		BBi	1982	Rosso/Nero	Nero	LHD				
42873		BBi	1982			LHD				
42875		BBi	1982	Bianco Avus	Tan	LHD		Los Angeles	US	Koenig conv
42931		BBi	1982	Argento Met	Nero	LHD				
42933		BBi	1982	Rosso Corsa	Nero	LHD				Koenig conv
42969		BBi	1982	Rosso/Nero	Nero/Crema	RHD	CPC 839Y		UK	
42971		BBi	1982	Nero Met	Nero	LHD				
43029		BBi	1982	Rosso/Nero	Tan	LHD			Canada	
43033		BBi	1982	Rosso Corsa	Tan	LHD				
43081		BBi	1982	Argento Met	Bordeaux	LHD				
43083	00263	BBi	1982	Rosso Corsa	Crema	LHD	S 9359 BBL	Barcelona	Spain	
43085		BBi	1982	Rosso/Nero	Crema	LHD				
43087		BBi	1982	Rosso Corsa	Crema	RHD			UK	
43089	00266	BBi	1982	Rosso/Nero	Crema	RHD	MSP 8Y		UK	
43091		BBi	1982	Argento Met	Nero	LHD	TFL 663		Belgium	
43153		BBi	1982	Rosso/Nero	Tan	LHD		Texas	US	US Legalised by AmeriSpec 07.88
43157		BBi	1982	Rosso/Nero	Nero	LHD				
43203		BBi	1982	Rosso Corsa	Crema/Rosso	LHD				Koenig conv
43215		BBi	1982	Rosso/Nero	Tan	LHD			Sweden	
43217		BBi	1982	Rosso/Nero	Nero	LHD				
43219		BBi	1982	Rosso/Nero	Nero	LHD		Monaco	France	
43221		BBi	1982	Nero Met	Nero	LHD				
43263		BBi	1982	Rosso/Nero	Crema	LHD		Florida	US	Koenig conv
43265		BBi	1982	Rosso/Nero	Nero	LHD		California	US	
43269		BBi	1982			LHD				
43339		BBi	1982	Argento Met	Nero	LHD				
43341		BBi	1982	Blu Sera Met	Nero	LHD	BS 25304		Switzerland	

BB512i	BB512i	BB512i	BB512i	BB512i	BB512i	BB512i	BB512i	BB512i	BB512i	BB512i	BB512i	BB512i	BB512i	BB512i
VIN #	ENG #	MODEL	YEAR	COLOUR	INTERIOR	DRIVE	REG No.	LOCATION		COUNTRY		COMMENTS		
43343		BBi	1982	Rosso/Nero		LHD								
43345		BBi	1982	Rosso Corsa	Tan	RHD	BXI 309			UK				
43351		BBi	1982	Rosso/Nero	Nero	LHD								
43419		BBi	1982	Azzurro Met	Crema	LHD		Bern		Switzerland				
43423		BBi	1982	Marrone	Tan	LHD	ZH 15694	Zurich		Switzerland				
43477		BBi	1982			LHD								
43481		BBi	1982	Rosso Corsa	Tan	LHD								
43491		BBi	1982	Rosso Corsa	Tan	LHD								
43493		BBi	1982	Argento/Nero	Nero	LHD		New York		US				
43561		BBi	1982	Rosso/Nero	Nero	LHD		Texas		US				
43565		BBi	1982	Rosso/Nero	Tan	LHD		California		US				
43567		BBi	1982	Argento Met	Nero	LHD								
43569		BBi	1982	Rosso/Nero	Nero	LHD								
43571		BBi	1982			LHD								
43625		BBi	1982	Rosso/Nero	Nero	LHD		California		US				
43635		BBi	1982	Rosso/Nero	Nero	LHD		Florida		US				
43649		BBi	1982	Verde Met	Tan	LHD								
43653		BBi	1982	Rosso Corsa	Tan	LHD								
43723		BBi	1982	Rosso Corsa	Nero/Grigio	LHD		Florida		US				
43725		BBi	1982	Rosso Corsa	Tan	LHD								
43727		BBi	1982	Rosso Corsa	Nero	LHD				Germany				
43729		BBi	1982	Rosso Corsa	Crema/Rosso	LHD								
43793		BBi	1982	Rosso Corsa	Nero	LHD		New Jersey		US				
43795		BBi	1982	Nero Met	Crema	RHD	XPF 278Y	Derbyshire		UK				
43797		BBi	1982	Bianco Avus	Tan	LHD								
43799		BBi	1982	Rosso Corsa	Tan	LHD		Florida		US				
43855		BBi	1982	Rosso Corsa	Nero	LHD		Florida		US				
43857		BBi	1982	Rosso Corsa	Nero	LHD								
43859		BBi	1982	Rosso Corsa	Tan	LHD		California		US				
43941		BBi	1982	Rosso/Nero	Nero	LHD								
43943		BBi	1982	Rosso Corsa	Tan	LHD		Oklahoma		US				
44015		BBi	1982	Rosso Corsa	Crema/Rosso	RHD	LBH 319Y			Australia				
44021		BBi	1982	Rosso/Nero	Nero	LHD		New Jersey		US				
44023	00039	BB/LM	1982	Rosso Corsa	Nero	LHD	N/A	Conneticut		US				
44033		BBi	1982	Rosso Corsa	Tan	LHD		California		US				
44035		BBi	1982	Rosso Corsa	Tan	LHD				US				
44089		BBi	1982	Rosso Corsa	Nero	LHD							Koenig conv		
44093		BBi	1982	Rosso Corsa	Tan	LHD								
44097		BBi	1982	Argento Met	Grigio Scuro	LHD								
44099		BBi	1982	Rosso Corsa	Nero	LHD				Germany			Koenig conv		
44101		BBi	1982	Rosso Corsa	Tan	LHD								
44171		BBi	1982			LHD								
44231		BBi	1982	Rosso Corsa	Tan	LHD								
44233		BBi	1982	Rosso/Nero	Nero	LHD		Rhode Island		US				
44237		BBi	1982	Rosso/Nero	Nero/Rosso	LHD		Los Angeles		US				
44241		BBi	1982	Rosso/Nero	Nero	LHD								
44243		BBi	1982	Rosso Corsa	Tan	LHD		Colorado		US				
44257		BBi	1982	Rosso Corsa	Tan	LHD								
44295		BBi	1982	Rosso/Nero	Nero	LHD								
44313		BBi	1982	Argento Met	Nero	LHD	CQS 612			Belgium				
44315		BBi	1982	Argento Met	Nero	RHD	TLR 4			UK				
44317		BBi	1982	Blu Sera Met	Crema	LHD								
44321		BBi	1983	Rosso Corsa		LHD								
44323		BBi	1983	Rosso Corsa	Tan	LHD		Texas		US				
44325		BBi	1983	Rosso Corsa	Tan	LHD								

	BB512i	BB512i	BB512i	BB512i	BB512i	BB512i	BB512i	BB512i	BB512i	BB512i	BB512i	BB512i	BB512i	BB512i
VIN #	ENG #	MODEL	YEAR	COLOUR	INTERIOR	DRIVE	REG No.	LOCATION	COUNTRY	COMMENTS
44327		BBi	1983	Rosso Corsa	Tan	LHD			US	
44387		BBi	1983	Rosso Corsa	Tan	LHD				
44389		BBi	1983	Rosso Corsa	Bordeaux	LHD		North Carolina	US	Original Colour Nero Met
44395		BBi	1983	Rosso Corsa	Tan	LHD		Florida	US	
44453		BBi	1983	Argento Met	Bordeaux	LHD		Florida	US	
44455		BBi	1983	Rosso/Nero	Nero	LHD		Alabama	US	
44459		BBi	1983	Nero Met	Nero	LHD				
44461		BBi	1983	Rosso/Nero	Nero	LHD				
44499		BBi	1983	Rosso/Nero	Nero	LHD		Michigan	US	
44539		BBi	1983	Rosso Corsa	Crema	LHD		Alabama	US	
44543		BBi	1983	Nero Met	Nero	LHD			US	
44545		BBi	1983	Rosso/Nero	Nero	LHD		Ohio	US	
44577		BBi	1983	Rosso/Nero	Nero	LHD				
44579		BBi	1983	Rosso/Nero	Tan	LHD				
44593		BBi	1983	Rosso/Nero	Tan	LHD		California	US	
44611		BBi	1983	Rosso/Nero	Bordeaux	LHD				
44661		BBi	1983	Rosso/Nero	Nero	LHD				
44663		BBi	1983	Nero Met	Crema	LHD				
44665		BBi	1983	Bianco Avus	Bordeaux	LHD				
44669	00395	BBi	1983	Rosso Corsa	Tan	LHD		California	US	
44671		BBi	1983	Argento Met	Nero	RHD	JDC 4		UK	
44714		BBi	1983	Rosso/Nero	Nero/Grigio	LHD				
44719		BBi	1983	Rosso/Nero	Nero	LHD		Texas	US	
44755		BBi	1983	Rosso Corsa	Blu Scuro	LHD			Holland	
44757		BBi	1983	Rosso/Nero		LHD				
44761		BBi	1983	Rosso/Nero	Nero	LHD		Indiana	US	
44763		BBi	1983	Grigio Ferro	Bordeaux	LHD				
44809		BBi	1983	Rosso Corsa	Nero	LHD		Oregon	US	
44811		BBi	1983	Rosso/Nero	Nero/Grigio	LHD	2BKE985	San Francisco	US	
44815		BBi	1983	Rosso/Nero	Nero	LHD	5JKO92	California	US	
44879		BBi	1983	Bianco Avus	Nero	LHD				
44881		BBi	1983	Rosso Corsa	Nero	LHD				
44899		BBi	1983	Rosso Corsa	Nero	LHD		Sendai	Japan	5.6 Ltr Eng, Twin KKK Turbo, Intercooler, Est 650 BHP
44909		BBi	1983	Rosso Corsa	Nero	LHD				
44937		BBi	1983	Rosso Corsa	Tan	LHD		Switzerland		
44941		BBi	1983	Rosso/Nero	Nero/Rosso	LHD		California	US	
44943		BBi	1983	Rosso Corsa	Nero	LHD				
44991		BBi	1983	Rosso Corsa	Tan	LHD				
44993		BBi	1983	Rosso Corsa	Tan/Rosso	LHD				
44995		BBi	1983	Rosso Corsa	Nero	LHD		Paris	France	
45043		BBi	1983	Bianco Avus	Nero	LHD				
45045		BBi	1983			LHD		Texas	US	
45047		BBi	1983	Rosso Corsa	Tan	LHD		California	US	
45049		BBi	1983	Nero Met	Crema	LHD		Singen	Germany	
45051		BBi	1983	Nero Met	Crema	LHD		Florida	US	
45053		BBi	1983	Bianco Avus	Crema	LHD				
45055		BBi	1983	Nero Met	Bordeaux	LHD				
45057		BBi	1983	Rosso Corsa	Tan	LHD		California	US	
45121	00518	BBi	1983	Rosso Corsa	Nero/Grigio	RHD	APA 15Y	London	UK	
45123		BBi	1983	Nero Met	Tan	LHD		Texas	US	
45125		BBi	1983	Rosso Corsa	Tan	LHD	VD 276938		Switzerland	
45129		BBi	1983	Rosso Corsa	Tan	LHD	SZ 20459		Germany	

BB512i	BB512i	BB512i	BB512i	BB512i	BB512i	BB512i	BB512i	BB512i	BB512i	BB512i	BB512i	BB512i	BB512i	BB512i
VIN #	ENG #	MODEL	YEAR	COLOUR	INTERIOR	DRIVE	REG No.		LOCATION		COUNTRY		COMMENTS	
45131		BBi	1983	Rosso Corsa	Tan	LHD								
45133		BBi	1983	Rosso Corsa	Crema/Tan	LHD								
45135		BBi	1983	Rosso Corsa	Nero	LHD					Switzerland			
45153		BBi	1983	Rosso Corsa	Tan	LHD			Texas		US			
45221		BBi	1983	Nero Met	Tan	LHD	TI 19 U				Switzerland			
45229		BBi	1983	Rosso/Nero	Nero	LHD			Arizona		US			
45273		BBi	1983	Nero Met	Tan	LHD			California		US			
45275		BBi	1983	Rosso Corsa	Nero/Rosso	LHD					US		Targa conversion	
45277		BBi	1983	Rosso Corsa	Tan	LHD								
45279		BBi	1983	Argento Met	Crema	LHD					Italy			
45281		BBi	1983	Grigio Ferro	Nero	LHD								
45283		BBi	1983	Argento Met	Blu Scuro	LHD								
45339		BBi	1983	Rosso/Nero	Nero	LHD	J45 019J		Pennsylvania		US			
45341		BBi	1983	Rosso/Nero	Tan	LHD			California		US			
45343		BBi	1983	Rosso Corsa	Tan	LHD			Florida		US			
45347		BBi	1983	Rosso Corsa	Crema	LHD								
45349		BBi	1983	Argento Met	Tan	LHD								
45399		BBi	1983	Rosso Corsa	Nero	LHD					US			
45403		BBi	1983	Bianco Avus	Tan	LHD								
45405		BBi	1983	Nero Met	Nero	LHD								
45409		BBi	1983	Rosso Corsa	Tan	LHD			California		US			
45413		BBi	1983	Rosso Corsa	Nero	LHD					Germany		Koenig conv	
45417		BBi	1983	Rosso Corsa	Crema/Rosso	RHD	512 BGH				UK			
45441		BBi	1983	Nero Met	Nero	LHD								
45447		BBi	1983	Rosso Corsa	Nero/Rosso	LHD			Vermont		US			
45449		BBi	1983	Rosso Corsa	Tan	LHD			Texas		US			
45439		BBi	1983	Rosso Corsa	Tan/Nero	LHD					France			
45451		BBi	1983	Rosso Corsa	Crema	LHD								
45521		BBi	1983	Nero Met		LHD								
45603		BBi	1983	Rosso Corsa		LHD								
45615		BBi	1983	Argento Met	Blu/Crema	LHD								
45617		BBi	1983	Rosso Corsa	Crema	LHD								
45623		BBi	1983	Rosso/Nero	Nero	LHD			California		US			
45627		BBi	1983	Rosso/Nero	Nero	LHD					US			
45629		BBi	1983	Rosso Corsa	Nero	LHD			Florida		US			
45691		BBi	1983	Rosso Corsa	Nero	LHD								
45693	00274	BBi	1983	Rosso/Nero	Tan	LHD			Ohio		US			
45697		BBi	1983	Nero Met	Tan	LHD			California		US			
45729		BBi	1983			LHD								
45733		BBi	1983	Rosso Corsa	Tan	LHD			Florida		US			
45735		BBi	1983	Nero Met	Bordeaux	LHD	HA DN 512				Germany			
45807		BBi	1983	Rosso Corsa	Crema	RHD	FCW 735Y		Derbyshire		UK			
45811		BBi	1983	Rosso Corsa	Nero/Rosso	LHD			Tennessee		US			
45813		BBi	1983	Rosso Corsa	Tan	LHD								
45815		BBi	1983	Rosso Corsa	Tan	LHD					US			
45875		BBi	1983	Nero Met	Nero	RHD					HK			
45879		BBi	1983	Rosso Corsa	Nero	LHD								
45881		BBi	1983	Rosso Corsa	Nero	LHD			Rhode Island		US			
45927		BBi	1983	Rosso Corsa	Tan/Rosso	RHD	FLY 19				UK			
45929		BBi	1983	Rosso Corsa	Tan	LHD								
45931		BBi	1983	Rosso Corsa	Tan	LHD								
45937		BBi	1983	Rosso Corsa	Tan	LHD					US			
45997		BBi	1983			LHD								
45999		BBi	1983	Rosso Corsa	Nero/Rosso	LHD								
46005		BBi	1983			LHD								

BB512i	BB512i	BB512i	BB512i	BB512i	BB512i	BB512i	BB512i	BB512i	BB512i	BB512i	BB512i	BB512i	BB512i	BB512i
VIN #	ENG #	MODEL	YEAR	COLOUR	INTERIOR	DRIVE	REG No.	LOCATION	COUNTRY	COMMENTS
46073		BBi	1983			LHD				
46075		BBi	1983	Rosso Corsa	Nero	LHD				
46077		BBi	1983	Rosso Corsa	Tan	LHD				
46109		BBi	1983	Rosso Corsa	Nero/Crema	LHD				
46111		BBi	1983	Rosso Corsa	Nero	LHD				
46113		BBi	1983	Rosso Corsa	Tan	LHD		Arizona	US	
46115		BBi	1983	Rosso Corsa	Nero	LHD				
46117		BBi	1983	Rosso Corsa	Tan/Rosso	LHD		Nevada	US	
46119		BBi	1983	Rosso Corsa	Nero	LHD		Florida	US	
46161		BBi	1983			LHD		California	US	
46187		BBi	1983	Rosso Corsa	Tan	LHD		Florida	US	
46189	00545	BBi	1983	Rosso Corsa	Tan	LHD	512 BOXR	Washington	US	
46237		BBi	1983	Rosso Corsa	Crema	RHD	APM 550Y		UK	
46239		BBi	1983	Argento Met	Nero	LHD		Texas	US	
46243		BBi	1983	Rosso/Nero	Bordeaux/Nero	LHD		Oklahoma	US	
46249		BBi	1983	Blu Sera Met	Tan	LHD				
46315		BBi	1983	Rosso Corsa	Crema/Zegna	RHD	FWD 753Y	Lancashire	UK	
46317		BBi	1983	Grigio Ferro	Bordeaux	LHD		California	US	
46321		BBi	1983	Rosso Corsa	Nero	LHD	188 BDJ 92		France	
46323		BBi	1983	Argento Met	Nero	LHD				
46325		BBi	1983	Nero Met		LHD				
46327		BBi	1983	Rosso Corsa	Nero/Grigio	LHD				
46391		BBi	1983	Marrone	Tan	LHD			Japan	
46393		BBi	1983	Rosso Corsa	Tan	LHD		Ohio	US	
46433		BBi	1983	Rosso Corsa	Tan	LHD				
46461		BBi	1983	Nero Met	Nero	LHD		California	US	
46503		BBi	1983	Rosso Corsa	Tan/Nero	LHD	10 TVO 61	California	US	
46509		BBi	1983	Rosso/Nero	Tan	LHD		Denver	US	
46511		BBi	1983	Rosso/Nero	Nero	LHD		Conneticut	US	
46513		BBi	1983	Nero Met	Nero	RHD	WVT 67		UK	
46519		BBi	1983	Rosso Corsa	Tan	LHD				
46545		BBi	1983	Rosso/Nero	Nero	LHD			US	
46549		BBi	1983			LHD				
46639		BBi	1983	Blu Chiaro	Crema	RHD	A209 HPK	Surrey	UK	
46641		BBi	1983	Rosso Corsa	Nero/Rosso	LHD				
46643		BBi	1983	Rosso Corsa	Nero	LHD				
46663		BBi	1983	Rosso Corsa	Nero	LHD		California	US	
46647		BBi	1983	Rosso Corsa	Crema	LHD		Nevada	US	
46707		BBi	1983	Rosso Corsa	Nero	RHD	96 F		UK	
46709		BBi	1983			RHD				
46711		BBi	1983	Rosso/Nero	Nero	RHD				
46753		BBi	1983	Rosso Corsa	Crema/Rosso	RHD	PUL 555Y	Surrey	UK	
46807		BBi	1983	Rosso Corsa		LHD				
46811		BBi	1983	Rosso/Nero	Nero	LHD		Paris	France	
46813		BBi	1983	Blu Sera Met	Tan	LHD				
46815		BBi	1983	Blu Sera Met	Crema	LHD		New York	US	
46817		BBi	1983	Nero Met	Nero	LHD				
46887		BBi	1983	Rosso Corsa	Tan	LHD		Florida	US	
46889		BBi	1983	Rosso Chiaro	Nero	LHD		New Jersey	US	
46891		BBi	1983	Rosso/Nero	Nero	LHD				
46893		BBi	1983	Rosso/Nero	Crema	LHD				Koenig conv
46937		BBi	1983	Rosso/Nero	Nero	LHD				
46939		BBi	1983	Blu Sera Met	Nero	LHD				
46941		BBi	1983	Rosso/Nero	Nero	LHD		Atlanta	US	
46943		BBi	1983	Rosso Corsa	Tan	LHD				

BB512i	BB512i	BB512i	BB512i	BB512i	BB512i	BB512i	BB512i	BB512i	BB512i	BB512i	BB512i	BB512i	BB512i	BB512i
VIN #	ENG #	MODEL	YEAR	COLOUR	INTERIOR	DRIVE	REG No.		LOCATION		COUNTRY		COMMENTS	
46945		BBi	1983	Rosso Corsa	Tan	LHD			Florida		US			
47013		BBi	1983	Nero Met	Tan	LHD			Florida		US			
47015		BBi	1983	Rosso Corsa	Tan/Crema	LHD								
47075		BBi	1983	Rosso Corsa	Tan	LHD			Florida		US			
47077		BBi	1983	Rosso/Nero	Nero	LHD								
47083		BBi	1983	Rosso/Nero	Tan	LHD					US			
47085		BBi	1983	Argento Met	Nero	LHD								
47185		BBi	1983	Rosso Corsa	Tan	LHD			Mississippi		US			
47191		BBi	1983	Rosso Corsa	Nero	LHD			Montreal		Canada			
47229		BBi	1983	Grigio Ferro	Tan	LHD								
47233		BBi	1983	Rosso Corsa	Tan	LHD			California		US			
47235		BBi	1983	Rosso Corsa	Tan	LHD			Vancouver		Canada			
47239		BBi	1983	Rosso/Nero	Nero	LHD								
47241		BBi	1983	Rosso/Nero	Nero	LHD								
47313		BBi	1983	Rosso/Nero	Nero	LHD								
47321		BBi	1983	Rosso/Nero	Nero	LHD								
47325		BBi	1983	Nero Met	Tan	LHD			Washington		US			
47413		BBi	1983			LHD			Rhode Island		US			
47417		BBi	1983	Bianco Avus	Tan	LHD			Florida		US			
47419		BBi	1983	Rosso Corsa	Tan	LHD								
47421		BBi	1983	Rosso Corsa	Nero	LHD								
47495		BBi	1983	Rosso Corsa	Tan	LHD								
47497		BBi	1983	Nero Met	Nero	LHD								
47499		BBi	1983	Rosso Corsa	Tan	LHD			Massachusetts		US			
47501		BBi	1983	Rosso Corsa	Nero	LHD					Netherlands			
47503		BBi	1983	Nero Met		LHD								
47505		BBi	1983	Rosso Corsa	Tan	LHD			Virginia		US			
47555		BBi	1983	Rosso Corsa	Tan	LHD					US		BB LM Prepared Engine	
47557		BBi	1983			LHD			Florida		US			
47559		BBi	1983			LHD								
47561		BBi	1983	Rosso Corsa	Tan	LHD								
47565		BBi	1983	Rosso Corsa	Tan	LHD			Florida		US			
47685		BBi	1983	Rosso Corsa	Crema	LHD			Los Angeles		US		Targa conversion	
47687		BBi	1983			LHD								
47689		BBi	1983	Rosso Corsa	Tan	LHD								
47691		BBi	1983			LHD								
47743		BBi	1983	Rosso Corsa	Tan	LHD			California		US			
47747		BBi	1983	Nero Met	Tan	LHD								
47751		BBi	1983	Bianco Avus	Blu Scuro	RHD	A664 TUV		Gloucestershire		UK			
47783		BBi	1983	Nero Met	Nero/Rosso	LHD								
47805		BBi	1983	Argento Met	Nero	LHD								
47807		BBi	1983	Rosso Corsa	Nero	LHD					Germany		Koenig conv	
47849		BBi	1983	Rosso Corsa	Tan	LHD								
47859		BBi	1983	Rosso Corsa	Tan	LHD					US			
47865		BBi	1983	Nero Met	Nero	LHD			Florida		US			
47867		BBi	1983	Rosso Corsa	Tan	LHD			California		US			
47869		BBi	1983	Rosso Corsa	Nero/Rosso	LHD			Mississippi		US			
47871		BBi	1983	Rosso Corsa	Tan	LHD								
47967		BBi	1983			RHD	A512 PHK				UK			
47969		BBi	1983	Rosso/Nero	Nero	LHD			Texas		US			
47973		BBi	1983	Rosso Corsa	Tan	LHD			California		US			
47975		BBi	1983	Rosso Corsa	Nero/Rosso	LHD			Conneticut		US			
47977		BBi	1983	Rosso Corsa		LHD								
47999		BBi	1983	Rosso Corsa	Tan	LHD								

BB512i	BB512i	BB512i	BB512i	BB512i	BB512i	BB512i	BB512i	BB512i	BB512i	BB512i	BB512i	BB512i	BB512i	BB512i
VIN #	ENG #	MODEL	YEAR	COLOUR	INTERIOR	DRIVE	REG No.		LOCATION	COUNTRY		COMMENTS		
48015		BBi	1983	Rosso Corsa	Crema	LHD			Missouri	US				
48029		BBi	1983	Argento Met	Bordeaux	LHD								
48049		BBi	1983	Rosso/Nero	Nero	LHD								
48051		BBi	1983	Rosso Corsa	Crema	LHD	ZH 390592			Switzerland				
48055		BBi	1983	Rosso/Nero	Nero	LHD			Colorado	US				
48059		BBi	1983	Rosso Corsa		LHD								
48093		BBi	1983	Blu Sera Met	Tan	LHD								
48099		BBi	1983	Rosso Corsa	Tan	LHD								
48101		BBi	1983	Nero Met	Nero	LHD								
48111		BBi	1983	Rosso Corsa	Crema	LHD	AN 84 BXR		California	US				
48147		BBi	1983	Rosso Corsa		LHD								
48163		BBi	1983	Argento Met	Nero	RHD	A755 HPK		Surrey	UK				
48165		BBi	1983	Rosso Corsa	Tan	LHD			New York	US				
48167		BBi	1983	Rosso Corsa	Tan	LHD								
48169		BBi	1983	Rosso Corsa	Nero	LHD								
48171		BBi	1983	Rosso Corsa	Crema	LHD	ARMEN		California	US				
48173		BBi	1983	Rosso Corsa	Tan	LHD								
48249		BBi	1983	Blu Sera Met	Tan	LHD								
48253		BBi	1984	Nero Met	Nero/Grigio	LHD			Florida	US				
48255		BBi	1984	Rosso Corsa	Tan	LHD			Colorado	US				
48257		BBi	1984	Rosso/Nero	Tan	LHD			New York	US				
48319		BBi	1984	Nero Met	Nero	LHD			Texas	US				
48321		BBi	1984	Rosso Corsa	Tan	LHD								
48323		BBi	1984	Rosso/Nero	Nero	LHD			Connecticut	US				
48325		BBi	1984	Rosso Corsa	Nero	LHD			California	US		Original Colour Argento		
48327		BBi	1984	Rosso Corsa	Tan	LHD			Callifornia	US				
48329		BBi	1984	Rosso Corsa	Crema/Zegna	RHD	BOX 666V		Lockerbie	UK				
48407		BBi	1984	Rosso Corsa	Tan	LHD			Florida	US				
48409		BBi	1984	Rosso/Nero	Nero	LHD			Illinois	US				
48411		BBi	1984	Rosso Corsa	Crema	LHD			California	US				
48413		BBi	1984	Rosso/Nero	Nero	LHD								
48415		BBi	1984			LHD								
48417		BBi	1984	Rosso/Nero	Nero	LHD	PF ZX 12			Germany				
48419		BBi	1984	Nero Met	Tan	LHD								
48495		BBi	1984	Rosso Corsa	Tan	LHD								
48499		BBi	1984	Rosso Corsa	Tan	LHD			Texas	US				
48501		BBi	1984	Rosso Corsa	Tan	LHD								
48505		BBi	1984	Rosso/Nero	Nero	LHD			Nevada	US				
48507		BBi	1984	Argento Met	Tan/Rosso	LHD				US				
48523		BBi	1984	Nero Met	Nero	LHD								
48563		BBi	1984	Rosso Corsa	Tan	LHD								
48565		BBi	1984	Rosso Corsa	Tan	LHD			New Jersey	US				
48567		BBi	1984	Nero Met	Tan	LHD			California	US				
48571		BBi	1984	Rosso/Nero	Nero	LHD								
48659		BBi	1984	Argento Met	Nero	LHD				France				
48663		BBi	1984	Rosso Corsa		LHD								
48665		BBi	1984	Rosso Corsa	Crema	LHD			California	US		Featured in Road & Track Article		
48723		BBi	1984	Rosso Corsa	Crema	LHD	VTH 8255		North Carolina	US				
48725		BBi	1984	Nero Met	Nero	LHD			Los Angeles	US				
48727		BBi	1984	Rosso Corsa	Tan	LHD			New York	US				
48729		BBi	1984	Rosso Corsa	Crema	LHD			South Carolina	US		Original Colour Nero Met		
48731		BBi	1984			LHD								

BB512i	*BB512i*	*BB512i*	*BB512i*	*BB512i*	*BB512i*	*BB512i*	*BB512i*	*BB512i*	*BB512i*	*BB512i*	*BB512i*	*BB512i*	*BB512i*	*BB512i*
VIN #	ENG #	MODEL	YEAR	COLOUR	INTERIOR	DRIVE	REG No.	LOCATION	COUNTRY	COMMENTS
48817		BBi	1984	Rosso Corsa	Bordeaux	LHD				
48821		BBi	1984	Bianco Avus	Tan	LHD				
48823		BBi	1984	Rosso/Nero	Nero	LHD				
48887		BBi	1984	Rosso Corsa	Tan	LHD		Florida	US	
48915		BBi	1984	Nero Met		LHD				
48941		BBi	1984	Rosso Corsa		LHD		California	US	
48945		BBi	1984	Argento/Nero	Nero	LHD	4GRM504	California	US	
48949		BBi	1984	Rosso Corsa	Tan	LHD		Washington DC	US	
48951		BBi	1984	Rosso Corsa	Tan	LHD		California	US	
49023		BBi	1984	Rosso Corsa	Tan	LHD			Canada	
49025		BBi	1984	Rosso Corsa	Nero/Rosso	LHD				
49027		BBi	1984	Rosso Corsa	Tan	LHD				
49029		BBi	1984	Argento Met	Bordeaux	LHD				
49037		BBi	1984	Argento Met	Nero	LHD				
49097		BBi	1984	Argento/Nero	Nero/Grigio	LHD		New York	US	
49105		BBi	1984	Rosso Corsa	Nero	LHD				
49107		BBi	1984	Rosso Corsa	Nero	LHD				
49135		BBi	1984	Rosso Corsa	Tan	LHD				
49169		BBi	1984	Rosso Corsa	Nero	LHD		Georgia	US	
49171		BBi	1984	Rosso Corsa	Nero	LHD				
49173		BBi	1984	Rosso Corsa	Tan	LHD		New Jersey	US	
49175		BBi	1984			LHD		Ontario	Canada	
49217		BBi	1984	Rosso/Nero	Tan	LHD		Maryland	US	
49219		BBi	1984	Rosso Corsa	Tan	LHD		Maryland	US	
49253		BBi	1984	Rosso Corsa	Tan	LHD				
49255		BBi	1984	Rosso Corsa	Tan	RHD	B914 OSA		UK	
49257		BBi	1984	Argento Met	Nero	LHD		Florida	US	
49259		BBi	1984	Rosso Corsa	Crema	LHD			US	
49261		BBi	1984	Rosso Corsa	Crema	LHD		New York	US	
49309		BBi	1984	Nero Met	Tan	LHD		Los Angeles	US	
49311		BBi	1984	Rosso/Nero	Nero/Rosso	LHD		Illinois	US	Heavily Modified
49313		BBi	1984	Rosso Corsa	Tan	LHD				
49315		BBi	1984			LHD		Florida	US	
49317		BBi	1984	Rosso Corsa	Tan	LHD	BOBS BB	Oklahoma	US	
49419		BBi	1984			RHD	BOX 1N		UK	
49421		BBi	1984	Rosso Corsa	Tan	RHD		Australia		
49423		BBi	1984			RHD			UK	
49425		BBi	1984	Rosso Corsa	Tan/Nero	RHD	B376 VLJ	London	UK	
49427		BBi	1984	Blu TdF	Nero	LHD				
49465		BBi	1984	Nero Met	Tan	LHD				
49467		BBi	1984	Nero Met	Nero	LHD		California	US	
49473	00792	BBi	1984	Rosso Corsa	Tan/Rosso	LHD	F512 BB	North Carolina	US	
49493		BBi	1984	Argento Met	Nero	LHD				
49539		BBi	1984			LHD				
49541		BBi	1984	Rosso Corsa	Tan	LHD		California	US	
49575		BBi	1984	Argento Met	Nero	LHD				
49577		BBi	1984	Rosso Corsa	Tan	LHD	NA7 62C	Florida	US	Original Colour Argento/Nero
49579		BBi	1984	Rosso Corsa	Grigio	LHD				
49585		BBi	1984	Nero Met	Nero/Rosso	LHD				
49587		BBi	1984	Rosso Corsa	Tan	LHD				
49699		BBi	1984	Rosso Corsa	Tan	LHD		California	US	
49701		BBi	1984	Rosso Corsa	Nero	LHD	ZH 139200	Zurich	Switzerland	
49703		BBi	1984			LHD				
49705		BBi	1984	Rosso Corsa	Crema/Tan	LHD		Texas	US	

BB512i	BB512i	BB512i	BB512i	BB512i	BB512i	BB512i	BB512i	BB512i	BB512i	BB512i	BB512i	BB512i	BB512i	BB512i
VIN #	ENG #	MODEL	YEAR	COLOUR	INTERIOR	DRIVE	REG No.		LOCATION	COUNTRY		COMMENTS		
49707		BBi	1984			LHD								
49709		BBi	1984	Rosso Corsa	Tan	LHD								
49729		BBi	1984	Rosso Rubino	Crema	LHD								
49799		BBi	1984	Nero Met	Tan	LHD								
49803		BBi	1984	Rosso Corsa	Crema	LHD								
49805		BBi	1984	Nero Met	Crema	LHD			New York	US				
49891		BBi	1984			RHD	RS 6			UK				
49893		BBi	1984			LHD								
49895		98145.452	1984	98145.452	98145.452	98145.452			98145.452	98145.452				
49897		BBi	1984	Argento Met	Nero	LHD			California	US				
49899		BBi	1984	Rosso Corsa	Crema	LHD								
50011		BBi	1984	Rosso Corsa	Tan	LHD			California	US				
50013		BBi	1984	Rosso Corsa	Crema/Rosso	LHD	KS 0615			Germany				
50015		BBi	1984			LHD								
50019	00862	BBi	1984	Nero Met	Nero	LHD			Virginia	US				
50021		BBi	1984	Rosso Corsa	Tan	LHD			California	US				
50077		BBi	1984	Rosso Corsa	Tan	LHD								
50081		BBi	1984	Rosso/Nero	Nero	LHD			Canada	US				
50083	00859	BBi	1984	Rosso Corsa	Crema	LHD				US				
50111		BBi	1984	Nero Met	Nero	LHD			California	US				
50181		BBi	1984	Argento/Nero	Nero/Grigio	LHD			Pennsylvania	US				
50183		BBi	1984			LHD								
50185		BBi	1984	Rosso Corsa	Crema	LHD								
50187		BBi	1984	Rosso Corsa	Tan	LHD								
50281		BBi	1984	Rosso Corsa	Tan	LHD			Texas	US				
50283		BBi	1984	Nero Met	Crema	LHD	VC 423583			Italy				
50285		BBi	1984	Rosso Corsa	Tan/Nero	LHD			California	US				
50287		BBi	1984	Nero Met	Nero	LHD								
50349		BBi	1984	Rosso Corsa	Tan	LHD			California	US				
50351		BBi	1984	Blu TdF	Crema/Blu	LHD				US				
50353		BBi	1984			LHD								
50355		BBi	1984	Rosso/Nero	Zegna Cloth	LHD			Pennsylvania	US				
50357		BBi	1984	Grigio Ferro	Crema	LHD								
50359		BBi	1984	Rosso Corsa	Tan	LHD			California	US				
50437		BBi	1984	Rosso Corsa	Nero	LHD								
50469		BBi	1984	Nero Met	Nero	LHD								
50471		BBi	1984	Rosso Corsa	Tan	LHD								
50475		BBi	1984	Rosso Corsa	Tan	LHD								
50477		BBi	1984	Rosso Corsa	Tan	LHD			Massachusetts	US				
50537		BBi	1984			RHD	B918 OVU			France				
50591		BBi	1984	Rosso Corsa	Tan	LHD			New Jersey	US				
50593		BBi	1984	Rosso Corsa	Tan	LHD			Ohio	US				
50595		BBi	1984			LHD								
50667		BBi	1984	Nero/Grigio	Bordeaux	LHD			Frankfurt	Germany				
50673		BBi	1984	Rosso Corsa	Tan	LHD	WND U1			Germany				
50675		BBi	1984	Rosso Corsa	Tan	LHD								
50743		BBi	1984	Rosso Corsa	Tan	LHD			Atlanta	US				
50745		BBi	1984	Rosso Corsa	Tan	LHD								
50749		BBi	1984			LHD								
50861		BBi	1984	Rosso/Nero	Tan	LHD			California	US				
50863		BBi	1984	Nero Met	Crema	LHD								
50865		BBi	1984	Rosso Corsa	Tan	LHD			Texas	US				
50959		BBi	1984	Rosso Corsa	Tan	LHD								
50963		BBi	1984	Rosso Corsa	Nero	LHD			Florida	US				
50965		BBi	1984	Rosso Corsa	Tan	LHD								

BB512i	BB512i	BB512i	BB512i	BB512i	BB512i	BB512i	BB512i	BB512i	BB512i	BB512i	BB512i	BB512i	BB512i	BB512i
VIN #	ENG #	MODEL	YEAR	COLOUR	INTERIOR	DRIVE	REG No.		LOCATION		COUNTRY		COMMENTS	
50969		BBi	1984	Rosso Corsa	Nero	LHD								
51071		BBi	1984	Rosso/Nero	Nero	LHD			Conneticut		US			
51073		BBi	1984	Rosso Corsa	Crema	LHD	076 BB		Collorado		US		Original Colour Nero Met	
51075		BBi	1984	Rosso Corsa	Tan	LHD								
51077		BBi	1984	Nero Met	Nero	LHD			Massachusetts		US			
51079		BBi	1984	Rosso Corsa	Crema	LHD					US			
51081		BBi	1984	Nero Met	Bordeaux	LHD								
51121		BBi	1984	Rosso Corsa	Tan	LHD			California		US			
51177		BBi	1984	Rosso Corsa	Nero/Grigio	LHD			California		US			
51179		BBi	1984	Nero Met	Tan	LHD								
51251		BBi	1984	Rosso Corsa	Tan	LHD								
51255		BBi	1984	Argento Met	Blu Scuro	LHD								
51257		BBi	1984	Rosso Rubino	Tan	LHD					Canada			
51259		BBi	1984	Giallo Fly	Nero	LHD								
51331		BBi	1984	Rosso Corsa	Tan	LHD			Rhode Island		US			
51333		BBi	1984	Nero Met	Crema	LHD			Marseille		France			
51335		BBi	1984	Rosso Corsa	Tan	LHD			Florida		US			
51337		BBi	1984	Nero Met	Tan	LHD								
51339		BBi	1984	Argento Met	Bordeaux	LHD			North Carolina		US		Original Colour Rosso Corsa	
51351		BBi	1984	Nero Met	Tan	LHD			Pennsylvania		US			
51411		BBi	1984	Rosso Corsa	Nero	LHD								
51413		BBi	1984	Nero Met	Nero	LHD					Germany			
51419		BBi	1984	Rosso Corsa	Tan	LHD			Tennessee		US			
51421		BBi	1984			RHD					Malaysia			
51507		BBi	1984	Rosso/Nero	Nero	LHD								
51509		BBi	1984	Rosso Corsa	Crema	LHD			Arizona		US			
51513		BBi	1984	Nero Met	Tan	LHD			Pennsylvania		US		Original Colour Grigio Ferro	
51515		BBi	1984			RHD					HK			
51573		BBi	1984	Rosso Corsa	Tan	LHD								
51607		BBi	1984	Argento Met	Nero	LHD					US			
51609	00957	BBi	1984	Rosso Corsa	Tan	LHD	3JOH963		California		US			
51611		BBi	1984	Rosso/Nero	Tan	LHD					US		Original Colour Argento Met	
51619		BBi	1984	Rosso Corsa	Tan	LHD			California		US			
51715		BBi	1984			LHD								
51723		BBi	1984	Rosso Corsa	Tan	LHD			Florida		US			
51725		BBi	1984	Argento/Nero	Bordeaux	LHD	64121		California		US		Ex AJ Foyt	
51745		BBi	1984								Holland		2004: Badly damaged in fire	
51747		BBi	1984	Rosso Corsa	Tan	LHD			North Carolina		US			
51751		BBi	1984			LHD								
51753		BBi	1984	Rosso Corsa	Tan	LHD			New York		US			
51845		BBi	1984	Nero Met	Tan	LHD								
51847		BBi	1984	Rosso/Nero	Nero	LHD			Massachusetts		US			
51869		BBi	1984	Rosso Corsa	Nero	LHD			Milan		Italy			
51871		BBi	1984	Rosso Corsa	Crema	RHD	B388 JPG				UK			
51873		BBi	1984	Rosso Corsa	Crema	LHD			Connecticut		US			
51925		BBi	1984	Rosso Corsa	Tan	LHD			California		US			
51969		BBi	1984	Rosso Corsa	Tan	LHD								
51993		BBi	1984	Rosso Corsa	Tan	LHD			New Jersey		US			
51995		BBi	1984	Nero Met	Tan	LHD								
52039		BBi	1984	Bianco Avus	Crema/Rosso	LHD								

BB512i	BB512i	BB512i	BB512i	BB512i	BB512i	BB512i	BB512i	BB512i	BB512i	BB512i	BB512i	BB512i	BB512i	BB512i
VIN #	ENG #	MODEL	YEAR	COLOUR	INTERIOR	DRIVE	REG No.	LOCATION	COUNTRY	COMMENTS
52061		BBi	1984	Rosso/Nero	Nero	LHD		Alabama	US	
52077		BBi	1984	Nero Met	Nero	LHD				
52081		BBi	1984	Rosso Corsa	Tan	LHD				
52083		BBi	1984	Rosso Corsa	Tan	LHD		California	US	
52151		BBi	1984	Rosso Corsa	Tan	LHD		Kentucky	US	
52183		BBi	1984	Rosso Corsa	Nero	LHD				
52203		BBi	1984	Rosso Corsa	Crema	LHD				
52207		BBi	1984	Rosso Corsa	Nero	LHD				
52209		BBi	1984	Rosso Corsa	Tan/Rosso	LHD		California	US	
52241		BBi	1984	Argento Met	Nero	LHD				
52259		BBi	1984	Grigio Ferro	Bordeaux	LHD				
52271		BBi	1984	Rosso Corsa	Tan	LHD				
52273		BBi	1984	Nero Met	Tan	LHD				
52293		BBi	1984	Rosso Corsa	Nero	LHD				
52295		BBi	1984	Rosso Corsa	Tan	LHD		Connecticut	US	
52297		BBi	1984	Rosso Corsa	Tan	LHD		Florida	US	
52299		BBi	1984	Rosso Corsa	Tan/Rosso	LHD		Tennessee	US	
52323		BBi	1984			LHD		California	US	
52339		BBi	1984	Rosso Corsa	Tan	LHD				
52417		BBi	1984	Rosso Corsa	Tan	LHD				
52445		BBi	1984	Rosso Corsa		LHD				
52525		BBi	1984	Rosso Corsa	Nero	LHD			Japan	
52529		BBi	1984	Rosso Corsa	Tan	LHD		California	US	
52561		BBi	1984			LHD				
52563		BBi	1984	Rosso Corsa	Nero/Rosso	LHD	R94 5EU	Florida	US	
52565		BBi	1984	Rosso Corsa	Tan	LHD				
52589		BBi	1984			LHD				
52607		BBi	1984			LHD				
52629		BBi	1984	Rosso Corsa	Nero	LHD		Paris	France	
52631		BBi	1984	Rosso Corsa	Nero	LHD		Rhode Island	US	
52655		BBi	1984	Rosso Corsa	Tan	LHD				
52657		BBi	1984	Rosso Corsa	Tan	LHD			US	
52659		BBi	1984	Rosso Corsa	Nero	LHD		Connecticut	US	
52773		BBi	1984	Rosso Corsa	Tan	LHD	CNTDRV 55	California	US	
52775		BBi	1984	Nero Met	Nero	LHD				
52783		BBi	1984	Rosso Corsa	Tan	LHD				
52795		BBi	1984	Rosso/Nero	Nero	LHD		California	US	
52813	01020	BBi	1984	Rosso Corsa	Nero/Grigio	LHD		Tennessee	US	
52815		BBi	1984	Rosso Corsa	Tan	LHD	DI 39313	New Orleans	US	
52817		BBi	1984	Rosso Corsa	Tan	LHD		Arizona	US	
52819		BBi	1984	Rosso Corsa	Nero/Rosso	LHD				
52885		BBi	1984	Argento Met	Bordeaux	LHD				
52933		BBi	1984	Nero Met	Nero	LHD			US	
52935		BBi	1984	Rosso Corsa	Crema	LHD		Tennessee	US	

Thanks to Steve Pickering for his chassis listing and registry input. Any amendments or additions should be sent directly to Steve - SLN831@aol.com"

Also, thanks to Lee Sanders for added information. Updates to Lee's BB register - lee@leesanders.com

Also note that Frank Masiarz runs a web-site devoted to BBs; http://www.masiarz.net/bb_resource/front.html

17257 with non-standard front air-dam (Reuben Kennedy)

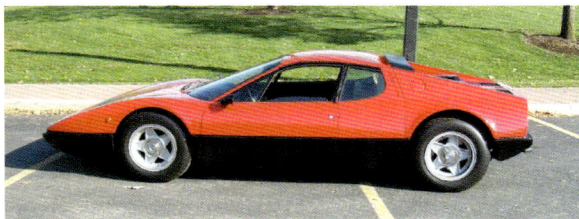

18745 displays it red-over-black colour scheme (Steve Biagini)

19343 showing the 365GT4/BB's triple rear light and exhaust treatment (Simon Campbell)

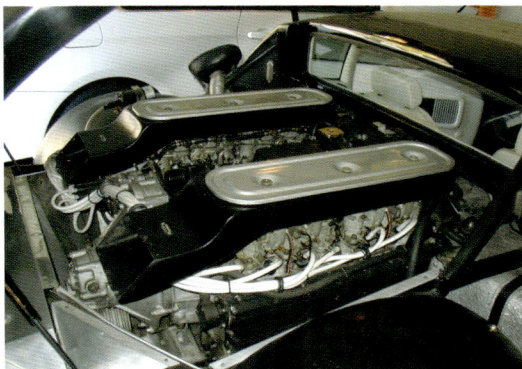

19865 - all black with white interior (Jesse Ingram)

20339 (Carl Jones)

20657 is a BB512 that was owned by a friend of mine. I can recall many exciting trips, especially to Goodwood and back, which was a mix of country roads and motorway blasts, in the days before speed cameras ruined everyone's fun. In the late 80s Ferraris were a rare sight on England's roads and I recall pulling into a petrol station where the attendant looked at the car, then the badge and asked, "Is this the latest Peugeot?" (NB Colln)

The conversion of 21873 into a BB/LM replica (Tom Wiggers)

Original body panels are from 26681 and are used as templates for the replica. (It would be a shame if they disappear onto the replica) (Tom Wiggers)

22153 at Donington Park test day (NB photo)

22543 braking hard for the Goodwood chicane.

24641 (Carl Jones)

Get me to the church on time? No problem in 25291. Incidentally, the bridesmaid in the photo is now Mrs. Hughes – (It's the car - Chicks love the car!) (Phil Hughes)

I admire the owner for using this car as intended (look at the stone chips on the front) (NB photo)

27001 shows off the triple carbs (Lee Sanders)

27941 (Carl Jones)

29897 (Carl Jones)

28235 pictured at the Goodwood test day (NB Photo)

28537 shows off its black seats with red inserts (Drew Altemara)

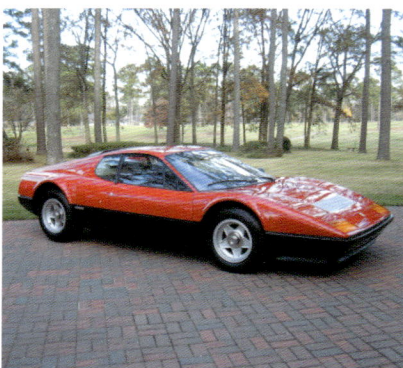

30311 One of the best drives of my life (NB photo)

30713 in all red, rather than the more usual red over black. This is an Amerispec conversion (Don Vollum)

35177 looks unusal in all white (NB Colln)

The original Certificate issued for 40565 by the factory (Dave Bendl)

Dave Bendl proudly displays his FCA Gold & Platinum award winning BB (Norbert Ertel)

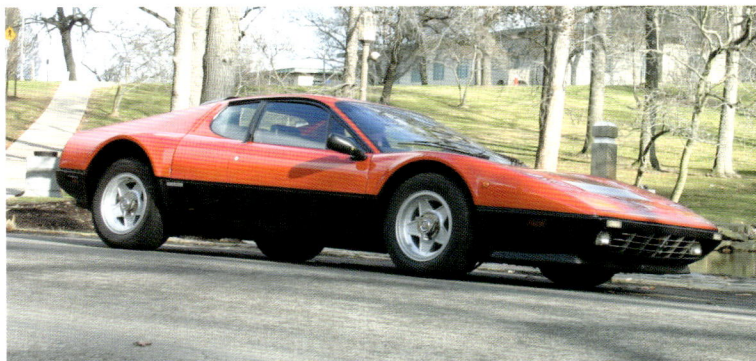

40661 (Bernie Kuhn)

40773 Beauty or the beast? (NB photo)

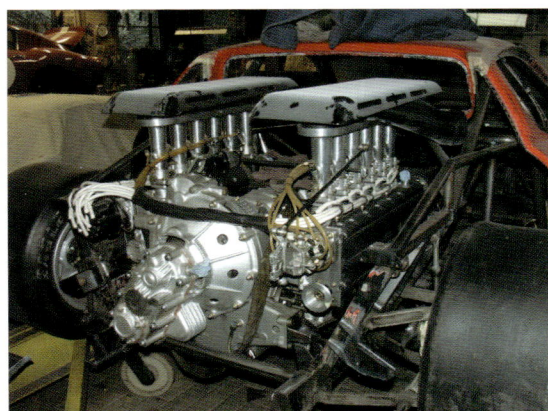

41041 in the process of being converted to another BB/LM replica (Tom Wiggers)

42213's BBi engine has a different apperance to the carburettor versions (Franklin Parker)

The BB's toolkit, for the owner who wants to do his own engine rebuild (Franklin Parker)

42509 started life in Zurich, and now has about 35,000kms on it (Paul Newman)

44755 (NB Colln)

46189 just looks great in any setting (Gary Reed)

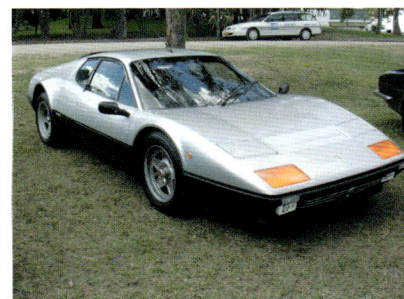

47085 (Carl Jones)

The sad remains of 51745 (NB Colln)

49317 in close-up (Robert Wakeling)

Technical Specifications (Official Ferrari figures*)

	BB	BB512	BB512i	BB/LM 80[1]
Bore	81	82	82	82
Stroke	71	78	78	78
Displacement – CCs	4390	4942	4942	4942
Maximum RPM	7700	6800	6600	7500
bhp	380	360	340	470
Carburation	4 x Weber 40IF3C	4 x Weber 40IF3C	Bosch K-Jetronic FI	Lucas FI
Front Track – ins	59	59	59.4	61.5
Rear Track – ins	59.8	61.5	61.9	67.4
Length – ins	171.65	173.25	173.2	187.3
width – ins	70	72	72	80
Height – ins	44	44	44.1	42
Wheelbase – ins	98.4	98.4	98.4	98.4
Weight – lbs	2472	3084	3305	2500
Maximum Speed – mph	188	176	174	191[2]

*These are official Ferrari figures, but power output and weight are questioned by Boxer owners.
US versions are heavier due to anti-smog equipment, larger bumpers etc.
[1] This information is representative of all the 1980 BB/LMs, and is taken from Ferrari build sheets (Scheda di Montaggio) and information from owners.
[2] This is with Le Mans gearing (from official Ferrari figures) although in reality higher speeds were reached by some BB/LMs at Le Mans

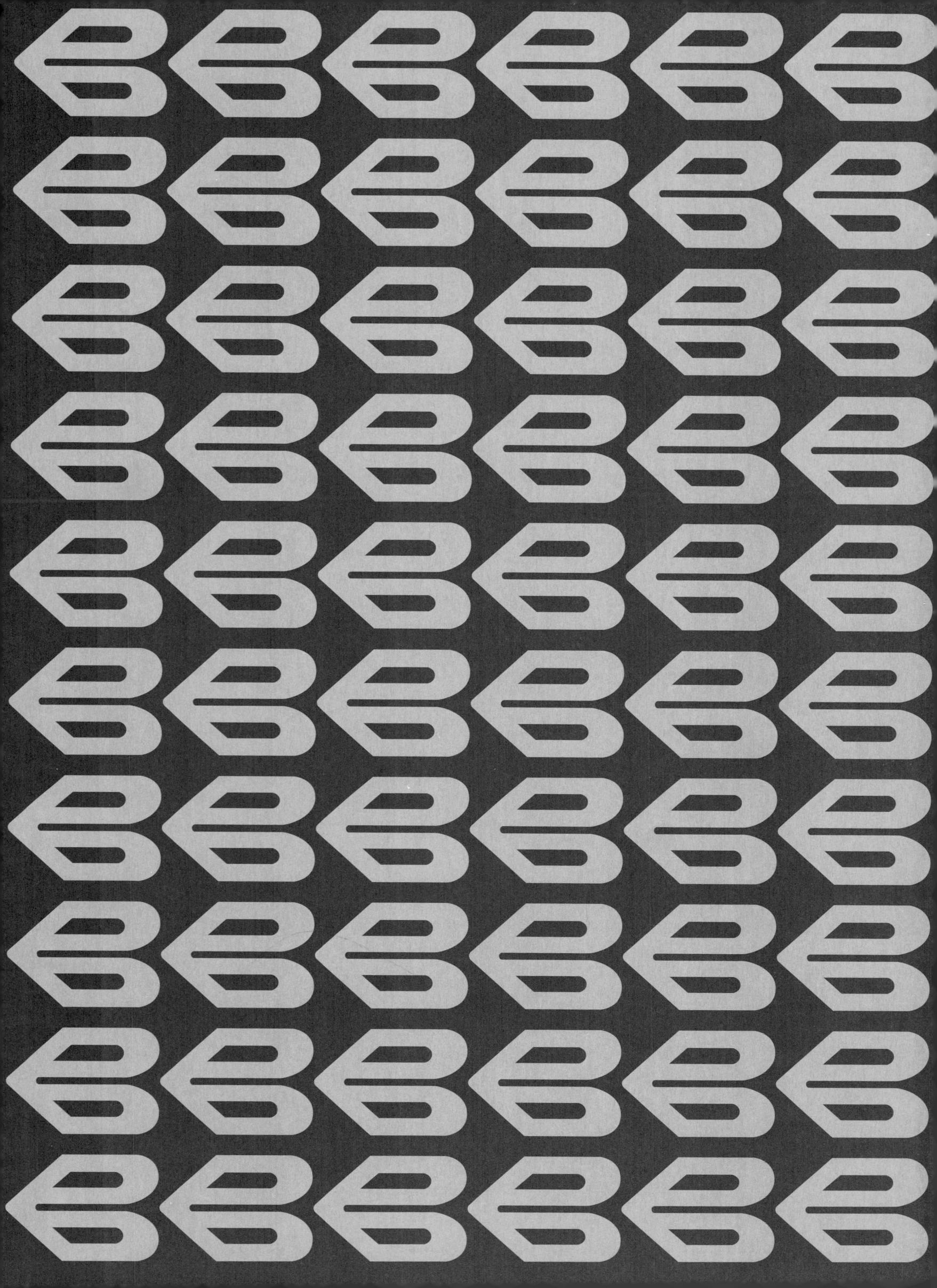

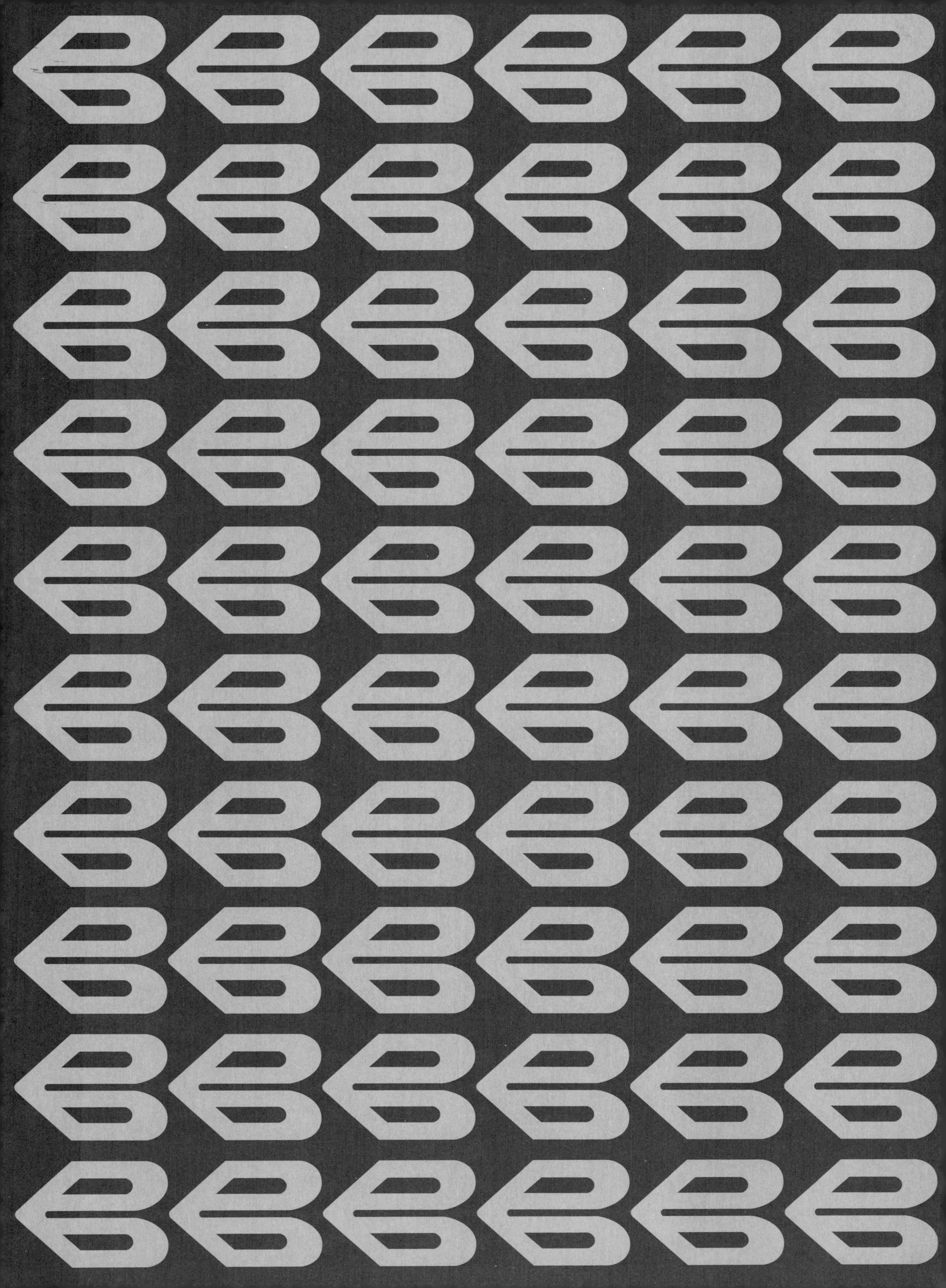